WITHDRAWN

THE VAMPIRE FILM

Also by James Ursini:
Preston Sturges
David Lean and his Films

Also by Alain Silver:
The Samurai Film
David Lean and his Films

The Vampire Film

James Ursini and Alain Silver

SOUTH BRUNSWICK AND NEW YORK: A. S. BARNES AND COMPANY
LONDON: THE TANTIVY PRESS

PARKLAND COLLEGE LRC

© 1975 by A. S. Barnes and Co., Inc.

A. S. Barnes and Co., Inc.
Cranbury, New Jersey 08512

The Tantivy Press
108 New Bond Street
London W1Y OQX, England

Library of Congress Cataloging in Publication Data

Ursini, James.
   The Vampire film.

   Filmography: p.
   Bibliography: p.
   Includes index.

1. Vampire films—History and criticism   I. Silver, Alain, 1947-   joint author.   II. Title.
PN1995.9.V3U77   791.43'0909'375   74-9301
ISBN 0-498-01429-0

SBN 0-904208-40-0 (U.K.)
PRINTED IN THE UNITED STATES OF AMERICA

This survey is respectfully dedicated to the memory of three creators of the vampire genre: Dr. John Polidori, Joseph Sheridan Le Fanu, and Bram Stoker, foremost among those who

> "Intrigue with the specious chaos,
>   and dispart
> Its most ambiguous atoms with sure
>   art."
>
> (Keats, "Lamia")

Contents

Preface	9
Acknowledgements	11

Part One: The Vampire in Film and Literature

CHAPTER ONE: Sources of the Vampire Lore in Film	17
I. The Vampire in Legend	17
II. Historical and Natural "Vampires"	26
III. The Vampire in Literature and the Arts	31
CHAPTER TWO: The Male Vampire	53
I. The Vampire Figure	53
II. Dracula	57
III. The Sympathetic Male Vampire	89
CHAPTER THREE: The Female Vampire	97
I. Elisabeth Bathory	97
II. Carmilla Karnstein	103
III. Other Daughters of Darkness	112
IV. Vampyr	118
CHAPTER FOUR: Emerging Traditions	123
I. Hammer and the Victorian Psychology	123
II. Mario Bava and the Baroque Image	133

Part Two: Filmography and Bibliography

Filmography	**145**
Bibliography	**231**
Index to Film Titles	**237**

Preface

The designation of this study as a "critical survey" is intended to characterise its self-imposed limitations. The authors have consciously chosen to treat films which they deem most significant not in terms of whole. Consequently, they have occasionally allocated space to a little-popularity or critical reputation but as expressions of the *genre* as a known title which evidences a novel or extraordinary approach and restricted their discussion of accepted "classics," hoping to reconstruct a conception of the "vampire film" that is truly representative of the richness and variety of all the motion pictures that fall into that category.

Acknowledgements

The authors wish to express their appreciation to: David Bradley, Ken Dixon, Jim Paris, and Adriana Nerey for assistance in researching the films and literature; to Jerry Fiore, Alan White, David Ichikawa, Les Otis, Timothy Otto, and Eddie Brandt for invaluable help in acquiring stills; to Elmer Silver for aid in preparing the final copy of the manuscript; and, most particularly, to Will Russell Plax for giving generously of his extensive knowledge of the *genre* in many hours of discussion and numerous pages of notes on specific motion pictures.

Stills courtesy of: Allied Artists; American International; Amicus; Azteca Distributing (U.S.A.); Columbia; Hammer; Metro-Goldwyn-Mayer; Paramount; Republic; Tigon; Twentieth Century-Fox; United Artists; Universal-International; Warners-Seven Arts.

THE VAMPIRE FILM

Part One
The Vampire in Film and Literature

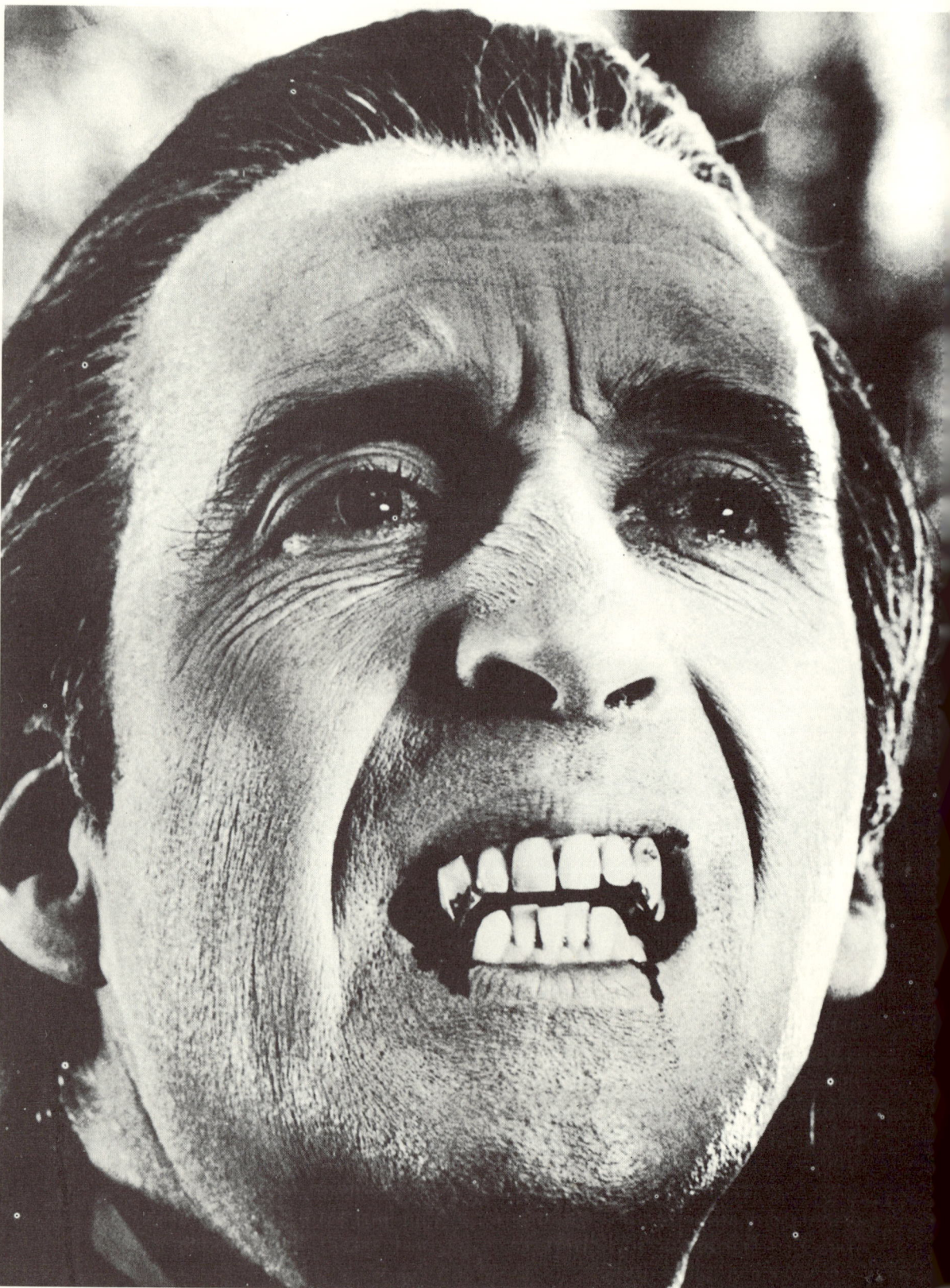

CHAPTER ONE

Sources of the Vampire Lore in Film

> When out of all my bones she had sucked the marrow,
> And as I turned to her, in the act to harrow
> My senses in one kiss, to end her chatter,
> I saw a gourd that was filled full with foul matter!
> I closed mine eyes, all my body shivering,
> And when I opened them, in the dawn's quivering,
> I saw at my side a puppet of derision
> Who had made of its blood too much provision,
> Then fragments of a skeleton in confusion
> That of themselves made a mere mist of illusion,
> Or of a sign-board at the end of a batten
> The winter wind swung, as it seemed, in Latin
>   Charles Baudelaire,
>   "Metamorphoses of the Vampire"

I. THE VAMPIRE IN LEGEND

In a previous study, "The Vampire: His Kith and Kin," it was my endeavour to trace back the dark tradition of the vampire to its earliest beginnings, until indeed it becomes lost amid the ages of a dateless antiquity, for this remarkable and worldwide belief was very present with primitive man, and is notably significant in the daily customs and practice, both tribal and domestic—more especially in the funeral rites and sepulchral houses—of furthest aboriginal and most savage indigene. Nor, owing (as I believe) to the fundamental truth, which, however, exaggerated in expression and communication, essentially informs the vampire-tradition did the legend die. As man marched towards civilization it persisted, losing much that was monstrous but none of the horror, for the horror was part of the truth.[1]

As Reverend Montague Summers, probably the foremost authority on the subject suggests, the roots of the vampire myth[2] go deep into man's

---

[1]. Montague Summers, "The Vampire in Europe" (London, 1929).
[2]. From the beginning it should be pointed out that the words "myth," 'lore," and "legend" are used in their strictest and most classical sense. For in most myths or legends factual bases or correlatives are present. The best example of this is probably the Arthurian legends.

written and oral history. Vampires and vampire-like phenomena are prevalent in almost every recorded culture with only minor variations in their subsidiary characteristics. In ancient Greece these creatures were given colourful names such as *Lamia, Empusa,* or *Strige*. The first two are most often females who are not only succubi (demons who have sexual relations with humans) but also blood-suckers and ghouls (devourers of corpses). *Lamias* are also associated with snakes. A *Strige*, on the other hand, has the ability to transform itself into a bird after sucking blood. In ancient Assyria and Babylon *Ekimmu* were the souls of the dead who had broken one or more of the numerous taboos and consequently were forced to wander the earth tormenting the living and drawing life from them. In Imperial Rome *Lemures* were like their Assyrian relatives, that is, spirits who tormented the living, often, according to Summers, "absorb[ing] the health and vitality" of their victims. In Druid Ireland blood-suckers were known and called *Dearg-duls*. In India a mythological figure called a *Baital* strikingly resembles the more familiar Eastern European-Balkans conception of a vampire, being a corpse reanimated by the *Baital* demon which can alternately assume a bat-like form. The *Vetala*, also Indian, is simply a blood-suckering hag. China's vampire, *Ch'ing Shuh*, also reanimates bodies and then devours humans, both living and dead, with lightning-like ferocity; it is reputed to be particularly horrifying in appearance. In contrast, Malaysian vampires are almost exclusively women—called *Langsuir, Pontianak,* or *Penaggalan*—and are often extremely beautiful. Africa has its blood-suckers as well—the spirits of dead sorcerers or medicine men *(Asbanbosam, Owenga, Otgiruru)*.

In the Christian West, the divergent characteristics and lore that surround the various species of the vampire *genus* begin to congeal into the myths growing out of Eastern Europe and the neighbouring Balkans—myths that ultimately exert the greatest influence on the rest of the West, and through film and literature, the world. The physical aspect, the powers, and the weaknesses of this Western vampire will be dealt with later. A brief list of its names may suggest this creature's proliferation in legend. In Greece: *Vrykolaka* (with variations on that name present also); in Bulgaria *Obour;* in Romania *Strigoi* or *Moroii*; in Hungary *Pamgri* or *Vampir*; in Russia *Upir* or *Oupyr* (among other names); in Serbia *Vlkodlak* or *Vampir*; in Morlacchia *Vukodlak*; in Germany *Vampyr* or *Nachzehrer*; in France *Vampire*; In Italy and Spain *Vampiro*; in Mexico *Vampiro* or *Ciuatateo*; and in English-speaking countries *Vampire* or in older script *Vampyre*. Even from this less than comprehensive list a sense of the universality of the vampire myth can easily be abstracted. The cultures alluded to above may be distinct in many other aspects but they seem to share an obsession with this figure, as archetype, as superstition, and as possible reality.

While no definition of "vampire" could encompass all the manifestations of this creature and its brethren, the best is probably Anthony Masters's in his book "The Natural History of the Vampire." Drawing on various encyclopedias and dictionaries, Masters generalises that:

> The vampire throughout the world can be divided into two basic manifestations. The spirit of a dead person [or demon] is the first and the second is a corpse, reanimated by his own spirit or alternatively by a demon, who returns to suck at the life of the living, depriving them of blood or some vital organ in order to maintain its own vitality.[3]

Such a definition is succinct yet comprehensive enough to cover the varied types that have been introduced; it is also one most likely to be accepted by researchers in the field.

Hypotheses Concerning the Prevalence of Vampire Legends

In trying to explain the vampire phenomenon and its universality theorists have formulated a number of hypotheses. First, there are those, like Dudley Wright or Montague Summers, who concentrate on collecting legends as well as more documentary evidence about vampiric phenomena. Though they are often reserved on the question of personal belief in vampires, their careful cataloguing of information, mostly in support of the existence of the "undead," leaves the reader with little doubt as to their view. This explanation of vampiric legends, then, is the simplest and yet for modern man, deprived of a Medieval faith in a cosmos inhabited by demons and angels, the most difficult to accept. In addition, much of the evidence quoted by these researchers is hearsay—based all too often on stories told to the author. There are exceptions, however, instances where the documentation is fairly impressive and a materialistic conception of reality most severely tested.

The second explanation, as advocated by more sceptical writers like Anthony Masters, addresses itself to man's traditional obsession in his folklore and art with blood and death. Ornella Volta in "Le vampire" and Masters in his book do a thorough job of tracing the evolution of blood cults. From pre-history, man has made the obvious connection between life and blood, so that the precious fluid has become the focal point of many rituals and taboos. According to Leviticus "the life of a living body is in its blood." In certain societies, women in men-

---

[3]. Anthony Masters, "The Natural History of the Vampire" (New York, 1972).

struation were secluded from the rest of the tribe for fear of the power of free-flowing blood. In some African tribes the spilling of even a drop of this liquid symbolic of the "life-principle" required immediate action. In battle the blood of fallen enemies has been drunk from time immemorial in order to acquire their strength. Blood has also been consumed to enhance prophetic powers: in "The Odyssey" the dead are given the power of speech after drinking the blood of sheep. The aphrodisiacal "virtues" of this fluid are also evident in ritual and especially in the cases of historical or natural "vampires," which will be discussed later. For now it should be pointed out that blood was often a necessary ingredient for philtres and that haematomania (blood obsession) is most often related to a sexual need. Organised religion, however, has probably had more to do with affirming the sacredness of blood than its more primitive counterparts. In the Old Testament, Jehovah warns against drinking blood so as not to partake of the life of a foreign body. In much of Christianity the blood of Christ, in the form of wine, is drunk to commemorate the Biblical dictate:

> Amen, amen, I say to you, unless you eat the flesh of the Son of Man, and drink his blood, you shall not have life in you. He who eats my flesh and drinks my blood has life everlasting. (John 5:54-56)

Blood sacrifices have also been common in man's relatively short chronology. The gods of diverse cultures and eras have been propitiated with blood, and not always that of animals. The Egyptians, the Aztecs, and Phoenicians, even the founders of Western civilization, the ancient Greeks, honored the cannibalistic practice of offering human lives to the gods. Even the therapeutic use of transfusions in modern medicine subtly re-states the cultural equation of blood and life.

Concomitant with blood cultism is man's natural fear of disease and dying. To the anthropologist, the vampire is just another mythic transformation that seeks to explain a death from unperceived or misunderstood natural causes. If the plague, pneumonia, smallpox, the "French pox" or venereal disease, and the contemporary catalogue of fatal maladies could not be fully comprehended medically in a given society, they could be feared metaphysically. Accordingly, an epidemic striking Sixteenth century Europe was not borne of rats or sexual promiscuity but of demons, witches, and vampires. To the Medieval and Renaissance minds in Europe and in many primitive societies today, the metaphysic of death and its aftermath ("the mysterious land of boundless possibilities where all phantasies are realised and all secrets revealed . . .")[4] was and is an impenetrable one that overshadows all

---
4. Ernest Jones, "On The Nightmare" (New York, 1951).

SOURCES OF THE VAMPIRE LORE IN FILM

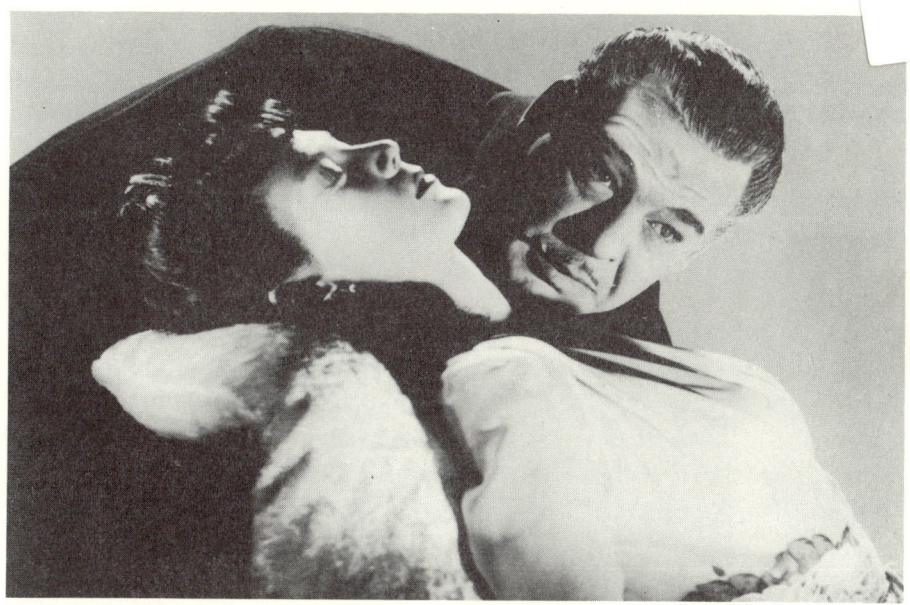

Lon Chaney Jr. and Louise Allbritton in SON OF DRACULA

facets of life. As Slochower puts it, "the knowledge of death is the most continuous, most persistent and inevitable, perhaps the most fateful trauma for man."[5] Ornella Volta takes this into consideration in her study and formulates a hypothesis regarding the vampire:

> By decreeing that only the soul has a right to immortality, a position has been created by which the body has also demanded its rights. By refusing to accept the limitations posed by physical death (and by not having the patience to wait for the Day of Judgment for a resurrection of the body) might not the vampire simply be seeking to demonstrate the possibility of survival for a body without a soul? How? By acquiring the soul and life of another through his blood.[6]

Aggravating this fear of death even further is another terror—one that only recently has been allayed by the widespread use of embalming and by medical advances, that is: the fear of being buried alive. Premature interment of plague victims in the Middle Ages and of cataleptics up to modern times was not an uncommon occurrence. Anthony Masters claims that "American statistics in the early 1900's show that not less than one case a week of premature burial was discovered." Masters, supported by Dr. H. Mayo's book "On The Truths Contained in Popular Superstition," promotes this statistic as one of

---

[5.] Harry Slochower. "Eros and the Trauma of Death," in "Death: Interpretations" (New York, 1969).
[6.] Ornella Volta, "Le vampire" (Paris, 1962). (English Translation by Raymond Rudorff).

the explanations for such vampiric phenomena as finding corpses in their coffins so well preserved, in distorted positions, or devouring their shrouds. Still Masters is hard-pressed to rationally explain the reports that these dead leave their graves and return without disturbing the ground or the fixtures of the crypt. He can only dismiss this as part of the mass hallucination symptomatic of vampiric lore.

A final body of conjecture on the origins of vampire legends is constructed by psychologists, most notably by Ernest Jones. They trace the lore back to one or a combination of the following: repressed sexual desires (often bordering on necrophilia); feelings of guilt towards and subsequent dread of the deceased; or a *liebestod* ("lovedeath") mentality. All of these are expressed, characteristically, in nightmares, many times accompanied by nocturnal emissions. And therein lies, they believe, the root of fantasies in which the dead suck vital fluids.

The Eastern European-Balkans Vampire and His Influence

As mentioned earlier, the image of the vampire which has been generated in the Western world and which dominates its folklore and art is basically derived from an Eastern European-Balkans tradition. For the most part the Eastern European-Balkans type of vampire is an

Herbert Lom as Van Helsing in EL CONDE DRACULA

"undead" (surviving after physical death) human corpse or possibly astral body, animated by the undead's own spirit (or in a few instances by a demon), which leaves its place of rest to visit the living and suck their blood. Further, in returning to the world of the living, the Eastern European-Balkans vampire often preys on his own relatives and loved ones, occasionally while having sexual intercourse with them. This fact is significant in psychological terms in relation to the love-dread attitude towards death and the departed which Jones among others discusses at great length. Adding even more to the ambiguity is the uncertainty as to whether the vampire returns to his loved ones out of affection, revenge, compulsion, simple unmitigated lust, or possibly some combination of these motives.

What can cause a person to turn into a vampire? The answer to this is as varied as the districts and peoples of Europe. The influence of the Greek Orthodox Church's thinking on the subject, even in Roman Catholic areas, has been most pronounced. Although the Roman Church has had no reservations about speaking its mind on the subject of witchcraft—witness the infamous "Malleus Maleficarum"—it has produced few official statements on vampirism *per se*. The obvious reason for this is that Western Europe, the centre of Roman Catholic power after the Schism and the Reformation, and England and North America as well suffered fewer "recorded" instances of vampirism than Eastern Europe and the Balkan countries. Consequently an obsession with eradicating sorcery and the black arts is manifested in these areas rather than concern with vampires. Whatever the case with the Roman Church, Greek Orthodoxy spoke dogmatically about vampirism. As Dudley Wright says:

> The Greek Church at one time taught that the bodies of persons upon whom the ban of excommunication had been passed did not undergo decomposition after death until such sentence had been revoked by the pronouncement of absolution over the remains, and that, while the bodies remained in the uncorrupted condition, the spirits of the individuals wandered up and down the earth seeking sustenance from the blood of the living.[7]

In addition, suicides, murderers, apostates, sorcerers, witches (if not already excommunicated), the unbaptised, a seventh son, a man born with a caul, a man with red hair, and generally debauchers, evil-doers, and blasphemers were considered among others qualified for the ranks of the undead after their human expiration.

The appearance and powers of these creatures is also too varied to

---

7. Dudley Wright, "Vampires and Vampirism" (London, 1924).

Christopher Lee as Dracula in **TASTE THE BLOOD OF DRACULA**

detail; but a general summary of the most common characteristics can be given. Ornella Volta quoting a work ventures an interesting appraisal of the appearance of a vampire: "In his "Encyclopaedic Dictionary of Medical Science," G. Tourdes enumerates the physical features of someone with an erotic temperament: 'a tapering face, sharp, shining teeth, an abundance of thick hair, a peculiar voice, aspect and expression and lastly, a typical odour (usually bad).' The Reverend Montague Summers remarks that his description might just as well be that of a vampire." In addition the vampire's skin is elastic and cold; his colour pale; his stare mesmerising; and when finished with a feast his body is gorged with blood. As regards his powers, the vampire is generally reputed to have the facilities of transmogrification—into a wolf, a bat, an insect, moonbeams, etc.—mesmerism, Herculean strength, invisibility, and control over natural forces. Through some preternatural power—possibly by projecting his astral body—the vampire also can leave and return to his grave without distrubting the ground. Vampirism, according to many, is also infectious, that is, the victim becomes an undead like his malefactor.

There are, of course, other attributes of vampires that have become very familiar, chiefly through literature and film, and yet are not catalogued above. The reason is that many of these traits have originated in obscure portions of Eastern European mythology and been developed and emphasised by Nineteenth and Twentieth century writers and filmmakers. For instance, the vampire's inability to be seen in a mirror and his need to return to his earth and coffin at certain times are both primarily Bram Stoker's creative extrapolations from myth for his novel "Dracula." Later, film-makers continued to interpolate this and have depicted vampires rushing back to their coffins every dawn in fear of destructive sunlight. Although the original Dracula's power could be reduced during the day and his coffin was necessary for transformation and reinvigoration over periods of time, he was a little more potent and flexible in his movements. It is true, however, in most Eastern European-Balkans legends that the apex of the vampires' powers comes during the night hours (effectively setting up the conflict between light and darkness).

The preventive measures which tradition asserts can be employed against a vampire are chiefly the following:
1. A stake—preferably made of aspen or whitethorn—through the heart
2. Decapitation
3. Consummation by fire
4. The corpse buried face down

5. Holy water or blessed articles (such as the crucifix), garlic, and thorny roses are considered only temporary deterrents.

II. HISTORICAL AND NATURAL "VAMPIRES"

I am not mad but at the moment of strangling, I understand nothing anymore. Once the deed is done I am satisfied and feel good. The idea never came to me to touch or keep the genital parts. It was enough for me to hold the woman's neck and suck her blood. Today I can't even remember what they looked like.[8]

In this section a notorious coven of criminals who are usually classed as historical or natural "vampires" will be briefly examined. Although it will be apparent in many of these cases that blood obsession *per se*, a usual prerequisite for a vampire, is not a factor (so that they seem closer to simple—if that word can be used—necrophiliacs, psychopaths, or ghouls) most researchers in the field have applied the term "vampire" to them and this categorisation is generally acknowledged.

1. Of all these individuals the most enigmatic is probably Gilles de Rais. Born in France in the early part of the fifteenth century, de Rais, who became a national hero fighting with Joan of Arc, was a noted scholar and a Marshal of France. During his early life his bravery and religious devotion were never in doubt; yet after retiring to his chateau—following Joan's death and the crowning of the Dauphin—he became involved in various bizarre practices. He began by using the blood of children (valued on account of its powers of transmutation) for alchemical experiments but soon was led into blacker rites, sodomy, and lust-murder. When he was finally brought to trial, de Rais neither expressed nor demonstrated remorse, going to the gallows with an untroubled conscience and an arrogance not uncommon to this type of "vampire." De Rais is reputed to have said that "the star under which he had been born destined him to accomplish feats that no one else could have accomplished . . ."[9] Perhaps the most lucid attempt at unraveling de Rais' character occurs in a fictional work, Joris Karl Huysmans' novel "Là-bas" (1891). The author suggests that de Rais, who plays an important role in the work, came under the influence of Joan's mysticism and was affected deeply by her death. "He is no longer the rough soldier, the uncouth fighting-man. At the same time when the misdeeds are about to begin, the artist and man of letters develop in Gilles and, taking complete possession of him, incite him, under the impulsion of a perverted mysticism, to the most sophisticated

---

8. Volta, "Le vampire," quoting Vincenzo Verzeni.
9. Volta, "Le vampire," quoting the trial records of Gilles de Rais.

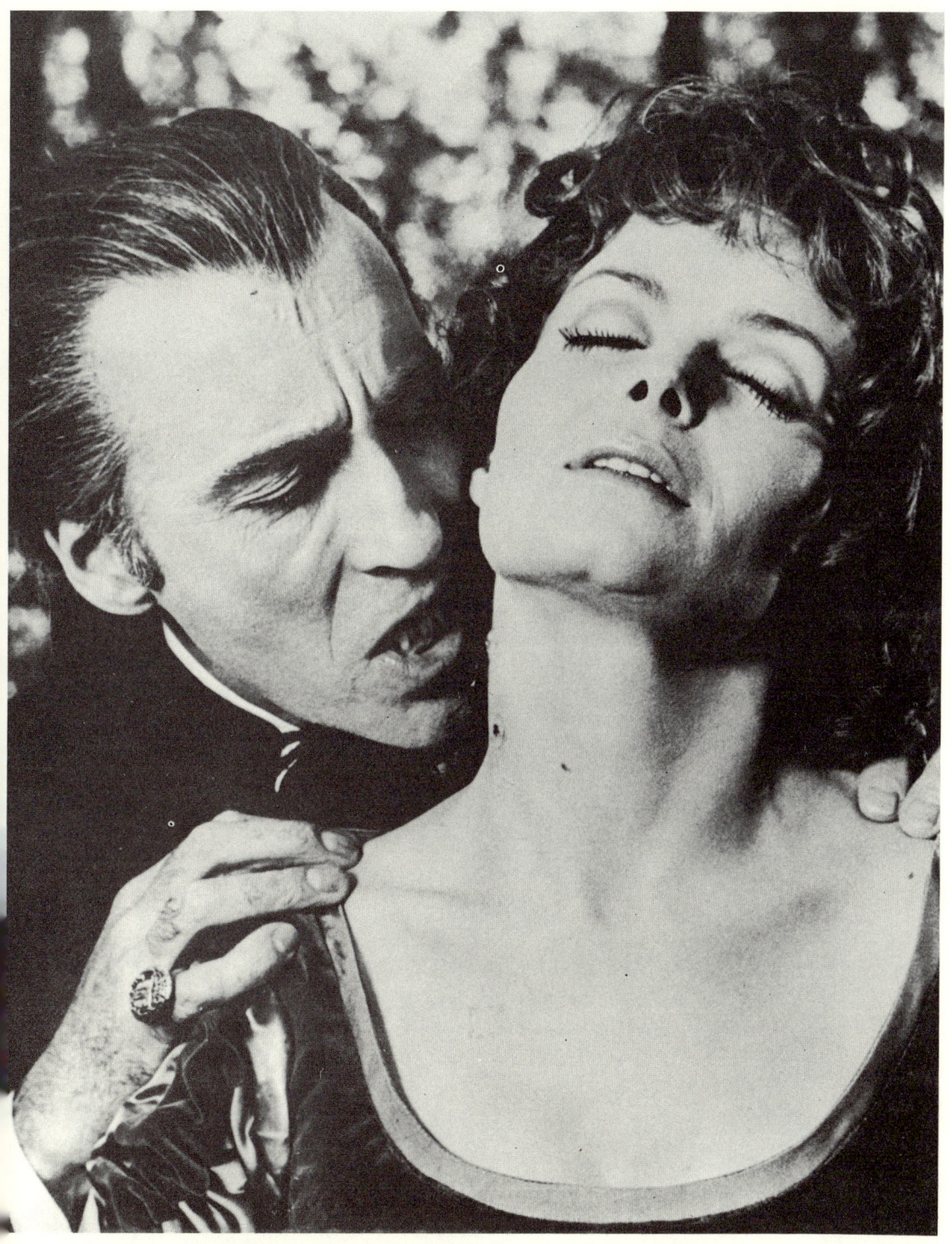

Christopher Lee and Isla Blair in TASTE THE BLOOD OF DRACULA

of cruelties, the most delicate of crimes. For he was almost alone in his time, this baron de Rais. In an age when his peers were simple brutes, he sought the delicate delirium of art, dreamed of a literature soul-searching and profound; he even composed a treatise on the art of evoking demons; he gloried in the music of the Church, and would have nothing about him that was not rare and difficult to obtain."

2. Gilles Garnier was a French "werewolf" of the late 16th century who was condemned to death for devouring the flesh and drinking the blood of young girls.

3. Clara Geisslerin was a German woman living around 1600 who was accused of drinking the blood of children, of fornication with the devil, and of other crimes of witchcraft. She died on the Inquisitional rack after "confessing" to all these crimes.

4. Elizabeth Bathory was a Hungarian noblewoman of the 16th Cen-

Some of the victims are discovered in COUNTESS DRACULA

tury who became infamous as the "Blood Countess." First introduced into the occult by her manservant Thorko, her high social position allowed her blood obsession—especially centered on young girls— to develop unhampered. It was further aggravated in the later years of her life when she discovered quite accidentally what she believed were certain restorative powers of blood rubbed into the skin. For ten years, from 1600 to 1610, Countess Bathory, with the help of her household servants, slaughtered and "milked" countless young women, reputedly as many as 600. Finally, in 1611, King Mathias II of Hungary investigated rumours of the atrocities and brought her to trial. Countess Bathory refused to appear at the tribunal but the evidence was so overwhelming against her that her appearance was deemed superfluous. She was imprisoned in her own castle where she died in 1614.

5. Antoine Leger, a French rapist and murderer, often ate the heart and drank the blood of his victims. He was guillotined in 1824.

6. Sergeant François Bertrand was known as "The Vampire" although his case is closer to those of lycanthropy and necrophilia. A soldier with a taste for corpses, his violations of graveyards around Paris went unchecked until 1849 when a trap was set for him by an enterprising police officer. He was captured, convicted and sentenced to a year in prison.

7. Vincenzo Verzeni was a young Italian laborer who in 1872 was tried for murder complicated by charges of corpse mutilation and the drinking of blood. He was sentenced to life imprisonment.

8. Dr. Richard von Krafft-Ebing in his work "Psychopathia Sexualis" relates an anonymous case of natural "vampirism." He gives the subject's initials as J.H.:

> J. H., aged twenty-six, in 1883 came for consultation concerning severe neurasthenia and hypochondria. Patient confessed that he had practiced onanism since his fourteenth year, infrequently up to his eighteenth year, but since that time he had been unable to resist the impulse. Up to that time he had no opportunity to approach females, for he had been anxiously cared for and never left alone on account of being an invalid. He had had no real desire for this unknown pleasure, but he accidentally learned what it was when one of his mother's maids cut her hand severely on a **pane of glass which she had broken while washing windows. While helping to stop the bleeding he could not keep from sucking up the blood that flowed from the wound, and in this act he experienced extreme erotic excitement, with complete orgasm and ejaculation. From that time on he sought, in every possible way, to see and, where practicable, to taste the fresh blood of females.**

9. Peter Kurten, also known as the "Vampire of Dusseldorf," possessed a classic Jekyll and Hyde personality. By day he was a plain,

well-mannered lorry driver; after dark he prowled the city in search of blood. His victims were usually raped and slashed across the throat so that their blood then gushed into his mouth. In addition, Kurten was infamous for writing macabre letters to his victims' parents. After being jailed for some nocturnal burglaries, Kurten's identity as the "Vampire" was revealed and in April 1931 he was condemned to death. One of his last statements is typical of the insular mania of the "vampire" psychopath: "You cannot understand me. No one can understand me."[10]

10. Fritz Haarmann's early life betrays an unstable and divisive family situation not unlike that of most of the other criminals in this study. Arguments between his parents and violent quarrels with his churlish father drove Haarmann to leave home and join the army. After a short period of service and a subsequent term in an asylum for child molestation, he opened a cook shop in a district of Hanover known for its homosexual inhabitants. With the help of a few friends (most notably Hans Grans), Haarmann began molesting and murdering young boys. What is even more gruesome to relate and what must have proved most unsettling, when it was ultimately revealed to the housewives of Hanover, is that the corpses of the boys he killed were often the source of the fresh meat for Haarmann's steaks and sausages. Haarmann and his accomplices were brought to trial in 1924 and the "Hanover Vampire" was condemned to death

11. We know more about Victor Ardisson, or "The Vampire of Muy," than any other natural "vampire" because of a doctoral thesis by Alexis Epaulard (filed in 1901). Ardisson was for all practical purposes never anything but a necrophile with a misdirected gentleness of manner. Unlike the others in this survey he rarely committed acts of violence. Instead he invaded cemeteries and indulged his fantasies on female corpses, often those of women he had fallen in love with in life. Some of these bodies were even stolen by Ardisson and lovingly preserved. After he was apprehended and confined to an asylum, he became the subject of many studies until his death.

12. In Magnus Hirschfeld's "Anomalies et perversions sexuelles" (Paris ,1935) the author records a case handled by Dr. Craven dealing with a Portuguese female considered an ideal natural "vampire." Here is an excerpt of the text:

> The thoughts and fantasies of the subject all moved around the idea of blood, which she expressed by means of blood-thirsty metaphors and

---

[10]. Volta, "Le vampire," quoting Kurten. See also Karl Berg's "The Sadist," a study of Kurten's psychopathia based on interviews with Kurten made during his incarceration.

SOURCES OF THE VAMPIRE LORE IN FILM

symbols. Blood for her is the symbol of love, hate, anger, and passion. She wants to know in what way human blood is different from animals' blood and has set herself this problem: what aspect would have if it were to lose its color?[11]

13. John Haigh, "The Vampire of London," is probably the most self-righteous member of this group. A religious fanatic, from a family of puritanically-minded practitioners, Haigh imagined himself as a Christ figure during his trials for murder in 1949. That he had killed and drunk the blood of nine victims did not seem to affect this perception of himself. From childhood he had dreams intermingling religious symbolism and blood lust, and as he grew older he began to enact "rites" inspired by these dreams. When captured and tried he expressed no remorse; quite the contrary, he proposed the erection of a monument to his memory. This admixture of religious fervour and vampiric perversion is eerily reminiscent of the first entry in this coven, Gilles de Rais, closing out the circle of arrogant psychopaths whose delusions of divine or Satanic mission, belief in preternatural powers, and insatiable bloodlust are emblematic of the natural "vampire."

[For more detail on vampires in history and legend see also the sections devoted to the various figures treated above in Montague Summer's two classics, "The Vampire: His Kith and Kin" and "The Vampire in Europe," Ornella Volta's "Le vampire"—although the English translation introduces numerous errors—and R.E.L. Masters and Eduard Lea's general survey "Sex Crimes in History" (New York, 1963)]

III. THE VAMPIRE IN LITERATURE AND THE ARTS

> When from this wreathed tomb shall I awake!
> When move in a sweet body fit for life,
> And love, and pleasure, and the ruddy strife
> Of hearts and lips! Ah, miserable me!
> (Keats, "Lamia")

1. Literature: Recognising the universality and antiquity of vampire legends, it is not surprising that some of the earliest literature which has come down to us should contain references to these creatures. In Euripides's play "Hecuba" the plot pivots on a blood sacrifice to the thirsty spirit of Achilles; in "The Odyssey" the dead speak to the hero after drinking blood; and in Summers's "The Vampire in Europe" the

---

[11]. Volta, "Le vampire," quoting Hirschfeld. The heroine of Octave Mirbeau's "Garden of Tortures" expresses very similar sentiments.

following dialogue from the "Ecclesiazusea" by Aristophanes is translated:

SECOND HAG: Come hither.
YOUTH (to the Girl) : O my darling, don't stand by,
    and see this creature drag me!
SECOND HAG: 'Tis the law drags you.
YOUTH: 'Tis a hellish vampire,
    Clothed all about with blood, and boils and blisters.

In the early history of vampire literature, the most frequently repeated story is from Philostratus's life of Apollonius of Tyana, a kind of "legendary" biography of the Greek sage including many apocryphal events. The narrative of Menippus and his love for a lamia is such a quasi-fable, made famous by Keats's use of the subject in his dramatic "Lamia" in the early 1800's. In both Keats's and Philostratus's versions Apollonius represents the forces of reason which are in opposition to the lamia's more libidinous and supernatural appeal. The differences between these two works—which are almost as vast as the years between them—are chiefly ones of moral attitude. When Philostratus's Apollonius finally dispells the illusions created by the lamia, breaking her hold over the young Menippus, it is a victory of Greek rationalism over the less sophisticated forces of the universe and the expression of the epistemological prejudices of Greek thought. On the other hand, Keats, rooted in a completely different set of values, makes manifest the more Romantic sentiments of his age and decries Apollonius's narrow rationalism (". . . who look'd thereon with eye severe,/And with calm-planted steps walk'd in austere") while sympathising with the lamia and Lycius—Keats's Menippus—in their search for love no matter how transitory or elusive. While Philostratus's tale concludes when the lamia is exposed as a flesh-devouring, bloodsucking demon who had no thought for Menippus except as victim, Keats's figure is banished like a "foul dream," her real intentions never clear and Lycius dying shortly after her disappearance.

Another ancient source for later vampire tales is recorded by Phlegon of Tralles, a freedman of Hadrian. Phlegon, supposedly speaking as an eye-witness, tells of the return of a young woman named Philinnion from the grave and how she visits a young man named Machates and has sexual intercourse with him until her parents intrude to her dismay and cut short her nocturnal excursions. In 1791 Goethe took this story by Phlegon and developed it into a poem called "The Bride of Corinth." Like Keats Goethe establishes a dramatic conflict between social repression and sexual instincts. The heroine dies of grief because her fanatically religious mother refuses to let her

Ingrid Pitt as Carla in THE HOUSE THAT DRIPPED BLOOD

marry the man she loves, so she returns to him as a vampire—with death acting as a catalytic release from the sublimations of the living.

Two other fairly ancient vampire stories are "Vikram and the Vampire or Tales of Hindu Devilry" and "A Vampyre of the Fens." The former is a Hindu legend composed in Sanskrit and is, according to the wife of the translator Richard Burton, "the germ which culminated in the Arabian Nights, and which inspired the 'Golden Ass' of Apuleius, Boccaccio's 'Decamerone,' the 'Pentamerone,' and all the class of facetious fictitious literature." Vikram is an Indian hero, not unlike King Arthur, who has promised to bring back Baital (the Indian demon who reanimates corpses and can take the form of a bat) to a Magician or Jogi. In order to delay this abduction Baital proceeds to relate a number of tales, mostly humorous. After these captivating narratives have run their course and the vampire's time is expiring, Baital gives Vikram a warning regarding the treachery of the Jogi (which proves accurate) and is released by Vikram. The second work is an Anglo-Saxon poem to which Dudley Wright alludes but exact information about the text and history of the poem is not available.

Without question, the most prolific period for vampire literature has been the last two centuries. It is no coincidence that this fascination with vampirism coincides with the growth of Romanticism, with that movement's emphasis on the irrational, the instinctual, and the emotional opening the door to the supernatural and its legends. One of the earliest and perhaps best works featuring vampirism in this period is "Thalaba the Destroyer" (1797) by Robert Southey. An epic heroic fantasy in verse, Thalaba's twelve books, which are set in the Near East, look back to stories in "The Arabian Nights," to "Beowulf" and "Orlando Furioso" and forward to "The King of Elfland's Daughter" and "The Lord of the Rings" in style, structure, and use of myth. It also contains a particularly vivid description of a visitation by a vampire (a vampire who takes the form of the hero's [Thalaba's] love Oneiza) :

> The Crier from the Minaret
> Proclaim'd the midnight hour.
> 'Now, now!' cried Thalaba;
> And o'er the chamber of the tomb
> There spread a lurid light
> Oneiza stood before them. It was She, —
> Her very lineaments,—and such as death
> Had changed them, livid cheeks, and lips of blue;
> But in her eyes there dwelt
> Brightness more terrible
> than all the loathsomeness of death.
> . . . 'This is not she!' the Old Man exclaim'd;
> 'A Fiend; a manifest Fiend!'
> And to the youth he held his lance;
> 'Strike and deliver thyself!'
> 'Strike her!' cried Thalaba,
> And, palsied of all power,
> Gazed fixedly upon the dreadful form;
> . . . He thrust his lance; it fell;
> And, howling with the wound,
> Its fiendish tenant fled,
> A sapphire light fell on them,
> And garmented with glory, in their sight
> Oneiza's Spirit stood.

By far, the most important vampire work of the early 19th Century was dominated by the figure and reputation of that arch-Romantic Lord Byron. "The Vampyre" was conceived on that now legendary June night in 1816 when Percy and Mary Shelley, Lord Byron and his mistress Claire Clairmont, and Dr. John Polidori gathered in a room of their Geneva chateau to amuse themselves with horror tales. On a suggestion from Byron each member of the menage decided to compose a horror story of his or her own. Mary Shelley's contribution became the novel "Frankenstein" while Claire Clairmont and Percy produced nothing of consequence. The situation with Byron and Polidori was a little more complicated. Polidori did publish in 1819 a story called "The Vampyre;" but in its original periodical version it was credited to Byron. Byron denied authorship and Polidori stepped into the void to assert that he was actually the author although he admitted that the original outline was Byron's. Why it was originally credited to Byron has never been fully explained; but the truth of the statement that the outline was Byron's was later verified when the poet published an excerpt from an unfinished novel of his own. This excerpt is unmistakably the core, in plot and characterisation, of Polidori's story. The main character of both the unfinished novel and Polidori's tale is a Byronic hero in its fullest dimensions: a mysterious figure whose magnetism draws people to him but whose secrecy and lonely brooding preclude relationships of any depth. The initial description of Lord Ruthven, the Vampyre, in the Polidori tale illustrates this:

> It happened that in the midst of the dissipations attendant upon a London winter, there appeared at the various parties of the leaders of the "ton" a nobleman, more remarkable for his singularities, than his rank. He gazed upon the mirth around him, as if he could not participate therein. Apparently, the light laughter of the fair only attracted his attention, that he might by a look quell it, and throw fear into those breasts where thoughtlessness reigned. Those who felt this sensation of awe, could not explain whence it arose: some attributed it to the dead grey eye, which, fixing upon the object's face, did not seem to penetrate, and at one glance to pierce through to the inward workings of the heart; but fell upon the cheek with a leaden ray that weighted upon the skin it could not pass.

In the story a young, idealistic man (Aubrey) falls under Ruthven's influence and eventually becomes his friend and travelling companion (the analogy here between the Polidori-Byron relationship and the Aubrey-Ruthven one is fairly clear). During their travels in Greece, they are ambushed and Ruthven is mortally wounded; but before he dies, he extracts a promise from Aubrey not to tell of his demise.

An uncomprehending Aubrey agrees. It is, however, a promise he comes to rue; for when back in London, Ruthven appears to claim Aubrey's sister. The half-mad young man is torn between love for his sister and his innate sense of honour. He only chooses too late. The last lines are: "The guardians hastened to protect Miss Aubrey; but when they arrived, it was too late. Lord Ruthven had disappeared, and Aubrey's sister had glutted the thirst of a VAMPYRE!"

There are a few interesting bits of mythology Polidori draws on or possibly creates for this story which are not common to Eastern European-Balkans vampire legend or to most vampire literature and films. They are the restorative powers of moonlight and the extreme vulnerability of the vampire, even to ordinary bullets. These bits of exceptional vampire lore are among the few Polidori uses in the work. Excepting his need for blood, a certain magnetism, and his revivification powers Ruthven is a most "human" vampire without many of the demonic qualities and potency of later figures.

Polidori's story was an immediate success inspiring scores of plays, poems and stories for decades. In fact, the only vampire story, in the first half of the century, to come close to this tale's popularity was a "penny dreadful" serial called "Varney the Vampyre." It was written by either James Malcolm Rymer or Thomas Peckett Prest (the question is still open) and contains over two hundred episodes which were released individually during the 1840's. Although, like many of the other "penny dreadful" serials of that period, it is at times poorly written and filled with inconsistencies and ludicrous twists of plot, the main character emerges as an engaging one. "Varney" introduces us to a tortured compulsive vampire who seems to be driven on by a will not his own. He is a sympathetic figure doomed to the "life" of the undead for heinous crimes (which are ambiguously delineated in the novel). Although he wreaks bloody havoc on a number of victims, Varney's introspection and sense of guilt are redemptive qualities and his situation cannot help but elicit empathy. In the final episode Varney, after a long confession, decides upon a way to end his "life-in-death." Standing at the mouth of a fissure in Mt. Vesuvius (with a guide alongside):

> 'You will make what haste you can,' said the stranger [Varney], 'from the mountain, inasmuch as it is covered with sulphurous vapours, inimical to human life, and when you reach the city you will cause to be published an account of my proceedings, and what I say, You will say that you accompanied Varney the Vampyre to the crater of Mount Vesuvius, and that, tired and disgusted with a life of horror, he flung himself in to prevent the possibility of a reanimation of his remains.' Before then the guide could utter anything but a shriek, Varney took one tremendous leap, and disappeared into the burning mouth of the mountain.

As both the evil and good of Pompeii were indiscriminately swallowed up, so is Varney.

With "Varney" the more intricate myths long associated with the legendary vampire are absorbed into formal fiction. Like Lord Ruthven, he has magnetism, strength, and the ability to be revived by moonlight; but, in addition, the author added elements of colour derived from Eastern European lore. Vampirism becomes infectious in this novel, as the victim too becomes one of the undead, and, more significantly, the stake is introduced as a way of laying a vampire to rest.

At about the same period two Russian writers were also producing vampiric stories. they were Nikolai Gogol and Alexis Tolstoy. Gogol published a story called "The Viy;" written in his usual sardonic style, it is the tale of a young philosopher who must keep vigil beside the coffin of a vampiric witch and who is finally killed by a Satanic monster called a"Viy." Alexis Tolstoy—not to be confused with his more famous cousin Leo—produced a series of stories in a more serious vein (though they are not without their own humour). "The Vampire," "The Family of a Vourdalak," "The Reunion after Three Hundred Years," and "Amena" make up an uneven quartet which is most memorable for flights of expressionistic symbolism. The landscape of Tolstoy's stories is one where dream and reality interplay without regard for territorial rights. For instance, the hero of "The Vampire" is tormented by visions which lead him to suspect his love's relatives of vampirism, while "Amena's" main character, an early Christian, is led by a lamia to renounce his faith and friends in exchange for her illusory charms.

As the sun of Romanticism began its descent in the second half of the 19th Century, a stylistic transformation occured. Out of the ashes of this earlier, more Byronic Romanticism grew a far more morbid and extreme movement in literature and art labeled "Decadence." One of its foremost spokesmen and practitioners was the Frenchman Theophile Gautier; and it is this same Gautier who wrote one of the most intriguing vampire stories of the century—"La morte amoureuse" (known variously in English as "Clarimonde," "The Beautiful Vampire," and "The Dead Leman"). "La morte amoureuse" is a richly textured, erotic tale the style of which is best described by Gautier himself in an essay on Baudelaire's works:

> The poet of the "Fleurs du Mal" loved what is improperly called the style of decadence, and which is nothing else but art arrived at the point of extreme maturity yielded by the slanting suns of aged civilizations: an ingenious complicated style, full of shades and of research, constantly pushing back the boundaries of speech, borrowing from all the technical vocabularies, taking colour from all palettes and notes from all keyboards, struggling to render what is most inexpressible in thought, what is vague

and most elusive in the outlines of form, listening to translate the subtle confidences of neurosis, the dying confessions of passion grown depraved, and the strange hallucinations of the obsession which is turning to madness. The style of decadence is the ultimate utterance of the Word, summoned to final expressions and driven to its lasting hiding-place. Unlike the classic style it admits shadow . . .

"La morte amoureuse" tells of an "obsession which is turning to madness" and towards death. It recounts the "fall" of a naive, young priest who beholds a beautiful woman—Clarimonde, an evil courtesan who has become a vampire—at his ordination and is immediately entranced by her aspect, as conveyed in Gautier's flowing, sensual prose:

> That woman was an angel or a demon, perhaps both; she certainly did not issue from the loins of Eve, our common mother. Teeth of the purest pearl sparkled in her ruddy smile, and little dimples appeared with each motion of her mouth in the satiny rose of her adorable cheeks. As for her nostrils, they were regal in their graceful and dignified shape, and indicated the noblest origin. A lustre as of agate played upon the smooth, glossy skin of her half-bare shoulders and strings of great blonde pearls, of a shade almost like her neck, hung down upon her bosom. From time to time she elevated her head with the undulating grace of a snake, or of a startled peacock, and imparted a slight quiver to the high embroidered openwork ruff which surrounded her neck like a silver trellis work.

This obsession comes to dominate the priest's life, so that he soon finds himself more and more frequently "transported" to a voluptuous world where Clarimonde becomes his perverse and demanding mistress. He continues to live this dual life, unable to determine whether his romantic adventures are dreams or not. The resolution of this dilemma is left, as it is in Keats's "Lamia," to a severe rationalist— here the Abbé Serapion. Serapion discovers the tomb of Clarimonde and destroys her—and the young priest's illusions—with a spray of holy water.

In 1871 a novella entitled "Carmilla" was published. Its author was an Irishman, J. Sheridan Le Fanu, who specialised in tales of horror and the supernatural. "Carmilla," like its descendant "Dracula," is very much a product of the Victorian age. It has that same surface optimism, gentility, and balance which was conducive to much of the dull, stodgy fiction of the period. Even when the action verges on the violent or perverse there is always a clear-cut division between good and evil; and, of course, evil is vanquished. But just below that surface, often not very far below, lurks the darker, pessimistic, and sometimes decadent spirit which gave so much of Victorian art and culture its true depth and feeling. Le Fanu's plot centres on a young woman

Ingrid Pitt and Pippa Steele in VAMPIRE LOVERS

(Laura) who is visited by a lovely and mysterious dream image (Carmilla). In the course of the first person narrative—the novella operates within a broader tradition of journal fiction—events reveal that she is also Countess Millarca Karnstein, a vampire. In the final scenes her secret crypt is sought out and she is staked and decapitated. Already a set pattern in plot is being followed without much variation; but there is more. There are unusual subtleties here which are only discovered by studying the character of Carmilla. To begin with, Carmilla's victims are almost all females; moreover, she seems to fall in love with her victims beforehand (specifically, Laura and General Spielsdorf's niece). Finally, Carmilla is extremely sympathetic, in that she acts out of compulsion more than will—in this she is somewhat

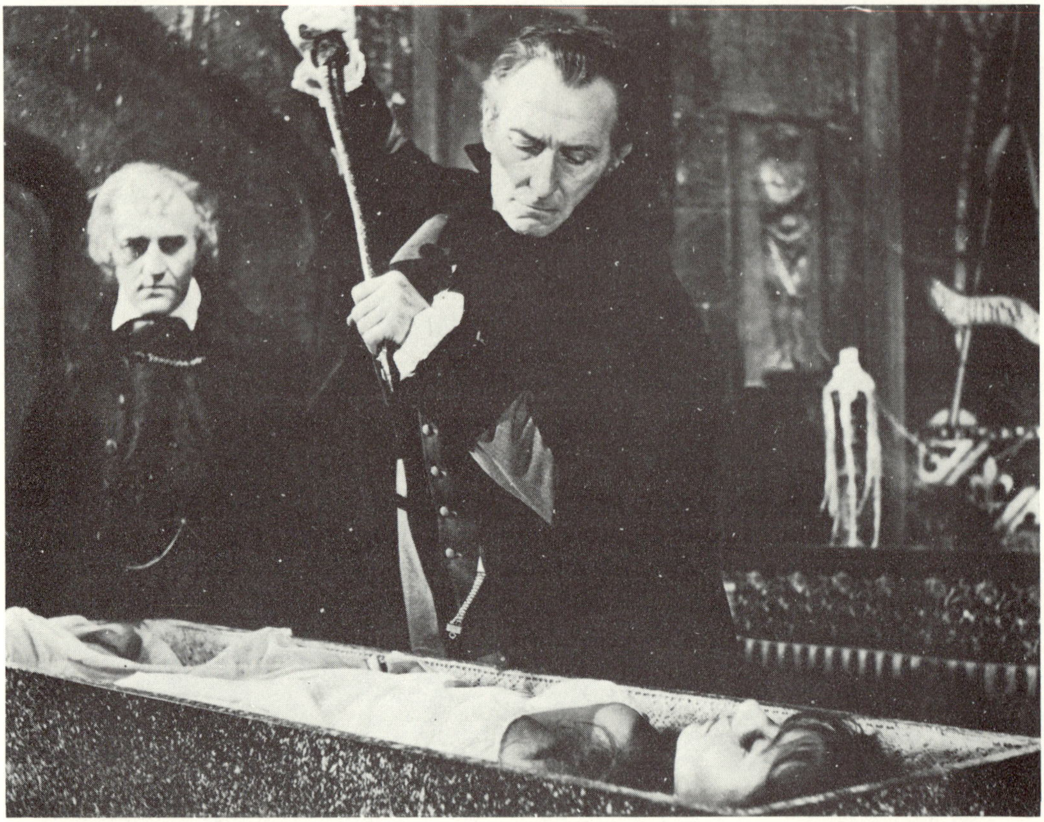

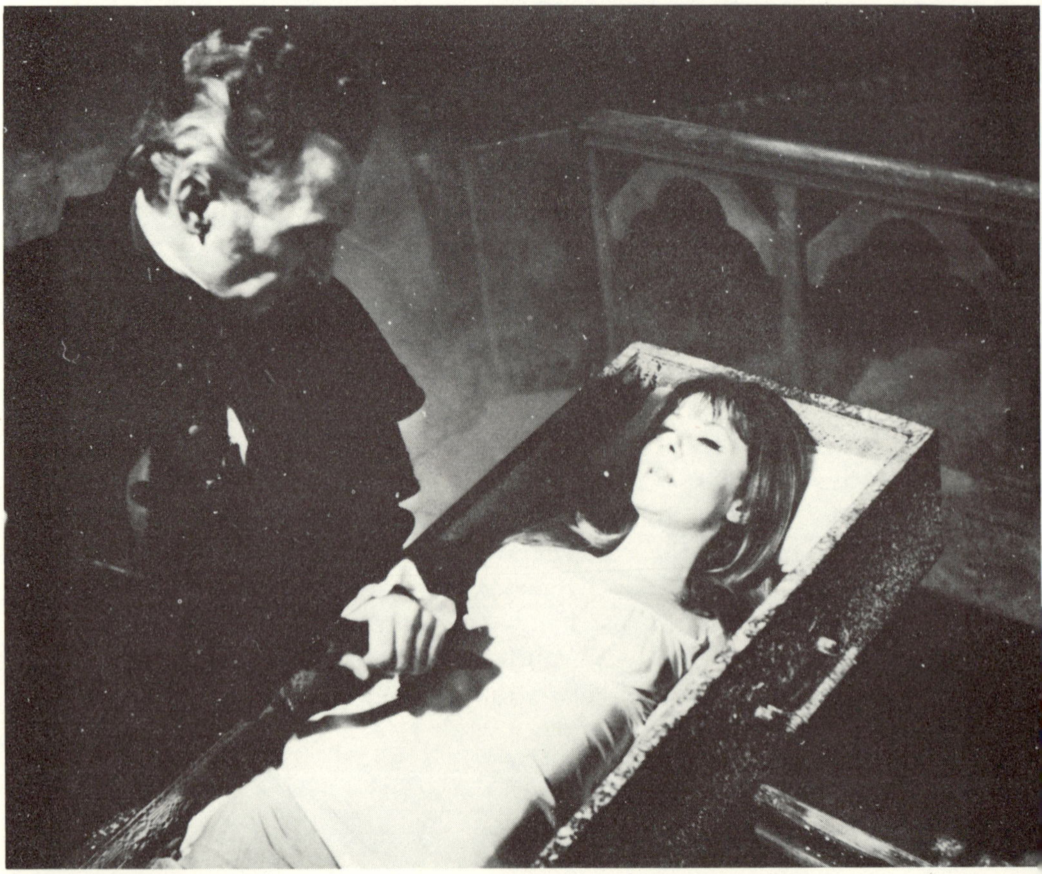

SOURCES OF THE VAMPIRE LORE IN FILM 43

reminiscent of Varney. This compulsiveness coupled with a thinly disguised lesbianism is expressed very well in the following passage:

> She [Carmilla] used to place her pretty arms about my neck, draw me to her, and laying her cheek to mine, murmur with her lips near my ear, 'Dearest, your little heart is wounded; think me not cruel because I obey the irresistible law of my strength and weakness; if your dear heart is wounded, my wild heart bleeds with yours. In the rapture of my enormous humiliation I live in your warm life, and you shall die—die, sweetly die—into mine. I cannot help it; as I draw near to you, you, in your turn, will draw near to others, and learn the rapture of that cruelty, which yet is love; so, for a while, seek to know no more of me and mine, but trust me with all your loving spirit.'

Bram Stoker's novel "Dracula" is, indisputably, the most influential work in vampire literature. With the book's publication in 1897, its predecessors in the genre were immediately overshadowed, and for a number of obvious reasons. "Dracula" represents the most involved interweaving of legends and myths that had been produced in the field. Stoker researched his subject thoroughly, seeking material in Transylvania and from eminent authorities such as Professor Arminius Vambery, who is alluded to in the book. In his research Stoker came upon the person of a Transylvanian ruler of the 15th Century—Vlad Tepes the Impaler, otherwise known as Dracula (meaning "son of the devil" or "son of the dragon"). This rather paradoxical character was reputed to be a mass murderer as well as one of the most celebrated defenders of Eastern Europe against the Turkish encroachment. But his virtues, like those of Shakespeare's Caesar, did not survive his death. They were submerged for centuries beneath a profusion of legends growing out of the facts of his atrocities. He became known within a few decades as a devil incarnate and ultimately a vampire. Building on the historical and legendary elements of this character, Stoker added even more to the myth by creating a Satanic figure who is almost invincible. His control over the elements, his polymorphism, his mesmeric faculty, his all-devouring blood lust can only be checked by someone who has studied his few weaknesses. Here Stoker establishes what has become the archetypal conflict in most of vampire literature and film to follow: between the scientist-doctor-scholar with occult knowledge and the

(Opposite: above and below)
Peter Cushing stakes Ingrid Pitt in VAMPIRE LOVERS

Peter Cushing as Van Helsing in DRACULA A.D. 1972

ravaging vampire. Stoker named his vampire stalker Professor Van Helsing and made him familiar with both the vampire and his vulnerability (namely periodic need to return to his native earth, fear of religious articles, and his susceptibility to staking, decapitation, and burning) so that he, in the final chapters, could bring about Dracula's destruction.

The stress in "Dracula," as in Le Fanu's novella, is again on the erotic. But, as in Carmilla, it is an eroticism veiled by Victorian manners and convention. An example of this is in the sensitive area of the author's idealisation of the women in his novel. The two heroines (Lucy and Mina) are representatives of the ideal Victorian woman, who is as J. H. Buckley has characterised her ". . . the pure . . . selfless center of a tightly closed domestic universe."[12] But this is only superficially true, in this novel and indeed in Victorian society itself. For

12. J. H. Buckley, "The Victorian Temper" (New York, 1964).

when the women come under the erotic-thanatotic spell of Dracula all the sexual drives, which had been so effectively repressed, are released. The attraction between the woman and the vampire in their actual encounters—for instance their fascination with Dracula's bestial *mien* or, more specifically, Mina's initiation drinking blood from his lacerated chest—are described in terms of dominance and submission. In the case of Lucy, the acquisition of a potent eroticism becomes a major factor after her death. The confrontation between the newly undead Lucy and Dr. Seward, Arthur, and Van Helsing gives an indication of the significance of sexuality in the vampire's "afterlife" while serving, incidentally, as an example of the excellence of Stoker's style when he is not attempting to mimic the mannered prose of the day:

> When Lucy—I call the thing that was before us Lucy because it bore her shape—saw us she drew back with an angry snarl, such as a cat gives when taken unawares; then her eyes ranged over us. Lucy's eyes in form and colour; but Lucy's eyes unclean and full of hell-fire, instead of the pure, gentle orbs we knew. At that moment the remnant of my love passed into hate and loathing; had she then to be killed, I could have done it with savage delight. As she looked, her eyes blazed with unholy light, and the face became wreathed with a voluptuous smile. Oh, God, how it made my shudder to see it! With a careless motion, she flung to the ground, callous as a devil, the child that up to now she had clutched strenuously to her breast, growling over it as a dog growls over a bone. The child gave a sharp cry, and lay there moaning. There was a cold-bloodedness in the act which wrung a groan from Arthur; when she advanced to him with outstretched arms and a wanton smile he fell back and hid his face in his hands. She still advanced, however, and with a languourous, voluptuous grace, said: 'Come to me, Arthur. Leave these others and come to me. My arms are hungry for you. Come, and we can rest together. Come, my husband, come!' There was something diabolically sweet in her tones—something of the tinkling of glass when struck—which rang through the brains even of us who heard the word addressed to another. As for Arthur, he seemed under a spell; moving his hands from his face, he opened wide his arms.

Ultimately, "Dracula's" enduring virtues lie in its immediacy, pacing, and in its power to evoke vivid moods. Like "Carmilla" the story is essentially told in first person narrative; but in Stoker's novel there is more than one narrator and so, through a series of letters, diaries and newspaper reports, the events (some of them the same) are recorded from different perspectives. The constant narrative rupture induced by this device is a key to the novel's genuine suspense, as the various perspectives gradually piece together the "reality" of the supernatural and seem to converge on the Borgo Pass for the climax of the

Bela Lugosi greets Dwight Frye in DRACULA (1931)

pursuit and the vampire's dissolution. To reinforce all this Stoker distills the essential mood from the somber style of the Gothic tradition. Dracula haunts medieval castles and abbeys dressed in penumbral attire, seeming to merge with the night; wolves and bats are his familiars and his home a coffin. All that the twentieth century has come to associate with the vampire, from his needle-sharp canine teeth to his retinue of gypsies is present and correct.

Shortly after the turn of the century and only a few years after "Dracula's" first printing, stories in sharp contrast to the "Stoker tradition" began to appear. First, writers introduced what can only be called "non-human" vampires. H. G. Wells did this in a tale about vampire vegetation called "The Flowering of the Strange Orchid" and so did E. F. Benson in "And No Bird Sings." H. P. Lovecraft went one step further and made his vampire inanimate: the story was "The Shunned House" and featured a "vampire building." In still another direction, writers such as Arthur Conan Doyle and Algernon Blackwood began to play with the idea of a "psychic vampire"— one who feeds off the brain waves or psychic energies of another. The notion was introduced in Doyle's "The Parasite" and in Blackwood's "The

A scene in the abbey from DRACULA (1931)

Transfer" but was not developed to any significant degree in the work of others. Perhaps the most enduring re-interpretation of the vampire was through the conceit of the man-eater into the body and soul of the *femme fatale*. As a result of a painting by Philip Burne-Jones and an accompanying poem by his kinsman Rudyard Kipling ("The Vampire"), the term came to represent a very human and non-supernatural creature who sucked the life out of her male lovers and then ruthlessly discarded them, a connotation which the word "vampire" has retained to this day.

There have been a few other landmarks of varying significance in vampire literature. Guy de Maupassant's frightening tale of mounting insanity deals with a rather non-substantial and invisible vampire called a "horla." F. Marion Crawford tells the story of a vampire suffering from unrequited love in "For the Blood Is the Life." Montague James made his contribution with "Count Magnus"—which Lovecraft praises highly in his essay on "Supernatural Horror in Literature"—and "An Episode of Cathedral History." E. F. Benson in a change of pace from his "non-human" vampires, delineates, in "Mrs. Amworth," a genuinely "human" vampire of the female sex.

And Luigi Capuana places his fiend in an Italianate setting in "A Vampire." Possibly the most creative use of the vampire myth in the early half of this century has been Clark Ashton Smith's in his tale cycle "Zothique." "Zothique" is an imaginary and imaginative view of the earth in its last days when "the coal-red sun" is "oblique" and "dead gods drink the brine." In this perishing world man again turns to the occult arts and to the ancient superstitions—vampirism among them. "He who loved the wild girls of Zothique shall come not back a gentler love to seek, nor know the vampire's from the lover's kiss. For him the scarlet ghost of Lilith from time's last necropolis rears amorous and malign." Smith paints with a vivid style similar to Gautier's a portrait of a luxuriant civilization peopled with vampiric succubi and those enraptured by their rapacious love.

Today vampire literature is being produced at a rate which is little short of astounding. Unfortunately, a good deal of this is pulp: paperbacks, comic books, and tabloids dealing with Dracula and/or other vampires are rife and usually of the lowest quality—rarely achieving even the competency of the "penny dreadfuls." There are, as always, exceptions: Richard Matheson in his novel " I Am Legend" has combined science fiction and vampire myths with interesting results. While more satirical writers like Robert Bloch have added touches of humour to the genre (as in "The Cloak") . Some other fascinating twists have been supplied by writers like Fritz Leiber who in "The Girl with the Hungry Eyes" combines a sardonic critique of society's modern advertising techniques with a stereotyped female vampire and Manly Wade Wellman who in "When It Was Moonlight" assumes the point of view of the vampire.

2. The Formal Visual Arts: Vampiric figures do not occur in the formal visual arts of painting and sculpture with the same regularity as in literature. Although there is a Babylonian sculpture of a vampire in the Louvre, most of the art works depicting vampires have been done in the last century—probably as a result of the fairly recent blossoming of surrealism and expressionism. These movements have provided a natural opening for the kind of fantasy treatment vampirism is inherently associated with. For example, Edvard Munch, the Dane, concentrated on sketches of bloody female vampires (e.g. "The Vampire") while his contemporary Max Ernst turned his surrealist leanings to more consciously symbolic paintings (e.g. "Une semaine de bonté"). Felicien Rops and Clovis Trouille, in Western Europe, took a slightly more outrageous tack in their depiction of similarly vampiric subjects. Trouille has been particularly drawn to saturated colours and outlandish humour in works like "Le rêve vampyr" and

"Mon tombeau" while Rops is famous for the eroticism and morbidity which he applied to the genre. The real center of activity in vampire art, however, has been in the pop category. Comic books, in recent years, have flooded the market with vampire issues. Though the illustrations are generally of uneven quality, there are exceptions. The "Vampirella" comics are a particularly good example: their illustrations are usually well-drawn and their multi-colour covers are, according to the publishers, their most important asset in sales. Finally, there are the T-shirts, posters, and even bottle caps which have been distributed in the last few years and which feature a vampire motif. The pop horror art market seems, at present, to have kept pace with the rise in popularity of both the occult arts and vampire films.

3. The Dramatic Arts: As mentioned earlier, Polidori's story "The Vampyre" caused such a sensation in Europe that it inspired a sequel of poems, stories, and plays for the next several decades. The earliest theatrical adaptation was staged in Paris by Charles Nodier and was itself a great success. At about the same time, J. R. Planché in London was producing his own "vampire drama" based more substantially on the Nodier piece than on the Polidori original. Planché, however, employed a more operatic format for his play and called it "The Vampyre or The Bride of the Isles." It, too, was a grand hit and, incidentally, developed a complex stage device known as the "vampire trap" door. In both these renderings, the once very human Lord Ruthven was transformed into a consummate, inhuman villain who receives his just punishment in the form of a lightning bolt. The public responded well to this less Byronic, melodramatic fiend, and adaptations of Nodier's play proliferated. In 1828, in Leipzig, "Der Vampyr" opened. This time Ruthven was an evil Wallachian nobleman who inhabited a Gothic manor and spoke with a thick Eastern European accent. This version was eventually brought to London and is purported to have inspired Bram Stoker's conception of Dracula. In 1851 the incredibly prolific Alexandre Dumas (père), not to be outdone by his contemporaries in any area, added to the list of Ruthven dramas yet another entitled "Le vampire," a play even more excessive and lacking in distinction than its predecessors. Inevitably, this saturation of the vampire theatre with Ruthven and his *semblables* compelled playwrights to seek a new approach to the situation—and satires were the result. A. E. Scribe, the master of the "well-made play," wrote such a comedy and called it, predictably enough, "Le vampire." In it he lampooned the character of Ruthven by having one of his *personae* masquerade as the Lord to the general consternation of the other characters. Similar burlesques were produced around the same time with varying success

—some, in Paris, even competed against each other in neighbouring playhouses.

Stoker's "Dracula" also left its mark in the theatre. The first to produce an adaptation of the novel was Stoker's mentor, the stage luminary, Henry Irving. In 1897, shortly after the novel's publication, Irving presented a version which lasted over four hours and consisted of more than forty scenes. The most famous dramatisation of Stoker's novel, however—one still produced today—came after the novelist's death. The adaptor and director was Hamilton Deane, who premiered his "Dracula" in June of 1924. Much shorter than the Irving version and confined in its action to the London portions of Stoker's story, this play was so successful that in 1927 Deane exported it to America. John Balderston collaborated on the American playscript (which was not significantly different) and the newest "Dracula" had its New York premiere in October of 1927. The actors engaged to portray Dracula and Van Helsing were Bela Lugosi and Edward Van Sloan—both of whom were brought to Los Angeles for the Universal film adaptation in 1931. Although the American production was another financial and critical triumph, Deane preferred to go on tour with a new company, which he did for a number of seasons.

In recent years there have been periodic theatrical versions of classic vampire stories, but none with the impact of the Nodier and Deane plays. One notably innovative and recent exception is the New York E.T.C. Company of Cafe La Mama's staging of "Carmilla." This multimedia chamber opera with rock-jazz-classical score and an emphasis on the erotic-lesbian elements of the original is remarkably faithful to Le Fanu in characterisation, plot, and dialogue and may be the only adaptation in any medium which has successfully transliterated the dual drives of the novella. The piece is so stylised that only the two principals, Laura and Carmilla, are ever present in full stage reality (the others being incorporated quite literally into the decor, their heads visible as decorative parts of a high-backed sofa on which Laura and Carmilla sit). The sexuality as well as the parasitic aspects implicit in this absence of others is given physical and emotional release in the energetic semi-arias which these two sing from their perpetual stage centre position. In scenes such as the destruction of the vampire (seen on film projected above the actors) viewed simultaneously as premonition and real event (in past and/or future) by the two women, the opera works with time in a manner beyond Le Fanu and accurately captures, where he could at best suggest, the anguish of not merely perpetual life but perpetual re-living which is peculiar to the vampire myth.

CHAPTER TWO

The Male Vampire

And day and night she's followed him
His teeth so bright did shine,
As he led her over the mountain,
Did the sly, bold Reynardine
     Anonymous Ballad

His face was a strong—a very strong—aquiline, with high bridge of the thin nose and peculiarly arched nostrils; with lofty domed forehead, and hair growing scantily around the temples but profusely elsewhere. His eyebrows were very massive, almost meeting over the nose, and with bushy hair that seemed to curl in its own profusion. The mouth, so far as I could see it under the heavy moustache, was fixed and rather cruel looking, with peculiarly sharp white teeth; these protruded over the lips, whose remarkable ruddiness showed astonishing vitality in a man of his years. For the rest, his ears were pale, and at the tops extremely pointed; the chin was broad and strong, and the cheeks firm though thin. The general effect was one of extraordinary pallor . . . The hands were rather coarse—broad with squat fingers. Strange to say, there were hairs in the centre of the palm. The nails were long and fine and cut to a sharp point. As the Count leaned over me and his hands touched me, I could not repress a shudder.
     Bram Stoker, "Dracula"

I. THE VAMPIRE FIGURE

Character Conventions. Synthesizing a set of conventional characteristics for the vampire in formal fiction is as difficult as positing the *sine qua non* of the vampire from the vast diversity of oral legend or of fact. As the individual work within the *genre* continues, it is inevitable that almost all the standard assumptions about the vampire be tested, that folk-tales and myths, literary, graphic, and cinematic traditions alike be broken down into component parts and form a nearly infinite range of inexhaustible potential for new combinations. In film particularly, the process of formulating a *genre* type is compounded even further by the medium's inherent multiplicity of verbal, visual and aural expressions. Obviously, the core of the fiction is the character of the vampire itself, whether described as a vortex of malevolence, lust, and savagery or, alternately, as the unwilling victim who becomes a tormented, driven, even tragic figure. But the fairly standard assumption that he or she, or perhaps more aptly it, is "undead" is still qualified by the lore from which the film-makers draw and expanded by the possibilities of narrative invention. As a result, the vampire in film remains a complex and curiously ambivalent figure, and when the usual icons are decomposed or discarded, when the teeth do not shine so brightly as the rakish Reynardine's, as difficult to penetrate as the phenomena surrounding him are rationally inexplicable.

It is equally clear that, in practical terms, the vampire is not that difficult to recognise. The Byronic figure, seductive, erotic, possessing a hypnotic power which makes its questionable charms seem irresistible to its victims is still the starting point for all but a few film characterisations. Most often, as the *revenant* in order to extend its existence

German Robles and Ariadne Welter in EL ATAUD DEL VAMPIRO

offers sexual pleasure and, coincidentally, appeals to the death wish of its prey, the dramatic interplay between the vampire and its lovers becomes a fusion of basic human instincts, not just self-preservative libidinal but also self-destructive, a ritual of "seeking to" as Freud suggests, "bring them back to their primeval, inorganic states."[1] The bride and groom of the vampire are, like the lists of unfortunates who have captured the fancy of the Greek gods, confronted by a potent metaphysical entity and, without the knowledge of ceremonial or symbolic defenses, killed by advances which are overwhelming by their sheer physical and sexual power. The key to the mythical qualities of Reynardine, Ruthven, Dracula and all those who follow after them in film is in this super-humanness. In a totemic sense these undead represent the arch-need of man to purge himself of his severest repressions, they are tokens through which vicariously the most sacred of taboos may be violated and sins that cry to heaven for vengeance committed. They rise up out of men's hidden fears *and* desires, glorying in their revulsive appetites and endowed with an epic quality like that of Milton's striding, primordial Death:

> To me, who with eternal famine pine,
> Alike is Hell, or Paradise, or Heaven,
> There best where most with ravin I may meet:
> Which here, though plenteous, all too little seems
> To stuff this maw, this vast unhidebound corpse.
> ("Paradise Lost" X, 597-601)

Most often then, the vampire is, like Satan, a ruthless stalker of men, attaining the life-blood of the body through the soul, possessing its lover in all senses of the word by instilling a cupidity for love and death in the mind of its object and simultaneously fulfilling it. The very nature of the undead state, willed or unwilled, violates not only the Christian concepts of life and afterlife but the dispassionate, intellectual notions of love as well. Small wonder then that Reynardine requires "concealment all from the pious men," because, for these most basic of reasons, the vampire is unnatural, sometimes definitely diabolical, and by virtue of its loathsome practices necessarily antithetical to society and its values.

Narrative and Visual Conventions

Beyond the character archetype which film has refined from a variety of sources, elements of the narrative and the *mise-en-scène*—from the locales, costumes, and make-up to the lighting and sound effects—have

---
1. "Civilization and Its Discontents".

also been conventionalised to varying degrees.

To begin with the vampire films are set, almost without exception, over the last one hundred and fifty years, which has come to mean that the action is set either sometime during the Nineteenth century or contemporary to the date of production—the former, as it happens usually being the case with European and Mexican productions (probably because of their more diverse architectural history and easier access to baronial houses, medieval churches, and other older structures) and the latter with American films. The implications of the period setting, which is by far the most frequently chosen of the two, are manifold in terms of specific imagery: Victorian cities with gas-lit, cobblestoned avenues and alleyways alternate with country manors and mountainous castles containing what H. P. Lovecraft has called the "dramatic paraphernalia" of fantasy in general:

> First of all the Gothic castle with its awesome antiquity, vast distances and ramblings, dark corridors, unwholesome hidden catacombs . . . and the infinite array of strange lamps, damp trap-doors, extinguished lights, mouldy hidden manuscripts, creaking hinges, shaking arras, and the like.[2]

Perhaps even more significant than these recognised icons, in relation to the expectations which the average viewer brings to the *genre*, is the notion that there was a general lack of sophistication in the 19th and early 20th centuries. Insulated from the people of that era by this sense of temporal, ethical, and practical distance the audience can accept and participate empathetically in the reality of that time's belief in vampires. Reinforcing this narrative assumption is a rather basic iconography. A traveller's reliance on horsedrawn conveyances, the necessity of passing through long stretches of open country and dense forests where night descends like a blanket, even in the towns and villages where a ground fog turns the high street into a sea of mist—everyday realities like these in a period context are suddenly rife with threatening elements, so that a shift to the still more alien locus of a mountain landscape or the high-vaulted cobwebbed interior of a *schloss* or tenebrous crypt becomes inevitably perilous, a clear sign to those having a minimal awareness of how the *genre* functions of imminent danger and perhaps approaching death.

As much as apprehension of dying or simple dread of the unknown engages the viewer's involvement with the narrative—and again the greater expressive impact of period makes it more acceptable to stage extremely melodramatic occurrences without testing viewer suspension

---

[2]. H. P. Lovecraft, "Supernatural Horror in Literature" in "Dagon" (New York, 1969).

of disbelief too severely—the converse, the fear that the vampire's audacity and power will preserve him from annihilation, has established a catalogue of events which are most likely to define the conflict between the human protagonist and vampiric antagonist. After the presence of the undead has been demonstrated—either directly by including an actual attack in the narrative or indirectly by the discovery of a blood-drained victim or victims—there normally follows an exhibition of the vampire's peculiar attributes (invulnerability to conventional weapons; preternatural strength; and/or metamorphoses into bat, wolf, etc.) common to legend but which only motion pictures, by means of special effects (bullets passing through to explode against the wall behind the figure; men and heavy objects being hurled aside like gimcracks; optical mattes and superimpositions achieving the change in form) can give those ascribed traits the impact of a high degree of graphic reality. After the particular protective devices—cross, wolfsbane, mirror, or whatever—are introduced, film is again uniquely capable of rendering the destruction of a vampire with grisly actuality, and the ritual of staking, burning, or beheading is usually enhanced by a visual contrivance which reduces the once-animated corpse to ashes or dust. Whether it is the illusion or the very melodrama of seeing these things happen on screen—with slight variations from the pattern in the face of innumerable repetitions of the basic scheme—they continue to elicit the most substantial viewer response, to constitute the narrative and visual foundations of the entire genre, which any individual motion picture may play with or against but cannot ignore.

II. DRACULA

Stoker's description of Count Dracula reproduced at the beginning of this chapter is the seminal portrait of that character from which all succeeding interpretations must theoretically be constructed; and yet it is quite apparent that the universally recognised film Dracula, who is in both attire and aspect the epitome of the male vampire, derives from other sources. Of all the incarnations of undead Transylvanian noblemen, from the spectral Max Schreck to the panther-like Christopher Lee, from slender, soft-spoken John Carradine to the heavy-set, belligerent Lon Chaney Jr., from the sinister German Robles in Mexico's *Nostradamus* series to the effete Robert Quarry as the campish Count Yorga, no other has so dominated the role and infused it with his personal mannerisms as the Hungarian, Bela Lugosi. It is somewhat ironic that Lugosi—who moved from the stage production to the film role because of Lon Chaney Sr.'s untimely death—should

Bela Lugosi as "Dracula" on the stage, circa 1928

Top: Lon Chaney as Count Alucard/Dracula with his wife, Louise Allbritton in SON OF DRACULA

Below: Christopher Lee in DRACULA—PRINCE OF DARKNESS

John Carradine in HOUSE OF DRACULA

so completely *become* Dracula, that the countenance and speech of this quasi-fictional Carpathian boyar[3] should be so irrevocably linked with Lugosi's pallid expressions and peculiar rendering of what Stoker dubbed a "strange intonation."[4] It could be argued that Schreck was more cosmetically terrifying, that Carradine has more grace, Chaney more brute force, Lee more erotic energy and sheer presence, that any of them were closer in some way to Stoker's original idea; but whenever a comic breaks into a vampire parody, the accent and florid gestures, the thick "Good Ev-e-ning," are unmistakably Lugosi's. The perpetuation of the Lugosi Dracula via televised airings of his old pictures and advertising in which mimics sell hair spray, throat remedies, and even hot dogs, and in the face of dozens of later *Dracula* adaptations, is so dominant a factor that a reader of the novel who has experienced all of this may try to visualize Stoker's own version

---

[3.] For details of Stoker's borrowing from the history of Vlad Tepes see McNally and Florescu's books "In Search of Draccla" and "Dracula: A Historical Biography."

[4.] No doubt accentuated by the fact that Lugosi's poor English compelled him to read his lines phonetically on stage and in the early films.

German Robles stalking his prey in EL ATAUD DEL VAMPIRO

of the character—stockier, older, with bushy grey hair, a moustache, and a "very strong" face—only to have the image of Lugosi, caped and top-hatted, coming out of the fog to mesmerise a doomed flower girl, force its way in.

This very genuine stereotypification of the Dracula figure adds to the list of expectations already associated with the *genre*, so that the dark clothes and full-flowing red-lined cape, the hair brushed back straight and flat from the forehead, the lips extraordinarily crimson and distended in an eerie smile which reveals abnormally long canines are specifically as common to the Hammer productions starring Lee as to the Lugosi vehicles made by Universal. Even Lee's most recent essay of the role in *Count Dracula (El conde Dracula*, 1971, directed by Jesus Franco), which claims to be a return to the novel's description, retains many of these aspects. Accordingly, the list of male vampires in motion pictures who adhere to the basic conception represented by Lugosi in the Thirties and Forties and by Lee since the Hammer series began is a lengthy one—Lugosi himself in *Dracula* (1931),

Mark of the Vampire, Return of the Vampire, and numerous cameos; Carradine in *House of Frankenstein, House of Dracula,* and *Billy the Kid vs. Dracula;* Chaney in *Son of Dracula;* Francis Lederer in *Curse of Dracula;* Lee in *Dracula* (1958), *Dracula, Prince of Darkness, Taste the Blood of Dracula, Dracula has Risen from the Grave, Scars of Dracula, Dracula A.D. 1972, Count Dracula,* and the comedy *Uncle Was a Vampire;* Robles as Nostradamus and Count Duval in a half-dozen titles; Quarry in *Count Yorga—Vampire, Return of Count Yorga,* and *The Deathmaster;* and finally Jack Palance in *Dracula* (1974) to cite only the most widely-seen films and discounting sympathetic portrayals which will be discussed later.

All this is not to say that the typing of the male vampire is total or rigid, that the characterisations of Dracula or the narrative and expressive values of the various films which feature him, by name or by implication, are of an inflexible sameness; but their diversity and invention are perhaps best explored and understood from the context of these well-established and truly world-wide (one has only to glance at the make-up of the title character of Japan's *Lake of Dracula* for confirmation of that) conventions of the genre.

Nosferatu

F. W. Murnau's *Nosferatu* (1922), the first film version of "Dracula," remains to this day the most imagistically unusual and expressionistic of all the adaptations.[5] The opening is a quote from Van Helsing [Prof. Bulwer] followed by a hazy panorama of Bremen with a church spire in the nearground, and the introduction of Harker [Hutter] and his wife, Mina [Ellen]. Besides the evocation of period, these shots set a tone, in the immediate tension between foreground and rearground and the array of detail in a deep frame, of unseen forces in contention, reinforced by the overt determinism of the dialogue ("Wait, young man—you cannot escape your destiny by running away"). Harker is dispatched by Renfield [Knock], a sinister bald-headed man in a tight fitting tail-coat who reads cabbalistic inscriptions, to Orlof's castle with an equally overt warning: "Do not be surprised if people speak of Transylvania as a land of phantoms." Harker's arrival in the land of phantoms—after he has consigned Mina to the care of Lucy Westenra [Annie Harding] and her husband—resembles the same scene in the novel, but is full of visual novelties from the simple insert of a lurking jackal to the use of under-cranking and a negative image as Orlof's

[5]. Murnau's Dracula is called Count Orlock or Orlof and the rest of the character names were also altered, which along with changes in the plot was designed to avoid legal difficulties since the producer did not have permission to adapt the Stoker novel then protected by unexpired international copyright. Certain English-language prints restored the original names—Harker for Hutter, Renfield for Knock, etc.—in the titles.

NOSFERATU: the vampire aboard the ship

funereal coach arrives to pick up Harker in a sustained long shot. Besides these manifestly surreal effects, Schreck's make-up—he resembles a giant bat with an oversized cranium, sunken eyes, a beak nose set above long crooked teeth, and tufts of white hair about his pointed ears—the shots of shadows cast by his thin body or gaunt hands with mandarin-like nails and back-lit views of his unnatural frame in Gothic archways become unsettling visual motifs. The many iris shots hint at enclosure, constriction of the image which graphically supports Orlof's unequivocal, "You cannot escape;" moreover, the Count's remark on seeing a miniature of Mina—"Is this your wife? What a lovely throat."—and the parallel montage between Mina's "somnambulistic dream" and Orlof's spectre looming over the hapless Harker combine to suggest the vampire's disquieting ability towards thought projection and mind control. Murnau's stylisation persists long after the plot disjointedly interfaces with the novel: more undercranking as Orlof leaves for Bremen with a load of coffins and slaughters the crew of the schooner that transports him during a gale; Van Helsing lecturing on the Venus fly-trap intercut with Renfield catching flies in a sanatorium; Mina reading a letter from Harker along the beach, where the same onshore winds which carry Orlof towards the city have bent the cemetery crosses to the ground.

The shift away from Transylvania and the intrinsic temporal distortions to the psycho-sexual conflict between the undead and Mina inspires an extrinsic change in pacing. As the plague spreads over Bremen and rats follow in Orlof's wake, Murnau orchestrates his self-styled "symphony of terrors" with fluctuating tempos, employing long takes and compositions of depth and great contrast for the processional lines of dead but shorter cuts as the escaped Renfield is pursued down narrow alleyways and across the rooftops. Orlof watching Mina's room from the window of a house across the street stands rigid and unblinking; while she paces frenziedly, having gained possession of the "Book of the Vampire" which Harker found at Castle Orlof, and prays for strength to sacrifice herself to end the chain of vampiric killings. The film's final effect is pressed into service after Orlof is seduced into remaining with her until after sunrise: he writhes and disintegrates as the light strikes him; Mina expires as well.

Coming as it does at the head of a very long list of films, *Nosferatu* can only be situated generically in retrospect. Thematically, Murnau discovers the potential of narrative distortions and externalised dream states from the beginning, using *mise-en-scène* to alternately condense and expand certain events—both interiorly when he tampers with camera speed and exteriorly in the selection and duration of shots in

NOSFERATU: Nina by the ocean

NOSFERATU: Orlof is caught by the first rays of the sun

his editing scheme—to detach his narrative cleanly from the convention of realism and relocate it elsewhere. While Murnau's visual contrivances—the undercranking; the negative insertions; doors opening by themselves; the dissolution of the vampire—have not all become part of the lexicon of the *genre's* recurring special effects, his choice of an extra-normal style for such a subject, that was already well-grounded in the various horror and fantasy films made before *Nosferatu,* bridged that tradition and all subsequent vampire films. One addition to the Stoker plot—the vampire's fatal susceptibility to sunlight, whereas the novel's character was able to emerge during the day suffering only the impairment of certain faculties such as transformation—has since become a generic constant which is seldom violated. More significantly, Murnau's expressionistic frenzy demonstrated that an exposition and treatment of the Dracula figure which is essentially visual can easily be as dramatic in engendering suspense and eliciting viewer response as the dialogue confrontations of the popular Deane-Balderston play.

The Expressionistic Tradition in America

Tod Browning's *Dracula* (1931), the earliest sound film in the *genre,* represents its first synthesis of stage and cinematic traditions. Browning "opens up" the play as soon as the titles fade with a process shot of a stagecoach in the narrow defile of the Borgo Pass; but the immediate connotations are not particularly ominous. Inside the conveyance a bespectacled tourist placidly leafs through a guidebook, and the

Bela Lugosi and Helen Chandler in DRACULA (1931)

broadlit location exteriors appear relatively free from threat. Renfield (fulfilling the part played by Harker in the analogous portion of the novel) is isolated visually from the others by a panning shot as he dismounts at the way-station, but this remains undeveloped as a verbal exposition supersedes—"It's Walpurgis Night. The night of evil. Nosferatu," and, "At the Castle there are vampires: Dracula and his wives. They take the form of the wolves and bats and feed on the blood of the living." The peasants' exaggerated warnings and repeated signs of the cross might normally be neutralised by Renfield's undiminished resolve to proceed to Castle Dracula ("That's just superstition . . . it's a matter of business with me"), but for the fact that the evocation of the *genre* has already directed viewer expectations in a certain direction.

The remainder of the prologue is a justifiably classic introduction of the Dracula figure: the emergence of the vampire and his wives from the subterranean coffins; the hovering bat which leads Renfield's carriage up to the Count's fortified mountain lair; the huge oaken door which opens with a cracking sound that suggests centuries of disuse and within the disarray and debris through which rats and armadillos forage; finally, Dracula himself descending the stairs with a candle that casts a feeble light over the massive stonework and solemnly intoning, "Listen to them, the children of the night. What music they make!" Karl Freund's photography—which never manages to hit Lugosi squarely with an eye-light—is remarkably controlled in this and other large interiors, on the one hand rendering the great hall with a somber expansiveness and on the other creating a suffocating intensity in the chambers upstairs, as Dracula hungrily watches his prey squeeze a drop of blood from a cut finger, a sequence which ends in a sustained shot after the stifled Renfield faints and the wives approach only to be turned back by Dracula who then bends to the prostrate man's neck.

Little of the rest of the film compares with this first portion. Visually, the few conspicuously stylised usages—the shadow of the dead schooner captain lashed to the wheel, reminiscent of *Nosferatu*; the craning shot across the sanatorium lawn up to and through the window of Renfield's room; the glimpse of Dracula and Lucy, after she has become "the bloofer lady," prowling in the park hedges—stand out without much effect, dispersed as they are between long dialogue scenes staged in medium and medium close shot. Even the return to architectonic vastness in the concluding sequence at Carfax Abbey is flattened by full-light and lenses of greater focal-length. Throughout the narrative, the most extraordinary events are reported rather than visualised—"He came to me; he opened a vein in his arm and made me drink"—as Browning is content to cutaway at the critical moment of every attack and indulge in ironic touches (as when Harker seeing the wounds on Mina's throat asks, "What could have caused them, Professor?" or the maid announces "Count Dracula" in voiceover before Van Helsing can reply). The ability to hypnotise and assume a bat-like shape are givens which are never reinforced by means of convincing optical work—the bat hovering outside Lucy's window returns to human shape through the benefit of a cut to the sleeping woman and a pan back to Lugosi at the foot of the bed—and never achieve even the understated impact of the simple device earlier in the film that has Dracula slip through a cobweb on the stairs of his castle, which the corporeal

Renfield cannot penetrate, to occasion a sardonic observation: "A spider spinning his web for the unwary fly. The blood is the life, Mr. Renfield." Even the hint of weariness which Dracula lets slip at the opera—"To die, to be really dead, that must be glorious . . . there are worse things awaiting man than death."—bespeaks a certain consciousness of lingering humanity on his part which is never amplified in later scenes. In a film which is already excessively verbal, Dracula, given increasingly to casual observations rather than action and more often spoken of than he is present on screen, assumes an off-handed haughtiness in his encounters with Van Helsing; although the latter interpreted by Edward Van Sloan with stolid determination and armed with wolfsbane, mirrors, and crosses is more than a fair match and wrests an admission of that ("Your will is strong, Van Helsing") and a wry compliment ("For a man who has not lived even one lifetime, you are wise, Van Helsing") from his adversary.

Perhaps the root difficulty with this *Dracula* is that even though modern (1931) London and Transylvania are thoroughly camouflaged, Van Helsing's dismay that "the strength of the vampire is that people will not believe in him" and his assertion that "yesterday's myth is today's science" are too insistent, too much the pronouncements of a Nineteenth century man undercut by a contemporary context of which he is markedly unaware. His single-minded combat with the undead is encapsulated but unable to carry the entire film. Mina's precipitous eroticism, transferred from Lucy in the novel, is introduced in the last reel; the laying to rest of "the bloofer lady" is not even included in the narrative. After an overabundance of static scenes, the film is stripped of a climax as Van Helsing stakes Dracula off-screen, with only a dull thud and a groan bearing witness to the event.

Browning followed *Dracula* with *Mark of the Vampire* (1935). Again there are the Eastern-European setting, the knowing professor, and some exquisitely Baroque images of dark figures moving through obscure passageways or of Luna flying with ragged silk wings like some decayed waterfowl, photographed by James Wong Howe with as much bravura as the menacing prologue of the earlier film. Again also there is reliance on expository dialogue, unavoidably so in the disclosure that all of it has been an elaborate sham to trap a commonplace murderer, which dissipates almost totally the iconic potential that has been built up.

In many ways, Robert Siodmak's *Son of Dracula* (1943) represents the liberation of the Dracula figure from these traditional, stagebound constructions. To begin with, the vampire itself is reduced to a subordinate role; but vampirism as a moral and ontological question becomes thematically central. While Count Alucard—a crude Dracula anagram—is treated more as a phenomenon than an actual personage, his scenes remain the expressive core of the film. His initial appearance is part of an elaborate craning shot, which—in contrast to the example of this technique in *Dracula*—pulls back from a dance in a country estate, travelling across a terrace and garden and stops abruptly on a high angle medium close shot of Alucard gazing at the house, a revelation which is sudden and startling despite the anticipatory camera movement, almost as if the figure had drawn attention to itself or somehow intruded into the frame while remaining immobile. Established by the dynamic of this shot as a force to be reckoned with, Alucard momentarily spreads his cape, compresses his massive form into that of a bat, and departs. The vampire's first nocturnal rising is equally impressive: a coffin breaks the surface of the swamp water, a mist seeps out from beneath the lids, congeals, and becomes the vampire who then propels the strange vessel forward by some psycho-kinetic command towards an eager victim awaiting him on the bank (the shot is taken from over Alucard's shoulder, floating silently with him across the pond).

Kay Caldwell, Alucard's willing victim, is less obsessed with him than with the freedom from death which he symbolises. Inheriting a Southern plantation house after her father is killed by Alucard, she rejects her former lover and marries the Count in order to become undead and immortal herself. After Frank Stanley, the discarded suitor, inadvertantly shoots her, when the bullets he intends for Alucard pass through his insubstantial "body" and into hers, she is reanimated and appears to him, in jail for her murder, to explain the premeditation behind her actions ("Frank, isn't eternity together better than a few years of ordinary life?") and to convert him to vampirism. This sequence of impacted narrative ironies which reduce the Dracula figure to something of a cipher for Kay Caldwell's aspirations towards eternal life speculates ambitiously on the notion of immortality so pivotal to the myth of the vampire.

Eventually, Frank eliminates Alucard by burning his coffin full of native earth hidden in a viaduct, then he immolates Kay in an upper room of her house. As the natural equilibrium of a complete and genuine cessation of life is restored, the staging which concludes the film—cross-travellings to underscore the once arrogant vampire's impotent terror on descrying the fiery coffin; a close shot of him rim-lit by the flames as he screams, "Put it out!"; a pan, after he staggers and collapses, from the sunbeams which penetrate the sod roof down to his skeletal hand. Or in the final scene, the tissue of gauze draped

THE VAMPIRE FILM

Robert Paige mourns his love Louise Allbritton in SON OF DRACULA

around the bed and framed in the foreground, which is parted by the fire and falls away to reveal Frank flanked by men who have followed him from jail before a travelling forward moves in to isolate him in close-up staring desolately at the pyre, also draws back from the qualified reality of special effects to the more natural expressions of lighting and camera movement, from the myth itself to the tragic dimensions of misguided belief in the promise of that myth.

While both *Dracula* and *Son of Dracula* are contemporary in their setting, so that strictly speaking they initiate the tendency towards updating traditional material peculiar to U.S. productions, a condition roughly analogous to that of a period locale is achieved in these pictures not only through stylisation of image and decor but also by avoiding many temporal indicators. Little more than an occasional auto horn on the soundtrack or the fashion of the costumes betray the 1930 London *Dracula,* and the situation of the action in the back country and marshland of the South similarly insulates *Son of Dracula* from the pressing realities of war-time 1943.

When the expressionistic approach fostered in pictures such as these

THE MALE VAMPIRE

by Universal studios ended in the late Forties, the vampire film in America went into a dormant stage. Curious *genre* experiments such as the vampire Western, *Curse of the Undead* (1959) in which the title figure, dressed all in black, is vanquished in a gunfight by an opponent with silver bullets in his revolver; quasi-science fiction in films like *The Vampire* (1957); or the "shadow-of-a-doubt" vampirism of *Return of Dracula* (1957) in which a Dracula figure impersonates the Eastern-European cousin of a small-town family to gain a secure base of operations but is unmasked by a suspicious teenage daughter—all these contributed to a confusion and breakdown of *genre* expectations built up by earlier releases. Not until the 1970's—ten years after the revival of the vampire film began in Europe and Mexico—did the undead return to the screen in the United States in sufficient numbers to reconstitute a *genre* identity.

Count Yorga, Vampire (1970) relocates an undead Transylvanian nobleman in the conspicuously modern precincts of Los Angeles, opening with a title sequence which follows his coffin from a docked freighter onto a flatbed truck, then over freeways and through business districts to his new home. Although that home is a large estate surrounded by park land, and the vampire himself recalls in dress and make-up the

Michael Pate as the vampire with Kathleen Crowley in CURSE OF THE UNDEAD

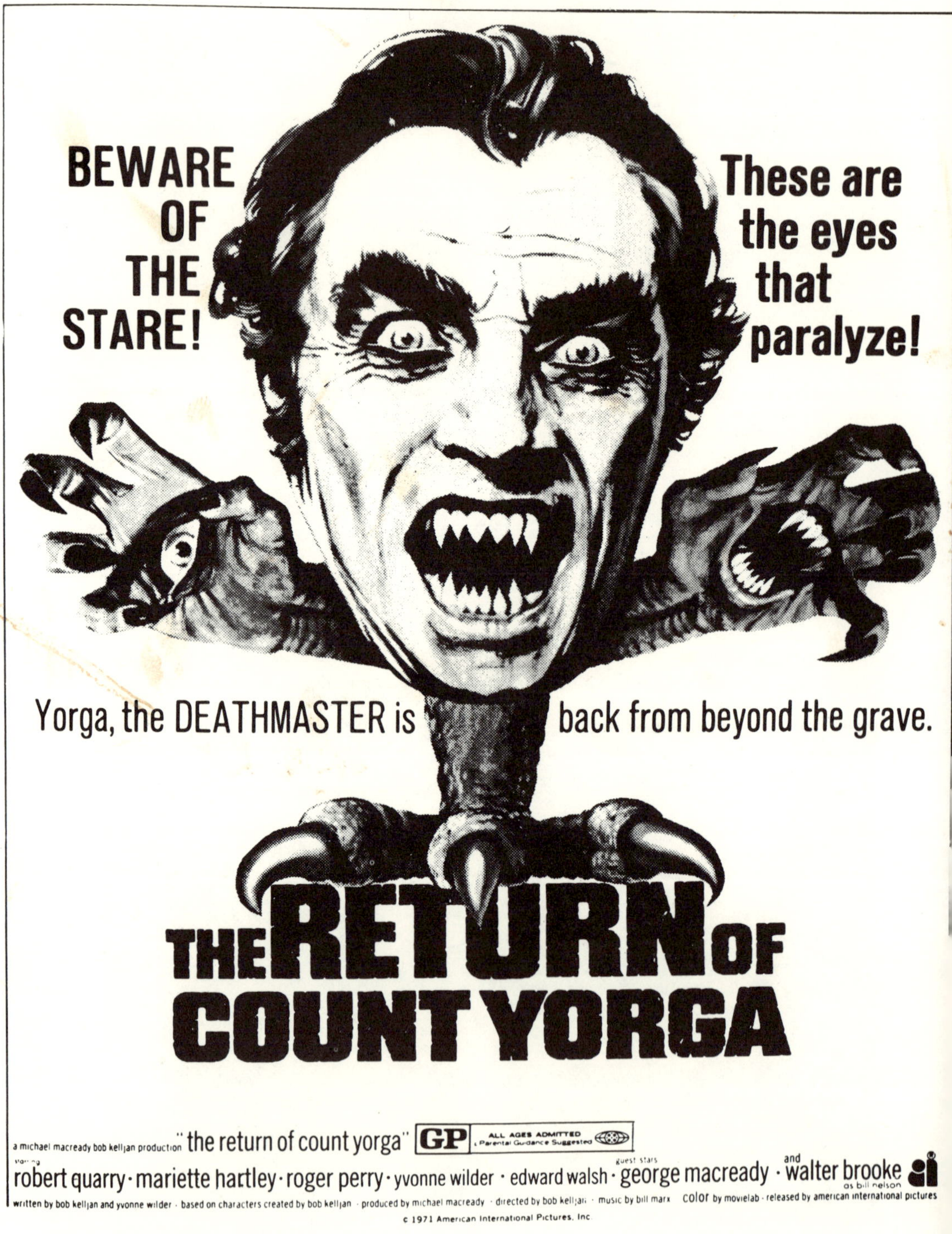
BEWARE OF THE STARE!
These are the eyes that paralyze!
Yorga, the DEATHMASTER is back from beyond the grave.
THE RETURN OF COUNT YORGA
a michael macready bob kelljan production "the return of count yorga"
GP
ALL AGES ADMITTED
Parental Guidance Suggested
starring
robert quarry · mariette hartley · roger perry · yvonne wilder · edward walsh · guest stars george macready · and walter brooke as bill nelson
written by bob kelljan and yvonne wilder · based on characters created by bob kelljan · produced by michael macready · directed by bob kelljan · music by bill marx color by movielab · released by american international pictures
c 1971 American International Pictures, Inc.

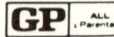

THE MALE VAMPIRE

prominent features of Lugosi, Chaney, or Carradine, the narrative consciously plays against both the anachronism of his appearance and speech and the obvious fact that he "looks," as someone is made to remark early in the film, "like a vampire." The challenge to his antagonists when faced with the realisation that he is precisely what his stereotyped aspect would suggest then becomes not merely to find the wherewithal to defeat him—their skepticism about the "normal" methods, about the efficacy of garlic or a cross makes them hesitant to rely on such silly or apocryphal remedies against a being which had been classed with unicorns and dragons in their belief—but also to remain convinced themselves while persuading others of the accuracy of their perceptions. "You've got to be kidding—a vampire!" is the kind of modern response which must almost of necessity occur somewhere in the course of the dialogue. *Count Yorga* approaches this inherent problem of having to address viewer disbelief, undiminished by any sense of pastness in the narrative and undistracted by a strong, mythic iconography, rather obliquely by retreating into parody and puns and by exploiting the alternate distractions of sex and violence—typified in Yorga's unexpected assault on a couple in a parked van. The characters' own disbelief continues to make them self-conscious, so that along

Roman Polanski and Jack MacGowran in clothes stolen from two vampires in DANCE OF THE VAMPIRES

John Beal and Lydia Reed in THE VAMPIRE (1957)

with the audience they cannot fully shake the impression of being only a step away from the ridiculous, from absurdity and buffoonery such as that of the inept Prof. Abronsius and Alfred in Roman Polanski's *Fearless Vampire Killers* (*Dance of the Vampires*) (1967). Ultimately, this vacillation between seriousness and satire in *Count Yorga* (which is common to other titles such as *Blood of Dracula's Castle* or *Scream, Blacula, Scream*), this situation of the picture being midway between the clear comedy of a film like Polanski's and a straight treatment reduces its integrity both as drama and as genre piece to the point where it loses its interior reality.

A more direct confrontation of the paradox of the modern-day vampire is illustrated in recent productions like the made-for-television *The Night Stalker* (1972) or *Grave of the Vampire* (1974). The former retains the essential demonic Dracula figure, "Janos Skorzeny," whom the plot eventually discloses as a Rumanian of relatively recent (1899) birth who also happens to be a voracious undead. His powers, in terms of *genre* precedents, are literally awesome. Equally invulnerable to a hail of police bullets or a battering with nightsticks, he overcomes dozens of men in a raid on a blood bank and in a later pursuit through surburban backyards. In both instances, the juxtaposition within the frame of helmeted, uniformed police with the gaunt, dark form of the vampire, illuminated by gunbursts as he throws men aside like rag dolls, sets up an opposition of iconic readings—that is, pragmatically omnipotent police versus mythically omnipotent vampire—which simultaneously tests and supports this hybrid of *genre* types. The viewer encounters this vampiric presence like the used-car dealer in the film does—"Something inside says don't mess with this guy. He's a creep . . . with those red eyes and that voice"—on a visceral level of raw strength and graphic violence.

The Night Stalker like *Son of Dracula* is less concerned with the persona of the vampire than it is with the abstract, mythic implications of his existence. The narrative framework—an ostracised reporter's diary-form recollections which flashback to a series of murders in Las Vegas—assumes a point-of-view which is already convinced of the authenticity of that existence; and yet Kolchak, the reporter, has both a detached precision—his voiceover account introduces scenes with a detailed journalistic chronology ("Sunday, approximately two-thirty A.M., the corner of Fremont and Central . . .") and description of events—and a sardonic style (one victim is simply "125 luscious pounds minus twelve pints of blood") to go with his straw hat and brash manner, to guarantee a minimum of continuing viewer identification with his predetermined perspective. While the narration and dialogue play with the question in the abstract (can vampires exist? if so, how?) during the press conferences and Kolchak's arguments with his editor, the visuals treat the actual attacks or the coroner's examination as occurrences without need of qualification, as things real because they are on the screen, while preserving the referent of Kolchak's point-of-view for certain puzzling details (the viewer like him can never do more than speculate, not having seen the action, on whether the second woman's body was thrown a hundred yards into a dry creekbed), so that the film's own base reality of image never questions the verisimilitude of vampirism. And while the plot may be full of modern conceits (the blood bank; the vampire keeping a hostage alive on plasma in order to have a ready supply of blood in his house), it is by and in the presence of more traditional objects (cross, stake, the coffin of earth, even the isolated rented house heavily-curtained against the intrusion of sunlight) that the vampire is finally trapped and executed.

Grave of the Vampire (1974) restores to the title figure a character function equal in importance to that of the non-vampire antagonists. Again the fact that it is contemporary—the film has a prologue that takes place in the Forties but is predominantly set in the present—

compels a certain amount of self-consciousness about the subject matter but not much compared to either *Count Yorga* or *The Night Stalker*. The undead of this film was a sorcerer and premeditated murderer in his first life and continues so in his vampiric phase, which he camouflages by working as a professor of the occult (night classes only), who occasionally practices what he teaches on his women students. The more interesting personage, however, is his son, conceived in rape, half human, half vampire (he is weaned on his mother's blood and survives to adulthood by eating raw meat), and bent on finding and killing his father in a situation charged with Oedipal connotations. By underlining the character conflicts and, fatalistically, by delaying the full inheritance of the son's proclivity to vampirism until after he has overcome his sire, this motion-picture, like *The Night Stalker*, succeeds to a great degree where *Count Yorga* and other productions fail, in transcending and reinterpreting many of the more rigid conventions of the genre.

Nostradamus

In 1956, the Mexican film industry began production of a cycle of vampire films which carry on the eclectic and extravagant expressionism of Universal studios. Beginning with *The Vampire* (*El vampiro*, 1956) the films freely recruited elements from the catalogue of both sublime and ridiculous *genre* conventions. Dense ground fogs and manor houses flanked by spectral forests are the locations for the operations of such undead noblemen as Count Duval in *The Vampire* and Count Swobota in *World of the Vampires* (1960). While the former portrays the vampire as a blood-sucking gigolo who uses his erotic appeal to captivate and live off the maiden aunt of the heroine and who is easily reduced to smouldering remains by a semi-comic doctor, *World of the Vampires* imposes its particular lore on a revenge narrative—the vampire has come to the new world to annihilate the descendants of a family which persecuted his ancestors in Hungary—including a Transylvanian melody with "certain combinations of notes" which raise the dead and play as much havoc with a vampire's senses as the sight of a cross. Both Duval and Swobota wear the classic make-up and the formal suit with high-collared cape, which inspires admiration for their "mysterious" good looks in women and contempt in men ("Jealous? Of a man who dresses as if he were at a carnival"). While there is generally a competent deployment of standardised visual usages in these films' art direction and cinematography—a travelling into a victim in bed and pan to her window is followed by a shot of Count Swobota standing amid some ruins and summoning her hypnotically; continued intercutting as she rises and walks, windswept and anxious, through the woods, while he waits with a keylight on his eyes reminiscent of *Dracula*—there are also glaring lapses in production value, such as the ludicrous, over-sized rubber masks and gloves worn by Swobota's fur-covered bat-like minions.

This dichotomy between levels of expression, between the imaginative and the banal, is nowhere more apparent than in the Santo series, featuring a masked wrestler in a succession of real-life matches with vampires and associated fiends. *Samson Versus the Vampire Women (Santo contra las mujeres vampiras*, 1962), for example, focuses on a blood cult of female undead who dress in white robes (resembling the gowns of the wives in *Dracula*) which mysteriously change colour to black when they enter their coffins. Interspersed with scenes in which Santo single-handedly overcomes these vampire women and their henchmen—including a finale in which he takes a torch and incinerates a line of them lying in propped-up wooden boxes in a sustained medium shot accentuated by the fetishistic use of flame which has been a motif throughout the film—are shots of the hero driving to the rescue in his sports car and even a number of prolonged bouts between Santo and human opponents in the arena, which bear no relation to the rest of the plot.

The most detailed and consistent of the Mexican Dracula prototypes is Nostradamus, also featured in a series of motion pictures in 1960. Fully as arrogant as any American or European vampire, Nostradamus dresses with a continental flair, sporting a black homburg and a neatly-trimmed steel-grey moustache and van dyke and with the lining of his cape folded back over his shoulders like small white wings. In *Curse of Nostradamus (La maldicion de Nostradamus)*, the first of the films, the vampire introduces himself under the pseudonym of Erikson to a Van Helsing analog named Professor Dolenz whose assistance he requests for a "revindication" of the prophesies of the 16th Century astrologer Michael Nostradamus, later revealed to be his father. The repeated zoom-ins to the face of this figure as he promises to commit a dozen murders to extort Dolenz's cooperation and warns him that "You know nothing of my power, power to destroy the whole world," imply in an energetically visual way that he may indeed have more than an imposing presence to back up his threats.

While the plot of *Curse of Nostradamus* wanders through the first half of the proposed killings (the rest are consigned to a sequel entitled *Blood of Nostradamus* [*La sangre de Nostradamus*]), the *mise-en-scène* displays a remarkable consistency in supporting characterisation and exploiting *genre* expectations. Repeated low angle shots of the vampire sustain the feeling of his dominance over men and events introduced in the first scene. In his second meeting with Dolenz, close-ups of Nostradamus are countered with medium close shots of the professor, making him physically larger within the frame as he scoffs at the gun held by his human opponent: "You haven't got the courage ... you will find that I'm invulnerable to petty human aspirations." More derisive laughter is followed by extra close shots of Nostradamus's mouth ("So fire!") then the gun as it explodes, cutting back to medium shot as Dolenz empties the revolver and a reverse of the room with only the billowing draperies betraying the vampire's departure, unscathed. On a less complex level, a recurrent use of low-light and side-light for "unnatural" effect; the deceptive point-of-view travelling camera into the bedroom of Dolenz's daughter which the viewer takes to be the vampire but turns out to be the professor; the optical device which allows Nostradamus to assume a bat shape when repelled by the Antioch cross; even the simple close-up of the undead's eyes as he takes possession of a bookseller ("My spirit will enter your body") to whom he had brought a first editon of his father's book—all these visualisations produce an expressive ambience which distinguishes the film from the stale, strictly conventional images of most Mexican entries in the *genre*. Although Nostradamus is eventually reduced to crawling rat-like through the sewers and buried in a cave-in after Dolenz and his assistant have pursued him with platinum bullets through torch-lit stone corridors and pillared anterooms, this cultured, impeccably-groomed, and extremely conceited vampire who discusses the ineffable qualities of time and space as well as "petty human aspirations" proved different enough from the pasteboard Duval and Swobota to merit a resurrection so *Curse of Nostradamus* was followed by three sequels in the same year: (*La sangre de Nostradamus* [*Blood of Nostradamus*], *Nostradamus y el genio de las tinieblas* [*Genie of Darkness*], and *Nostradamus y el destructor de monstruos* [*The Monsters Demolisher*])

By the time of *Genie of Darkness,* the novelty of the characterisation had worn thin. The professor continued to track him and the vampire acquired new assistants to replace the collection of dwarves and hunchbacks lost in prior outings; but the critical pieces of parchment, the theft of the vampire's ashes, even the transformations have a mechanical sameness about them which merely accentuates the exhaustion of the character's potential. Only a scene in which he stands by laughing as a woman burns to death recalls some of the striking arrogance of the first film.

Christopher Lee in DRACULA—PRINCE OF DARKNESS

The Hammer Dracula

The only incarnation of the Dracula figure on film to have appeared in more productions or to survive more intervening years than Lugosi or the Robles Nostradamus is the Hammer Film version of Stoker's Count as played by Christopher Lee. Debuting in Terence Fisher's *Dracula* in 1958 Lee's interpretation has restored the demonic and bestial aspects of Dracula lacking in the Universal pictures, without diminishing the cunning and evil intelligence of the character. Hunted by a succession of able vampire-killers—most notably Fisher's Van Helsing in the first film and Father Sandor in *Dracula, Prince of Darkness* (1965, also directed by Fisher) —Lee's Dracula possesses a primitive and instinctual dynamism which severely tests the rational foundations of these men's belief. Although the vampire usually receives but a fraction of the screen time allotted to his opponents, he manages to create an aura of menace with his limited presence that hangs over the whole of the various films.

In his *Dracula,* Fisher indicates a return to the narrative organisation of the book (rather than the stage play which formed the basis of the 1931 adaptation) with a deceptive introduction of the Count himself. Appearing suddenly at the head of a broad flight of steps, he strides down threateningly towards Jonathan Harker who is aghast at what seems to be the prelude to an attack, only to proffer words of greeting and conduct him upstairs. Dracula's second appearance is more unsettling: as Harker is about to be bitten by one of his wives who has asked his help in escaping, the vampire emerges from a secret passageway, red-eyed and snarling, and flings the woman viciously to the floor. To complement what can only be termed—particularly when compared to the stylised rendition of the same scene in Browning's *Dracula*, this explicitness of action, Fisher discards the conventions of expressionistic lighting and the amorphous cobwebbed expanses of earlier films, choosing to break up his frame instead with the variations of colour and detailed furnishings.

In other respects, Fisher retains and embellishes the pre-existing iconography of the *genre*. The Van Helsing of *Dracula* logs his notes onto a crude dictaphone carried over from the novel, which machine specifically records his serious doubts as a scientific observer about the undead's ability to change his shape or dematerialise. However by *Brides of Dracula* (1960, directed by Fisher) the professor is forced to concede that the bat which assails him may be the altered form of a vampire. Van Helsing's caution, however, is based equally on his fear of the vampire as an entity and his academically-grounded reluctance to hypothesise on the limitations of the known and the unknown. Integral to Fisher's conception of Van Helsing is both a ruthless pragmatism and a troublesome curiosity about ontological secrets. His professor is a Nineteenth Century forerunner of modern para-psychologists whose enthusiasm for the unexplained carries him into the occult and whose questing disregard for risks is fortunately protected by a physical dexterity and an uncanny ability to improvise, so that in *Brides of Dracula* he finds the means to cauterise a vampire's bite by heating an iron in the forge of a stable and in the climax of the earlier film he defeats Dracula himself first by feigning a loss of consciousness when in the vampire's grasp and, after breaking free, by fashioning an improvised cross from the base of two candlesticks. This destruction of the undead at the end of *Dracula* is particularly striking in contrast to the anti-climactic finale of the Universal production: after the vampire is transfixed by the makeshift icon, Van Helsing lunges at a nearby window and tears down the curtain. The shaft of light outlined by the disturbed accumulation of dust catches Dracula's foot and reduces it to a mass of putrid flesh; Van Helsing circles around and forces the whole body back into the killing light, so that the corpse buckles and collapses like a punctured air bag then crumbles to a fine ash (as Stoker describes the dissolution) to be scattered by the wind. Everything is rendered with a careful attention to the graphic details of image and sound in a convincing mixture of physical combat and ritual far removed from the

Christopher Lee threatens his guests in DRACULA—PRINCE OF DARKNESS

Michael Gough and Peter Cushing find a victim in DRACULA (1958)

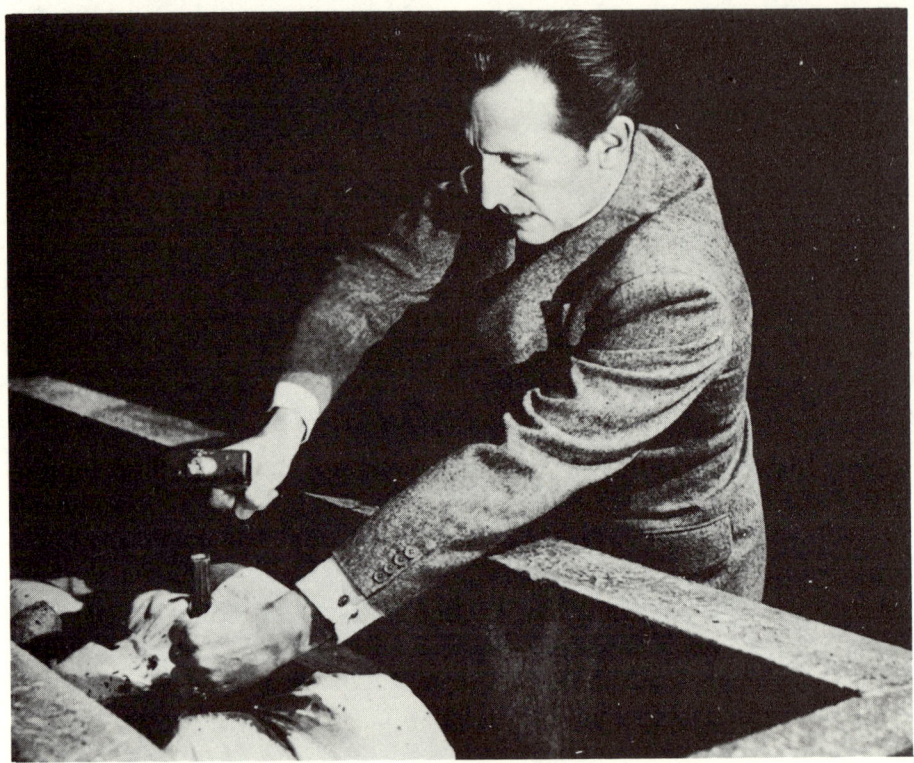

Peter Cushing at work in DRACULA (1958)

subdued, off-screen efficiency of Browning's Van Helsing. Moreover, the destruction of Dracula in the Hammer version comes after two earlier on-screen executions, the first by Harker of Dracula's wife (a staking which transforms her into a wizened corpse) and the second by Van Helsing of Lucy (the novel's erotic "bloofer lady," who the film's Van Helsing drives back into her crypt by branding her forehead with a cross and stakes her after sunrise), both of which are similarly direct in their use of special effects not to mention stage blood to underscore the grisly reality of piercing an undead—which screams out its hatred at the vampire-killer—and laying its soul to rest. But Fisher's violence is not gratuitous, not just a titillating bit of *grand guignol*. Like the savage eroticism which he associates with the vampire in *Dracula* and which Lee and later directors refine to the point where the responses of the young women in *Taste the Blood of Dracula* (1969) unmistakably suggest orgasm, the violence in the Hammer productions is a psychic release, an incontrovertible breakdown of the rational processes of the world and a substantive displacement of the filmic reality, throwing it and the viewer into a chaos which only ritual for

THE MALE VAMPIRE

the characters and catharsis for the spectators can restore to order.

Perhaps the most successful synthesis of the various generic elements among all the Hammer Dracula films is Fisher's *Dracula—Prince of Darkness*. Opening with a reprise of the last moments of *Dracula*, (vignetted by a diamond-shaped wedge of fog), this "prologue" incorporates a voiceover statement on Van Helsing's triumph:

> Here at last was an adversary armed with sufficient knowledge of the vampire to destroy him . . . thousands had been enslaved by the obscene cult of vampirism—now, the fountainhead himself perished.

Fisher's evolving notion of the vampire as a kind of aberrant but essentially natural phenomenon, as the germ of "an obscene cult" is introduced directly by means of this title and restated on several expressive levels. To begin with, the recapitulation of the concluding moments of the earlier film combined with the dispassionately-read commentary strips the event of almost all its mythopoeic potential, declines to romanticise or elevate Van Helsing's act to the level of anything more than execution of a criminal. In *Brides of Dracula*, the young male vampire is a spoiled son of aristocracy who profligacy and licentiousness eventually degenerate into what Van Helsing terms the "disease" of vampirism. In *Dracula* the emphasis on the bestial—low angle shots of the Count framed against the rapacious gargoyles which crown the battlements of his castle, Lee's hissing and growling—also hinted at a deteriorative or atavistic cause underlying the vampirism. In *Dracula—Prince of Darkness*, the narrative exposition and expressive imagery re-confirm this naturalistic point-of-view.

The film proper opens with a funeral procession for a young woman. In a long take around her bier, Fisher builds up tension as the dead woman's mother argues with several villagers and a local priest over the disposition of the body, as figures move from foreground to background then the camera pans with the crazed Frau as a man positions a stake over the girl's heart and raises a hammer. Before he can strike, a shot reverberates on the soundtrack. At the moment of maximum anxiety caused by the men's action and the unseen report of a firearm and sustained by the unbroken continuity of image, there is a cut to a low angle long shot of a mounted figure. This stylised introduction of Father Sandor as he rides out of the shadows to accuse the townspeople of "blasphemous sacrilege . . . and superstition," identifies him instantly as a dominant figure and, the viewer anticipates from convention, the representative of reason. Sandor is unusual in that he combines the function of priest (evident from his monkish garb) with those of hunter (the gun he carries) and scientist (his contempt for

From Terence Fisher's BRIDES OF DRACULA

the villagers' hysteria). While he scoffs at the local people's folk-tales and quaint defences against the unknown ("Garlic to keep out the bogie man"), he cautions the English tourists at the inn who plan to travel on to the next town at night to "at least, stay away from the castle." Such a warning, coming from a man who has confessed that "I enjoy shocking people's sensibilities, but I can be serious" becomes doubly portentous.

As the narrative focuses on two English couples—they have been abandoned by their coachmen at the crossroads near the castle which Sandor counseled them to avoid, and the brasher of the two men convinces the others to board a driverless carriage sent out to meet them—the indications of impending death become more overt. Despite this, Fisher pushes the viewer back into uncertainty by a misleading *mise-en-scène*. The dark silhouette which looms suddenly in the doorway inside the castle is revealed, when it steps into the light, to be nothing more than a servant of Dracula, however sinister. The supper and dialogue are full of ironies—the servant explaining that Dracula made provision to entertain guests after his death because "my master died without issue, sir . . . in the accepted sense of the word;" or the toast proposed by the Englishman, "Here's to him. May he rest in peace"—but Dracula fails to appear, and the expected attack on his guests is withheld. Eventually, the disturbingly "objective" travelling shots which explore the upper corridors after the visitors have retired—objective because they represent no character point-of-view, although the viewer may again be deceived into suspecting that it is the vampire moving down the halls—cedes to a subjective perspective as one of the men follows the servant through a hidden passage down to a cellar where he does discover the crested sarcophagus of Dracula. The camera moves with him as he walks around and examines it, finding it empty, then wanders into an adjoining room where he is stabbed.

Fisher's staging up to this moment has been consistently naturalistic —even the carriage without a driver is treated with an objectivity and lack of manipulation which differs markedly from analogous sequences in both *Nosferatu* and the Lugosi *Dracula*. Further, the handling of the re-animation of Dracula which ensues is the culmination of this detached expositional method, as the servant suspends the dead man's body over the ashen residue of the undead reposing in the funerary stone, punctures the neck, and lets the blood flow out and mix with the dry dust until a blue mist gathers in the well of the sarcophagus and a reformed hand with a red ring abruptly gropes out of it.

Having bridged the gap between the physical and metaphysical in this sequence, the succeeding events fall momentarily into a regular generic pattern. The wife of the sacrificial victim becomes Dracula's bride, while the other couple manages to escape under the protection of the cross; but the vampire pursues them to Sandor's monastery and in a context of increasing violence and defiance of conventional strictures on his behaviour, Dracula penetrates the consecrated building, forces the younger woman to drink from a self-inflicted wound in his chest (transposing a scene with Mina from the novel), and abducts her. In a precipitous conclusion, Father Sandor and her husband destroy his first victim who has become undead, his human servant, and the vampire himself as the monk's gun breaks the icy surface of the castle moat and the caped figure disappears beneath a floe.

Throughout *Dracula—Prince of Darkness*, Fisher refuses to reduce the conflicts to a level of abstraction. Sandor and the Dracula figure are opposed along a number of parallel lines, some of which are symbolic or allegorical, others moral or ethical; but neither impinge on the basic material reality of the frame. If anything the reverse is true,

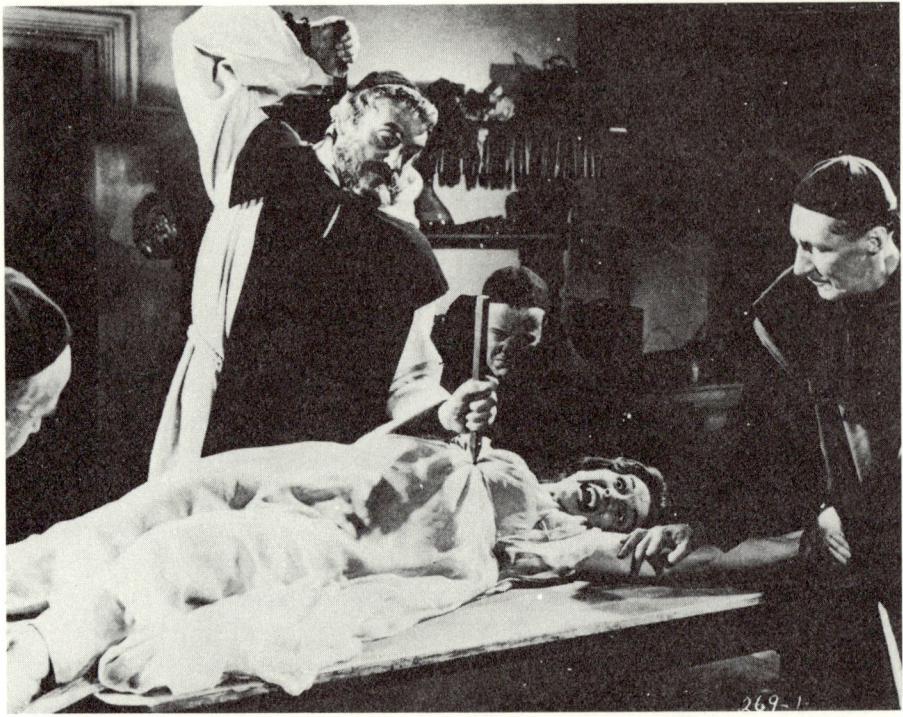
Andrew Keir stakes Barbara Shelley in DRACULA PRINCE OF DARKNESS

as Fisher's characters may produce the critical symbols from objects without inscribed meaning—as in Van Helsing's crossed candlesticks or the even bolder stroke at the end of *Brides of Dracula* in which a huge, fiery cross is fashioned from the burning blades of a windmill. Consequently, the struggles between the characters themselves cannot be generalised, for, developed as they are through a matter-oriented interpretation of the *genre's* iconic constructs and actualised in the minds and bodies of the participants, they define the Hammer Dracula and his antagonists with an immediacy and concreteness unparalleled in the *genre*.

Dracula 1974 Vintage

Dracula (1974, directed by Dan Curtis and written by Richard Matheson) is in many ways the most faithful and at the same time the most innovative film treatment of Stoker's novel. The earliest sequences between Harker and Dracula in the latter's castle are strikingly similar to the original both in their naturalness of exposition (Dracula recounting his personal history long into the night; or his very appearance, dressed in a simple grey frock coat and silk tie) and in their use

Christopher Lee and Peter Cushing in DRACULA A.D. 1972

of portents of impending disaster (the pack of wolves which surrounds the castle in the opening shots; the ghostly carriage ride). This sets up an immediate tension between surface appearances and what the viewer familiar with the *genre* knows are the sub-surface realities. Additionally, certain aspects of the novel which are rarely transliterated to the screen—for instance, Mina serving as a medium to track Dracula in the race back to the security of his homeland—are included, while other events are purely the invention of Curtis and Matheson (such as Dracula's freeing a wolf from the Scarborough Zoo to attack Arthur Holmwood).

Stylistically, the tone of the film is naturalistic. The use of titles ("Bistritz, Hungary, May, 1897") over shot to establish time and place suggests a quasi-historical or journal-like progression which resembles the novel. The images themselves are of interiors which are mostly full-lit, crypts where the detail of the Gothic arches and stonework is visible and not lost in *chiaroscuro*, and exterior scenes photographed under cloudy skies (Harker's arrival in Bistritz; the "Vesta" aground on the beach at Whitby), rain (Lucy's funeral), or a simulated moonlight—little which recalls the expressionism of previous adaptations. The acting as well is subdued, lacking in broad gestures or strange intonations. The unusual effects which are present become, in context, the more dramatically unsettling. The tilted angles which introduce numerous sequences become an unavoidably disturbing motif—particularly when the tilted shot is constructed from the strong, tipped verticals of a corridor or passageway—which figuratively externalise the metaphysical imbalance that hangs over the film as a whole. The elaborate camera movement when Dracula arrives in England—a side-travelling and pan around a dead sailor lashed to the schooner wheel in the foreground then a zoom into Dracula standing alone and windswept on the beach below with a single box of native earth at his feet—becomes in contrast to the earlier visual treatment of him doubly ominous.

Undoubtedly, what makes this film Dracula exceedingly different from both the Stoker conception and the other adaptations is the sympathy with which the title figure is treated. This is not to say that his demonic characteristics are underplayed. His blood obsession (typified in the scene in which Mina is compelled to drink from self-inflicted wounds in his chest); his arrogance ("So, you play your wits against mine, me who commanded armies hundreds of years before you were born"); his herculean strength (he overpowers at least a dozen men in his attack on an inn); his bestiality (he howls like a wolf, although he never transforms himself into any animal); and his mesmeric abilities (over both men and animals) are all present, true to certain conventions. But this Dracula suffers from a kind of existential anguish which draws him closer to the vampires treated in the next section than to Stoker's creation *per se*. He is to a great extent a Romantic figure, not merely in the Byronic mould but in the ironic suggestions of the large portrait of him (as Vlad Tepes) in the midst of battle astride a white horse and brandishing a scimitar (strongly reminiscent of Gericault's "Mounted Officer of the Imperial Guard") and in the flashbacks, from his point-of-view, to a woman who died during his natural life. In a very real sense, it is the burden of this past rather than his present vampirism which inspires Dracula's violent and irrational actions. He is distressed at the sight of blood when Harker cuts himself shaving less from any repressed desire to drink it than, it seems, from the realisation which it forces upon him that he is no longer human. A truer loss of control is evidenced in the mental disturbance of the flashbacks, which are brought on by the sight of a photograph of Lucy Westenra who resembles the woman in his fixated memory.

Dracula's "tryst" with Lucy on the lawn of her home in England combines the dynamic of cross-tracking (intercutting between a receding camera travelling back from her as she walks and a forward track from her viewpoint in towards him), which suggests in a direct visual way something of the magnetism of his being, the sexuality of their embraces, and her clearly orgasmic reaction to his bite with the sentimental associations of the music-box theme on the soundtrack, a melody first heard over his flashbacks and represents his former love. Consequently, his seduction and murder of Lucy is as much an attempt to recapture this lost love as it is to fulfill the needs of his "disease." When she becomes undead, he tries to rejoin her only to discover that she has been staked by Van Helsing. In a rage of despair—intercut with a final flash of memory back to the death of the woman in his first life—he demolishes the crypt then circles around inside it in a moment of impotence and frustration reminiscent of the closing shot of *Scream, Blacula, Scream* (both photographed from a high angle emphasising the futility of the figure's gestures). Even the final scene of his destruction—he is debilitated by sunlight and speared by Van Helsing but does not, as is traditional deteriorate into dust—ends with a travelling shot past his corpse into the portrait on the wall accompanied by a fanfare of martial music and a title explaining Dracula's historical "actuality" which mitigate the monstrousness of the character.

III. THE SYMPATHETIC MALE VAMPIRE

Africa, the dark land where voodoo drums beat in the night, where the jungles are deep and full of secrets and the moon that lights them is still a mystic moon. Africa, where men have not forgotten the evil they learned in the dawn of time. I always come back to Africa; but even here there is no rest for me. The path of time is curved upon itself like a circle, without beginning, without end. I must follow it forever. I cannot die. I cannot rest. I cannot rest. I cannot rest.
     (Webb Fallon in "The Vampire's Ghost")
"And I was once happy," he said mornfully, "once happy because I was innocent. Oh! gracious Heaven, how long am I to suffer?"
     ("Varney the Vampyre")

In distinct contrast to the Dracula figure is a much smaller group of male vampires whose roots go back to Lord Ruthven in "The Vampyre" and Varney in "Varney the Vampyre." Like Ruthven and Varney, these figures are driven by a disease of mind and body; and no matter how sedulously they try to rid themselves of the curse of the undead, they are always unsuccessful. One of the earliest examples of this type of vampire in motion pictures appears in *House of Dracula* (1945) Lawrence Talbot (the wolfman), Frankenstein's monster, and Dracula are all brought together in this, one of the last gasps of the Universal monster factory. The film-makers, in a final gesture, even allow Talbot

From Erle C. Kenton's HOUSE OF DRACULA

to be cured and redeemed. Although Dracula is not granted such an indulgence and perishes at the conclusion, the vampire is characterised as seeking a remedy for his affliction. But while undergoing the protracted treatment the "call of Thanatos" becomes too strong. Dracula's second fall into darkness comes as a woman plays Beethoven's "Moonlight Sonata," which he finds "breathes the spirit of the night . . ." Nonetheless, until the moment when the Romantic music precipitates a regression, this Dracula is portrayed as genuinely longing for release from his vampiric "malady."

In the same year Republic Pictures released an exceptional small-budgeted film called *The Vampire's Ghost*. Despite the limitations of minimal production values the filmscript (written by Leigh Brackett and John K. Butler) is an intelligent and restrained re-working of the vampire myth. *The Vampire's Ghost* disregards almost completely the immeasurable influence of the Dracula figure returning instead—much more decidedly than *House of Dracula*—to a pre-Stoker conception for its inspiration. Webb Fallon has, like Varney, suffered through several centuries as a vampire in reparation for a heinous crime. In his present "incarnation" he is the proprietor of a cheap bar and gambling hall in an African outpost. While he is generally liked and respected by the inhabitants, they are, needless to say, unaware of his periodic nocturnal wanderings in search of blood. Viewer empathy with Fallon is established from the first scene, when he breaks up a fight in his bar using his powers of mesmerism and thereby saves the life of the conventional hero (Roy). Despite the violent surroundings Fallon (as underplayed by John Abbott) is soft-spoken and unassuming; he is, in fact, a much more appealing character than the ostensible protagonist (Roy) to the point where Roy's fiancée begins to prefer Fallon. On a narrative level, there are further parallels with the histories of Varney and Ruthven. For instance, Fallon seems to operate equally well during the day or night with only his dark glasses suggesting any sensitivity to light. In addition, he has no need to return to his coffin for periodic resuscitation, although he is conventional in that he is impervious to bullets and can only be destroyed by fire, the stake, or a silver blade. However, when Fallon is stabbed with a silver lance by one of the more superstitious natives during a hunt in the jungle, he does not crumble to ashes like Dracula. Rather, like Ruthven, he enlists the aid of Roy—whose life he has saved a second time in the underbrush—and he is carried to a mountain-top where he can be revived by moonlight. This faculty of revivification by moonlight is something rarely seen in vampire films—a striking anomaly to say the least—which Fallon accomplishes by bringing the delirious Roy, like

Aubrey in "The Vampyre," under his hypnotic influence. Unfortunately for Fallon his all-too-human infatuation with Julie leads to his end. He kidnaps her and is followed into the jungle by Roy and a priest figure, Father Gilchrist. There he is slain by them in a traditional manner.

The title character of *The Vampire* (1957) is probably the most pathetic and unwilling vampire in film or literature. Combining the fifties vogue for science fiction with vampiric blood lust, this picture features a humanitarian doctor (Paul Beecher) who accidentally consumes some "vampire pills" developed by a fellow scientist, a situation made even more pathetic in that his young daughter unwittingly gives them to him. In the grip of an ironic, drug-induced personality split—killing by night and saving lives by day—his "angst" is like that of Talbot the wolfman in that, despairing of a cure, he seeks death.

Finally, this premise of the vampire himself as unwilling victim has been recently revived in American-International's Blacula films—*Blacula* (1972) and *Scream, Blacula, Scream* (1973). "Blacula" is the rather cynical sobriquet adopted by an African prince named Mamuwalde, who has been infected with vampirism after an encounter with

John Beal as Dr. Beecher in THE VAMPIRE (1957)

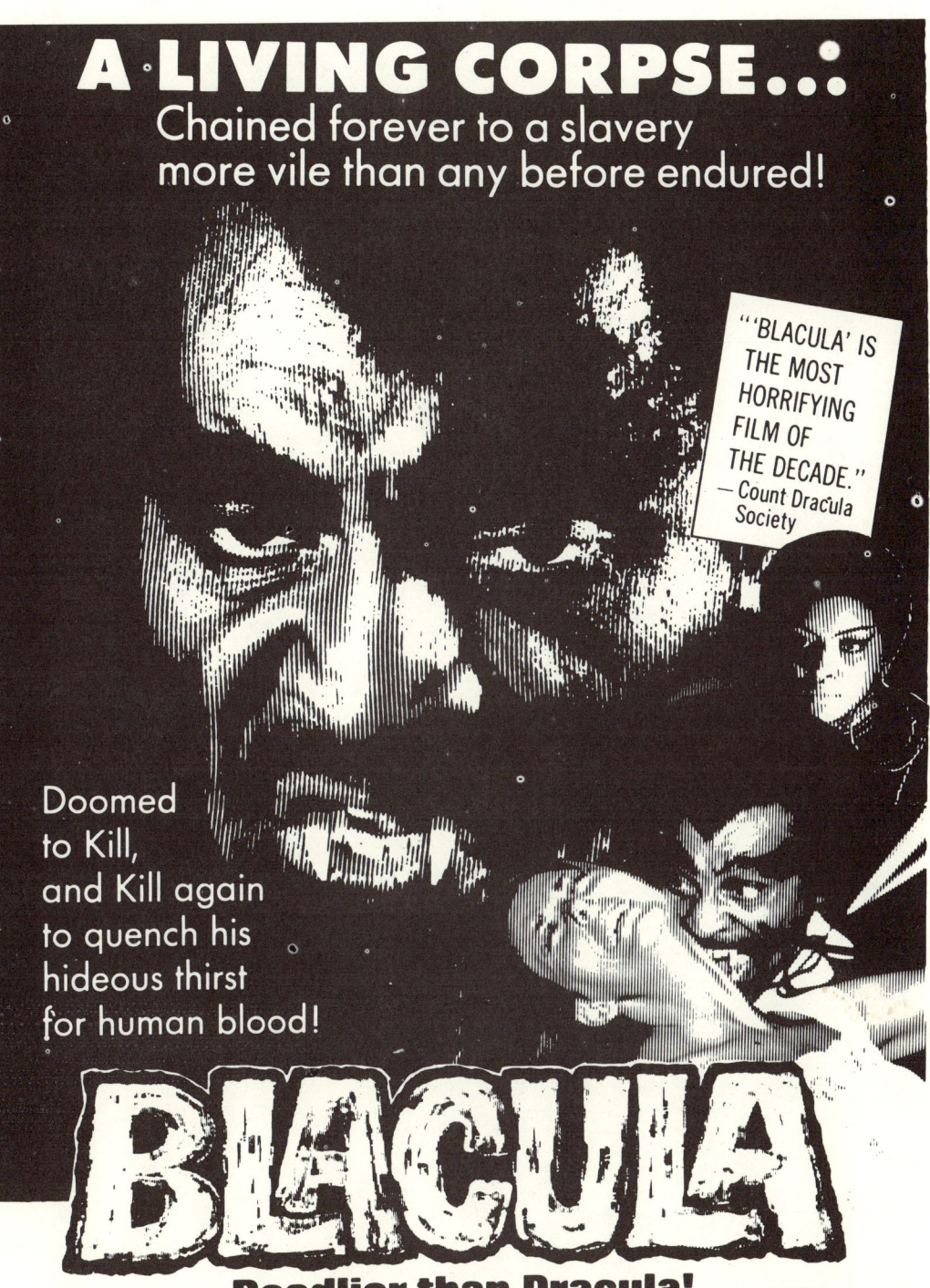

From William Crain's BLACULA

William Marshall and Pam Grier in SCREAM, BLACULA, SCREAM

The power of the cross in BLACULA

Dracula himself. Like his predecessors, Blacula is caught in a double bind between a desire for release and a compulsion to spread the vampiric plague, complicated in both films by the presence of love objects whom he does not wish to become his victims. In *Blacula*, he does turn the girl Tina into a vampire, but not until she is shot and vampirism seems the only way he can save her from complete death. When she is finally destroyed by those hunting Blacula, his instinct to continue "living" is so severely undercut that he walks out into the sunlight, and becomes a suicide in the manner of Varney.

In *Scream, Blacula, Scream* Mamuwalde is resurrected into a world even more alienating and unfamiliar than the one in the previous film. In one scene in particular, as he wanders the city streets and encounters two black pimps who laugh at his reprimands for exploiting their brothers and sisters and are as a result ruthlessly slaughtered, Blacula's outrage at society is explicitly stated. He does initiate a new search for a cure, participating in a voodoo ritual which the priestess Lisa—whom he has fallen in love with—performs, and nearly completes, before the police invade his house. In the final scene Blacula is found and staked. As he feels around the room in an agonised circle of frustration and despair, a freeze-frame from a high angle externalises his sensation of suspended, unending rage.

CHAPTER THREE

The Female Vampire

"I remember everything about it—with an effort. I see it all, as divers see what is going on about them, through a medium, dense, rippling, but transparent. There occurred that night what has confused the picture and made its colour faint. I was all but assassinated in bed, wounded here," she touched her breast, "and never was the same again."

"Were you near dying?"

"Yes, very—a cruel love—strange love that would have taken my life. Love will have its sacrifices. No sacrifices without blood."
Joseph Sheridan Le Fanu, "Carmilla"

None of these women approaches, so far as depth and sophistication of sadistic sexual perversion is concerned, Elisabeth Bathory . . . astonishingly white flesh, almost translucent, through which one could see clearly the delicate blue veins beneath; long shimmering, silken hair, black as the plumage of the raven; sensual, scarlet lips; great dark eyes, capable of doelike tenderness, but sometimes igniting into savage anger, and at others glazing over with the abandoned somnolence of intense sexual passion.
R. E. L. Masters and Eduard Lea,
"Sex Crimes in History"

I. ELISABETH BATHORY

Only recently has the Sixteenth century Hungarian Countess described above by Masters and Lea been reincarnated in films, the earliest of three motion pictures based on her life and legend having been released in 1970. The historical Elisabeth Bathory, wife of Count Ferencz Nadasdy, has been briefly detailed in an earlier chapter, and the fact most pertinent to this study is that among the other black practices she engaged in with her followers was the systematic torture of hundreds of young women, culminating with the Countess "milking" them

Ingrid Pitt as Countess Elisabeth Nadasdy reverts to her aged state at her wedding in COUNTESS DRACULA

of their blood to daub on her skin and restore its "translucence."[1]

Countess Dracula (1971, directed by Peter Sasdy) is not, despite its title, a conventional vampire film. For while it centres on the Countess's reputedly successful use of blood as an elixir of youth, Sasdy's adaptation of Bathory's life is a most literal and logically developed one which depicts her as a living woman rather than a blood-sucking vampire. Accordingly, *Countess Dracula* does not exploit the usual icons of the *genre* or adopt its pervasive style of expressionistic lighting and decor, deploying those elements instead as a general reinforcement to the authenticity of the narrative events and reserving the more extra-

---

1. Masters and Lea record that in the dungeons of her stronghold, Castle Csejthe, law officials eventually discovered a "herd" of young women quartered like cattle and kept ready to satisfy the Countess' obsession.

THE FEMALE VAMPIRE

Ingrid Pitt with her lover Nigel Green in COUNTESS DRACULA

ordinary handling for moments such as the Countess's transformations or to suggest her growing madness. The medieval art works which appear under the titles,[2] the portraits of Nadasdy ancestors, the scenes in the kitchen with their Breughel-like detailing (servants in drab homespun around the breakfast table, a pig being dressed and milk churning in the background), even the doddering scholar Fabio puttering in his library or the sequence in the tavern where light filters through grimy windows to cast broken patterns on the walls and white-painted men from the travelling circus carouse in turbans, feathers, and red capes—all these form a context of tangible reality, a

---

[2.] Including one of the real Elisabeth, called "The Blood Countess' and painted by St. Csok.

The rejuvenated Countess

verisimilitude which contrasts with the diffused landscapes and soft interior key-lights associated with the Countess's presence. As the grey-haired, deeply wrinkled woman of the opening scenes, garbed in faded black with veil and high collar, is transfigured by her fortuitous discovery of the power of blood, she is at the same time carried imagistically farther out of that reality, emerging from behind a screen of variously-coloured glass after her bath, golden-haired (strikingly contrary to descriptions of the actual countess) and attired in a blue peignoir which reveals a flesh that is indeed "astonishingly white."

Ultimately, in effects such as the montage of the old Countess stabbing a gypsy girl followed by a sudden red toning, freeze-frame, and dissolve to the young Elisabeth riding out of the castle or the simple tilted angles as the re-ageing woman frenziedly begs her discarded lover for help, Sasdy's stress is on the psychology and not the metaphysics of Elisabeth Bathory's aberration. Aside from the clear prerequisite that the blood be taken from a virgin—established when that of the local whore fails to have effect—nothing is specified of the alchemy which miraculously restores her beauty. Further, her personal vampirism is depicted as conditioned by aristocratic insensitivity rather than any incipient inclination to evil, so that she may even pray to God and finger a rosary while she waits anxiously for a new "object" to ritually immolate. With this preference for realistic detailing and visual understatement already demonstrated, Sasdy's staging of the final scenes becomes an effective mixture of ceremony and slaughter. The movement from the placid Titian blues and ochres of the wedding altar and the Latin reading of the priest to the sudden ferocity of the decaying Elisabeth's attack on her daughter and the stabbing of her youthful paramour externalises the opposing states of her mind. From a pan across the faces of village wives chanting "devil woman" below the castle ramparts, a cut inside reveals the Countess for the last time, walled up in her chamber, clad again in black, her visage more devastated by time than ever before, neither demon nor vampire, simply a madwoman.

A second adaptation of the Bathory character—produced in the same years as *Countess Dracula*—is more explicit in that it treats the Countess both as vampire and as sexual criminal. The central premise of *Daughters of Darkness* (*Le rouge aux levres,* 1970) is that the "Scarlet Countess"—the script's epithet for the historical Elisabeth—has somehow survived her incarceration up to the present time. Her face layered with heavy white make-up and sanguine lipstick (a visual pun on the French title), this Countess uses her real maiden name (Bathory) and makes little attempt to conceal either her inexplicable

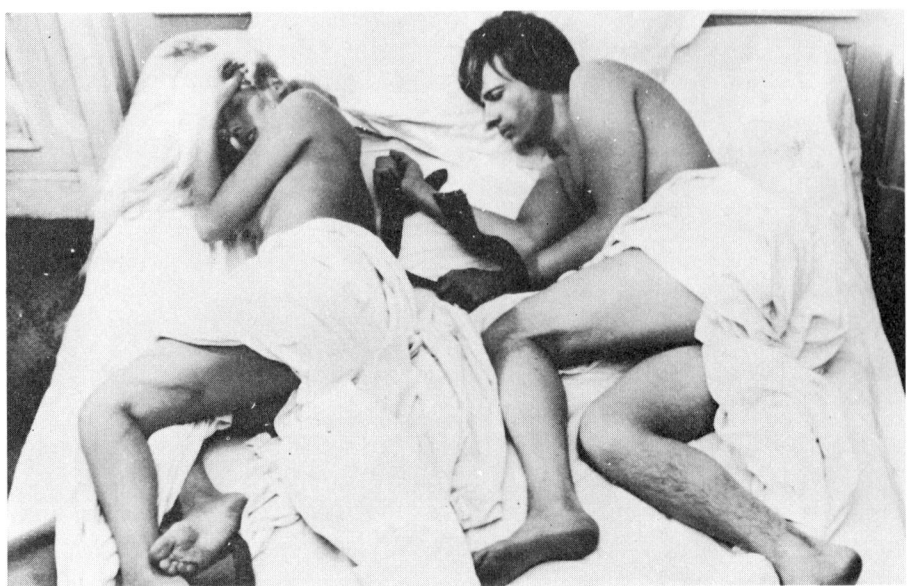
A sadistic couple in LE ROUGE AUX LEVRES

longevity (she tells the constable of a resort town she had visited forty years before that her secret is "diet and lots of sleep") or her proclivity for young women both as victims and sexual objects, even pausing midway through the film to discuss her medieval persona and how she drew "the blood of three hundred virgins to bathe in and drink." "To drink," because *Daughters of Darkness* describes Elisabeth Bathory as a vampire in the traditional sense, and while it emphasizes the erotic aspects of her blood lust, it concedes a sensitivity to water (her servant Ilona reacts violently to a shower) and daylight as limitations of her power. Elisabeth seduces rather than attacks her prey, gradually drawing the blood from a young bride she meets at the resort and hoping not to destroy her but to make her a companion undead. When the Countess herself "perishes," by being thrown from a car while racing home to avoid the sun and impaled on a tree branch, she evidences a faculty of metempsychosis very similar to that of Carmilla in Vadim's *Blood and Roses* which permits her to take possession of the body of her latest victim, who in turn assumes the pallid aspect and voice of the Countess and initiates a new cycle with another newly-wed couple as the film ends.

Ritual of Blood (*Ceremonia sangrienta*, 1973), as yet unreleased in the United States, restores the Bathory character to a period setting but obscures the question of her vampirism in much the same way as *Countess Dracula*. Although the film opens with the discovery of an authentic undead, who is staked and decapitated in hopes of terminating a plague of killings, the Marquise Elisabeth Bathory of this film is again fixated on blood only as a restorative of her youth. While her husband Karl does expire and become a *revenant,* she remains alive, entering into an arrangement with him whereby they "share" the young women he abducts to fulfill their respective needs. Eventually she destroys him out of jealousy, and, ironically, this murder cuts her off from the virgin blood. With a genuine emphasis on ritual—the narrative contains many scenes of incantations and castings by the Marquise and her counsellor sorceress as well as grisly stagings of blood-draining and torture eschewed by Sasdy in his version—and a stylistic stress on rich colours and *chiarascuro,* the overall portrait of the Bathory figure falls midway between the psychological realism of *Countess Dracula* and the unabashed eroticism of *Daughters of Darkness.*

II. CARMILLA KARNSTEIN

In 1871, Sheridan Le Fanu created in his Gothic novella of sixteen chapters the Countess Carmilla Karnstein. Under the guise of being a "discovered manuscript," it is not only an antecedent of the alternating first-person "diary" form which Stoker was to employ in "Dracula," but also the first major treatment of a female vampire in literature. Possibly Le Fanu knew of Bathory, for there are some resemblances between the two Countesses, but the noble rank and need for the blood of young women are of a superficial sort at best. The anagrammed antagonist of Le Fanu's fiction, Carmilla/Millarca/Mircalla is not a slayer of men. On the contrary, her conflicting impulses towards narcissistic love and annihilation compel her to seek out victims of her own age and sex, reflections of herself. The irony of Carmilla's affliction is not merely of one trapped in perpetual youth simultaneously forced to shun the daylight and to forego the patterns of normal existence, but, Le Fanu might allow, of a former victim caught in a cycle of having to relive with each new killing her own psychic destruction—an irony compounded by her awareness of playing a role.

Carmilla elucidates that dilemma in the lines cited at the beginning of this chapter, speaking of the "cruel love" which, later revelations make apparent, murdered her and issuing with a languorous fatality a warning to her "intended" of the impending re-enactment. That act of confession places Carmilla, at least in terms of the novella, with Lucy Westenra and others both male and female in a class of unwilling

Annette Vadim as Carmilla in ET MOURIR DE PLAISIR

THE FEMALE VAMPIRE

revenants, objects to be pitied rather than despised, to be executed but consolingly.

There have been a number of dramatic adaptations of Le Fanu's tale, each of them revealing different prejudices towards the original characters and themes. Le Fanu used understatement and pressed the reader into identifying with the somewhat innocuous Laura for suspense and *frisson*. The connotations of fatality and sexuality are not blatant but present nonetheless; and the images of bestiality, of breasts being pierced by two huge needles, were probably more acceptable to Victorian audiences in the context of supernatural horror. Beyond that, Le Fanu permits varying interpretations.

Consequently, in his film *Et mourir de plaisir* (*Blood and Roses*, 1960), Roger Vadim chooses to underscore the aspects of transference ("I live in you; and you would die for me . . . You must come with me, loving me, to death"). Vadim's Carmilla suffused with an incestuous energy that may lie hidden behind masks or explode in a fireworks display, never dies but draws the soul from a body and replaces it with her own in an eternal, parasitic transmigration. Although *Blood and Roses* uses only fragments of Carmilla's narrative line, the first-person viewpoint is carried over. It is, however, from Carmilla's perspective,

Elsa Martinelli and Mel Ferrer watch over Annette Vadim in ET MOURIR DE PLAISIR

Yutte Stensgaard in LUST FOR A VAMPIRE

becoming Georgia's—the equivalent of the novella's Laura—only after *she* has become Carmilla.

Excepting the one pursuit of a servant girl through the forest or the sight of Carmilla impaled on a fence post, Vadim avoids the *genre's* tendency towards violence and blood images; but ten years before *Countess Dracula,* he does evince a fascination with the psychology of vampirism as keen as Sasdy's. The dream states are not of "monstrous cats" but of women waiting listlessly in white corridors and of modern surgery, of fears not connected with distant castles and dungeon racks but with hospitals and operating tables, subverting the institutions of life-preservation and addressing death in a form that is most tangible to the viewer. Lacking the period setting, the present is stylised via the Italian manor with its antiques and faded oils and the forest with its night mist and carpet of leaves. On a narrative level, the costume ball and the visualisation of Georgia's nightmare in the unusual black-and-white waiting room produce moments of surrealism and anomaly within the assumed sense of contemporary actuality. These shifts in both narrative consciousness and expression, the displacement of reality by both masques (the ball) and reveries, the

Madeleine Smith, one of the victims in VAMPIRE LOVERS

change from colour to a world of greys, undercuts the stability of appearances in which the characters seek refuge in much the same way as vampirism being superstition threatens the rationalism of science. These events propel the film backwards figuratively into a dark age,

While the Carmilla of *Blood and Roses* pertains more to Vadim than to the novella; *Terror in the Crypt* (*La cripta e l'incubo*, 1963, directed by Camillo Matrocinque) transliterates it more exactly. The graphic, black-and-white aspect of the *schloss* and the ruined church, the cautious subjectification of Laura's dreams in slow, circular tracking shots, the emphasis of her fear of going insane—all expand the Gothic imagery and ambivalence of the original. The tension between Laura's fantasies and apprehensions and what Carmilla really is, belied by her moments of "normalcy," is restored—the final resolution is the revelation of the latter's true nature.

Terror in the Crypt begins in the midst of nightmare, a rapid montage as a woman leaps from a coach and pivots around a tree frightened by the vehicle's black shape: a close-up as she lies dead with her eyes open is followed by an extra long view of a castle, then a medium shot as Laura suddenly awakens in her bedroom and a fast zoom-in as she screams. The instantaneous effect is one of disjunction and continues as each succeeding dream is introduced into the narrative without any visual or aural qualifier to indicate that it is anything other than real. There is a confusion of the same sort of night-visions which Laura experienced in the novella with her waking state, coloured and made half-mad by those experiences.

The Carmilla-figure, here called Lyuba, arrives—again as in Le Fanu—in a runaway carriage and immediately is woven into the texture of Laura's dreams; but the audience as much as the dreamer is cut off from any indication of their cause. Visually, Laura alone and awake is linked with a kind of stasis (she is constantly introduced by high angle shots) and repressed energy (the dynamic yet limited action of the zoom shot), while Lyuba's presence—physical or psychic (when she impresses herself onto Laura's mind)—inspires movement in the form of pans and tracking shots. Laura and her governess turn to spells to try and rid her of her ailment; Lyuba remains a detached observer, playing a larger role in Laura's nightmares than in the rest of the film. This schematisation of Laura's growing insanity restores some of the subjective quality of the original work. Not only the dreams but nearly all the scenes which centre on Laura somehow reflect her inner thoughts and fears. The morbidity ("It's so beautiful here . . . here one could come for pleasure or for death") and sense of displacement ("In places like this, the past still seems to flourish . . . and I live more in the past than in the present") which surround her find equivalents in both the words and images, in a shot selection which fixes her to the ground but permits Lyuba to float over it, which externalises the former's sensations in the shock of quick cuts, the entrapment of tight close shots, the imbalance of off-angles, and the chaos of broken patterns of light.

In a way, the spectre of Lyuba and death represent freedom for Laura, a release from worldly care epitomised when both women hurry down the path to the ruined church at night, windswept and backlit, cutting a bold diagonal across the face of a dark landscape in

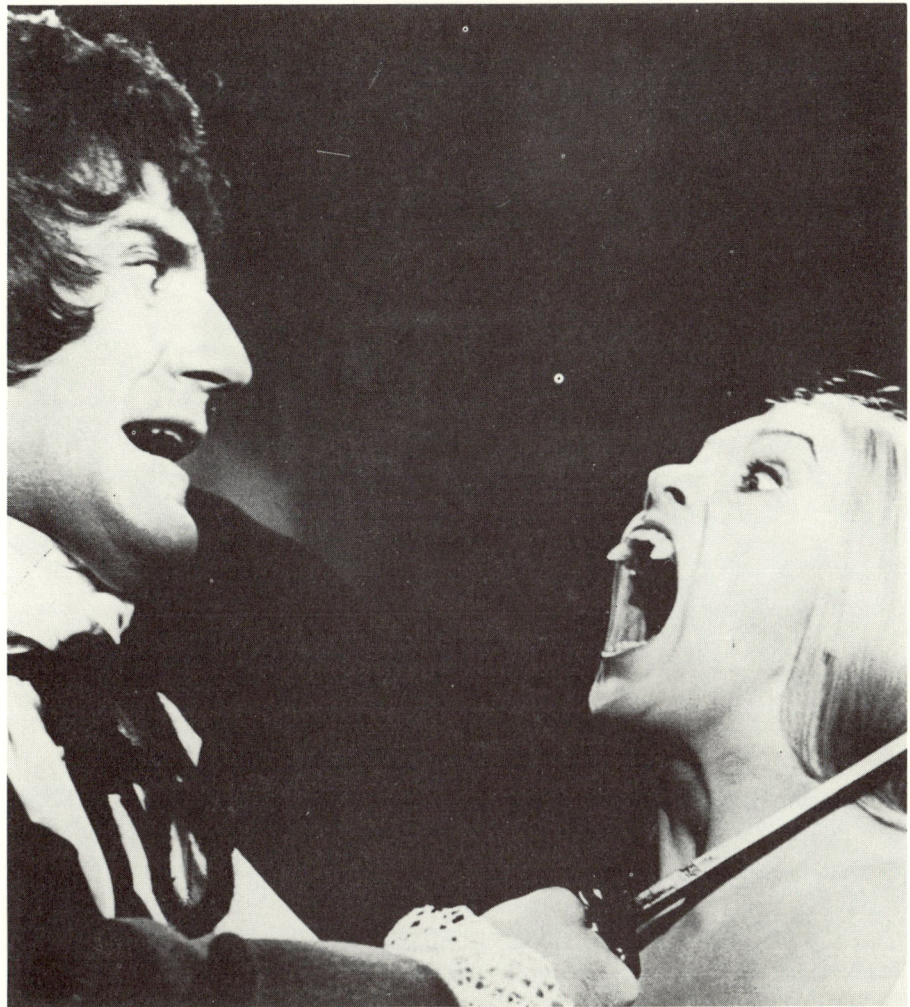
Douglas Wilmer revenges himself on Kirsten Betts in VAMPIRE LOVERS

their white nightdresses. The fact that Lyuba like Carmilla in *Blood and Roses* is suffocating her victim with the strength of her will is implicit in the narrative—*genre* convention tending to cast viewer suspicion on others than the stated heroine—and in the symbolic transformations of Laura's dream. The resolution, then, may be more confirmation than revelation. Appropriately all that remains of Lyuba, who has been more a stifling ghost in Laura's fantasies than anything substantial, after she has been shot with a wooden bolt and disintegrated, is an empty cloak which Laura removes from the earth.

Although both *Blood and Roses* and *Terror in the Crypt* have a highly developed narrative point-of-view, which filters the sexuality

Mike Raven and Yutte Stensgaard in LUST FOR A VAMPIRE

and mania of the sourcework through the subjective perceptions of predator as well as prey, both suffer the insertion of a male figure, which—even though the witch-hunter of the second film is drawn from the novella's "picture cleaner from Gratz"—is not present in the original and who to some extent in each film defocuses the sexual exchange between the two women. Self-love becoming love of the other, the projection of the potent vampiric consciousness onto the object and the latent carnality of that action, are treated mostly in a stylised or symbolic way in *Blood and Roses* and *Terror in the Crypt*. The former's close shot of the women's rain-wet faces as they kiss or, in the later film, the hand-holding strolls through the gardens and hesitant caresses are their strongest manifestations of the sexuality which is at the core of Le Fanu's work—clearly so in style and equally in the dramatic causality, past and present, of the narrative—and also of the most recent film adaptations.

Carmilla's lesbianism and Laura's qualified reciprocation of it is partially de-eroticised in all the film versions, but—in terms of scenes of physical interaction between Carmilla and her lover-victims—is least ambiguous in the two latest of them. Hammer's *The Vampire Lovers* (1970) and *Lust for a Vampire* (1971) represent in their way a

THE FEMALE VAMPIRE

Mike Raven and Barbara Jefford in LUST FOR A VAMPIRE

modern transliteration of the tradition in which Le Fanu laboured. Carmilla, as embodied by Ingrid Pitt—who portrayed Countess Dracula in the following year—is, more than the blondes Annette Vadim and Ursula Davis who had the role in the earlier productions, physically dissimilar to Le Fanu's description: "she was slender . . . her features were small and beautifully formed; her eyes large, dark and lustrous." But despite the fact that the Hammer Carmilla is full-bodied and lacking the sloe-eyed features of the verbal portrait, she possesses a consummate sexuality which she depends on more heavily than any cunning or unnatural strength to acquire blood and guard the secret of her affliction. Unlike the Carmilla of *Blood and Roses* or *Terror in the Crypt,* her communion with her victim is based more on a physical than mental control. Her blood-drinking begins as she bares and strokes the young woman's breasts, desensitising them to the sharpness of her fangs by inducing a quasi-orgasmic haze in the classic manner of the male undead. This Carmilla's prideful self-image, the view of herself as both master and malefactor, is also a state of mind more conventionally found in the male of the species.

Once having become what she is, the Hammer Carmilla seems to spends less time in remorse than in the pursuit of pleasures which are still available to her. In one sense, this kind of characterisation is farther removed from the novella than any previous, accentuating hedonism above compulsion as the principle motivating force and undermining much of the irony of the situation; but in a scene such as the observation of the village girl's funeral procession, in which Carmilla complains of how discordant the burial music is and deprecates the whole process ("What a fuss! Why *you* must die everyone must die. And all are happier when they do"), the emphasis shifts, so that her discomfiture may be caused either by the religious icons and chanting of the cortège or by the memory of her own death and melancholy over her loss of that "happiness" so that the ambiguity of the original is retained. Even with the added scenes of seduction and the overt staging of what remains essentially Le Fanu's plot. *Vampire Lovers* is far from purely exploitative. Carmilla's bath, for example, is not a *de rigueur* nude scene but a narrative event which sets up a situation in which Carmilla can first display her body then have her unwary host disrobe to try on one of the dresses she had laid out, insisting that to get the feel of the fabric she must wear nothing underneath, so that this episode ultimately becomes the first in the pattern of sensual manipulation which the vampire practices throughout the film.

Alhough the Hammer Carmilla is staked and beheaded at the end of the first film, she survives that quietus to return in a sequel; and this may, in the most pragmatic terms, account for why she is the least covert of female vampires, relying on her powers to seduce and destroy anyone who discovers her undead condition taking few other precautions. In turn, this arrogant and extravagant behaviour may explain why, of all the film versions of "Carmilla," *Vampire Lovers* most consistently brings the enigmas engendered by Le Fanu to melodramatic fruition.

III. OTHER DAUGHTERS OF DARKNESS

"I'm going out hunting vampires. Ha, ha, ha."
"Vampires, sir? I thought one hunted them with checkbooks."
"Don't be facetious, Hobbs."

(Dracula's Daughter)

While the historical and literary traditions represented by Elizabeth Bathory and Carmilla have only been brought to the screen in the picture goes back considerably farther in time and, as with the male last dozen years, the female vampire as the main character of a motion figure, includes both demonic and sympathetic characterisations.

Dracula's Daughter (1936) is, as the year and title may suggest, an

Gloria Holden hypnotises her young model in DRACULA'S DAUGHTER

informal sequel to Universal's *Dracula*. Although the Count's daughter, Maria, murders for blood—an early sequence demonstrates her mesmeric powers as she attacks a young man in the street—she is indifferent to her victims as sexual objects and considers herself an otherwise normal woman possessed by an hereditary disease. When the distractions of painting and a direct attempt to exorcise the influence of Dracula's parentage by stealing and burning his body in a moonlit ritual of elaborate incantations and rubrics prove unremedial, she seeks the help of a psychiatrist, planning to inspire either his love or his scientific curiosity ("There are more things in heaven and earth than are dreamed of in your psychiatry, Mr. Garth") to insure his silence. Because Maria is so painfully aware of her uncontrollable bestiality but so naive as to its necessary consequences—her conversations with her manservant underscore the futility of her attempts to sublimate and her hopes for a cure ("Sandor, what do you see in my eyes?" "Death")—and because the actual assaults are so stylised (she uses a ring to hypnotize her prey and the two sequences end before any actual blood-drinking with a subjective blurring as Maria advances on the man and a pan to the African mask on the wall of her studio when she attacks a young woman recruited by Sandor to pose for her), the female figure in *Dracula's Daughter* is more sympathetic than most.

The notion in film of the vampire as a demon or as a victim of its own evil desires finds an example much less frequently in women and then usually only in the form of minor or supporting characters. Such diverse titles as *Santo vs. The Vampire Women*, (see Chapter Two), *Vampyr,* and *Twins of Evil* constitute the isolated instances of female antagonists who are unmitigatedly evil. *Twins of Evil*, in particular, breaks down the schizophrenic impulses which often plague the unwilling vampire into two mentally opposed but physically identical

From LA NOCHE DE WALPURGIS

THE FEMALE VAMPIRE

The village beauty, played by Madeleine Collinson, finds an unsuspecting victim in TWINS OF EVIL

personages and develops as a central premise the assertion that "those who are truly dedicated will not die from a vampire's bite—they will become one of the undead."

At one point in *Dracula's Daughter* a police inspector has the brief conservation with his butler reproduced at the head of this section. In his own way Hobbs reflects the popular disbelief which underlies all films of the horror and fantasy *genre*, and against which many specific pictures from *Dracula's Daughter* to *The Night Stalker* have consciously played. As with the male figure, films centered on women which operate outside the normal iconography have an added burden in maintaining suspension of that disbelief. *Blood of Dracula* (1957) is, like *The Vampire*, a film which takes certain characteristics of the traditional undead and places them in a science-fiction context, specifically centering on an extraordinary situation at a girl's prep school where a chemistry teacher experiments on a pupil and changes her into a bat-faced monster who sucks blood, with whom a minimal amount of empathy is possible.

The Velvet Vampire (1971) is more of an analogue to *Count Yorga*, interesting both because the antagonist has no compunctions about the practice of her vampirism and also because it parodies certain aspects of the *genre*—ranging from simple homages such as an art exhibit in the "Stoker Gallery" and naming the woman vampire Diane Le Fanu to the more elaborate novelties of having her make her home in the desert or demonstrate a taste for raw chicken. The eclectic style of this film—day-lit desert landscapes and a final chase through downtown Los Angeles providing a contrast with low-lit interiors full of unnatural colours—encompasses some imaginative narrative turns (the vampire using her strength to overpower and kill an unsuspecting mugger which antedates a similar scene with the two pimps in *Scream, Blacula, Scream*; her body "floating" down an escalator in the chase scene in a manner reminiscent of *Son of Dracula*) but like *Count Yorga*, *The Velvet Vampire* never really comes to terms with the broader implications of the *genre*, never makes the female figure's vampirism more than an inexplicable aberration or, like her fondness for velvet, a fetish.

Celeste Yarnall as Diane Le Fanu in **THE VELVET VAMPIRE**

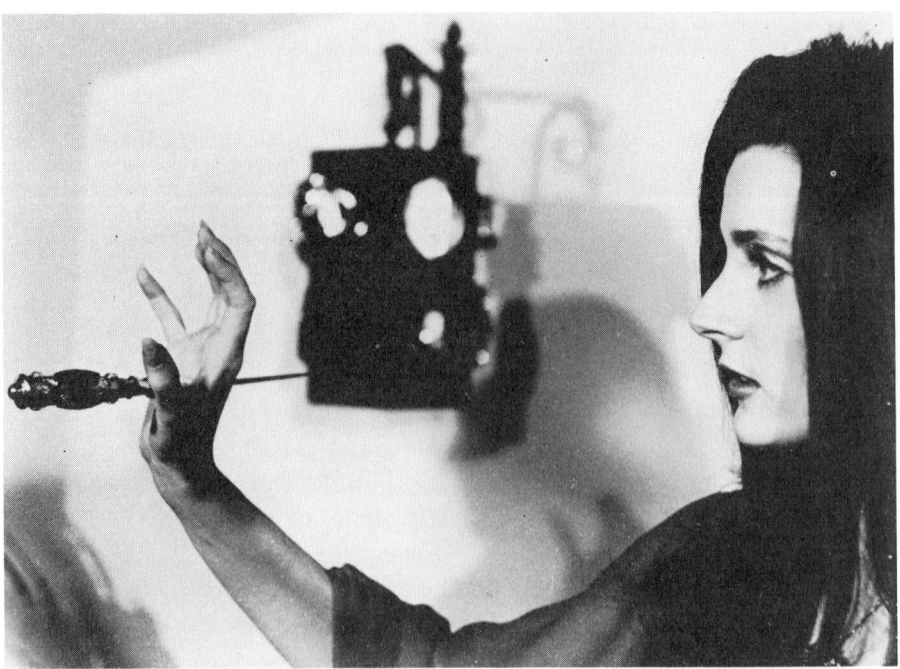

Celeste Yarnall seduces Sherry Miles in the VELVET VAMPIRE

IV. VAMPYR

Whether Carl Dreyer's *Vampyr* should even be classed with the other films of this chapter is unclear. Although the titles credit Le Fanu's "In a Glass Darkly" (a volume of tales containing "Carmilla") as a source, the conception of the female vampire which Dreyer brings to the screen bears little relation either to Le Fanu and the adaptations already discussed or almost any other figure in the whole of the *genre*. The entire film lies under a kind of expressionistic veil, much thicker than that of *Nosferatu* or *Dracula*, as the vampire (an old woman), the doctor in her service, and the various protagonists move with dance-like deliberation through a series of disconnected scenes. The very idea of the undead woman as a white-haired crone borrows more heavily from the lore of witchcraft and sorcery than that of vampirism—the figure in the film closely resembles the witch who is burned at the stake in Dreyer's *Day of Wrath*—and, excepting such secondary characters as the Baroness in *Brides of Dracula*, is without parallel in film.

Despite the fact that this withered succubus is more than anything else a personification of evil, a decaying body feeding on the young,

The skeletal hand in Gray's dream from VAMPYR

The vampire peers at Gray in the coffin from VAMPYR

Vampyr itself is less a horror film than a vivid nightmare of unforeseen images and events cut from the same fabric as the dream in *Blood and Roses* but less explicit, an ontology of terror which constricts and obscures material reality causing the viewer to puzzle over what traces of it do filter through. Characteristic of Dreyer as much as of the genre, the viewpoint is again that of the victim; for although an image like that of a skeletal hand poised to pour out the contents of a small vial may seem nothing more than an emblem of sensory delight—in having animated this bony thing or of intellectual delight in having the "magic" to animate it, when put in the context of an overall visual delirium, the shot reacquires a "sense" of its own. There are more direct examples of this subjective rendering of a vague, metaphysical malaise: a victim lying fully conscious inside a coffin and being carried to a gravesight; shots repeated to generate an aura of *déjà vu*. Even a statis shot such as that of a woman bound to a wrought-iron bench can be staged to suggest the rupture or perhaps transcendence of being caught in the vampire's grip: her black dress is set off from the white wall behind her; the uneven texture of that wall is accentuated by the shadow of the bench and unlit grey areas. Her hands are jerked behind her, bound and held to the iron by a two-foot length of rope which she

Leone bound to the bench from VAMPYR

The Doctor perishes in a deluge of flour, from VAMPYR

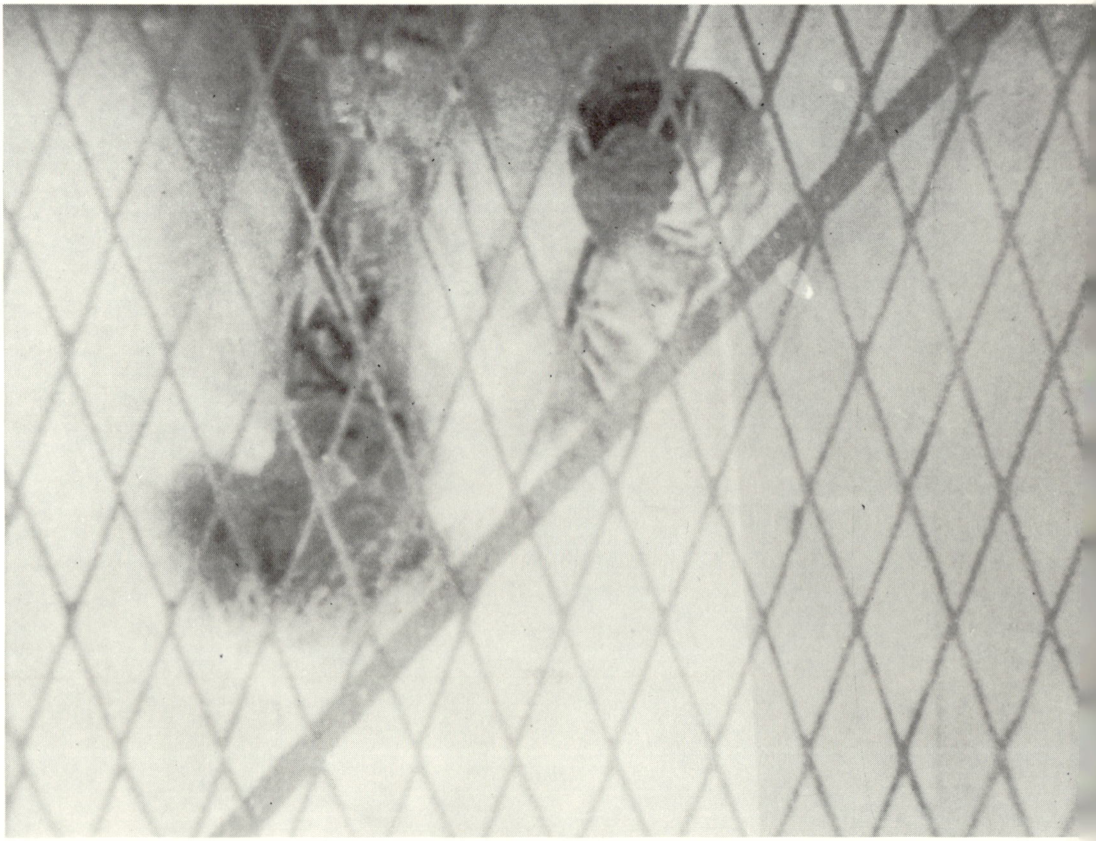

is drawing taut for no apparent reason. Her body lurches forward but her head is erect and she gazes ahead. What is most remarkable is that none of her discomfiture is apparent from her expression. Her body, which is alive, is reduced to a kind of inanimateness or numbness, even though her arms are twisted into angles not unlike the clawlike fingers of the bony hand. On the surface, her face and its serenity contradict her situation. Simultaneously, she cannot foresee and yet does foresee being untied, has a presentiment of such clarity that when she is freed she need not even glance at her rescuer. Like the bony hand the image requires penetration: it is not merely unreal but illusionary.

Accordingly, the conclusion of *Vampyr* is a perpetuation of all the earlier paradoxes. While a young couple wander through the woods, the doctor perishes. As the scenes shift back and forth, the light diffusing through the branches clutches at the couple annihilating the sharp line of their silhouette as it envelops them in hazy long shot; the flour tumbling down through an overhead sifter (shot subjectively so that the white powder pours through the wire mesh like the sun's ray through the branches outside) and clinging to his hair and whiskers envelops the doctor. Both move lethargically: he because of the physical impediment of the flour; they for unspecified reasons. The noise of the machinery alternates with the calling ("Halloing") on the lake, with the drums and violins on the soundtrack. From the low angle of the man with the lantern who sets the mill wheels in motion and traps the doctor, the scene cuts to a high angle of another man on a bank helping the couple to beach their boat. Finally, both are isolated, he in his white cage, they on the lake with its oppressive dimness, isolated from "land" as surely he is in his torrent of flour; and throughout, the facile symbol of the wheels grinding, reoccurs curiously explicit in the middle of it all. If this and, to a certain extent, the entire film deviate from the *genre* conventions in both narrative and expression, it is because Dreyer has gone beyond concerns of terror. The only terror is in the "dream in dream" tone of *Vampyr*, which goes beyond fantasy into a world where the fantastic imagines the real.

Christopher Lee as Dracula and Caroline Munro as Laura in DRACULA A.D. 1972

CHAPTER FOUR

Emerging Traditions

I. HAMMER AND THE VICTORIAN PSYCHOLOGY

> None of the group of beliefs here dealt with is richer or more overdetermined than that in the Vampire, nor is there one that has more numerous connections with the other legends and superstitions. Its psychological meaning is correspondingly complicated, and in the analysis of it we shall proceed from its most typical form. It may be said at the outset that the latent content of the belief yields plain indications of most kinds of sexual perversions, and that the belief assumes various forms according as this or that perversion is more prominent.[1]

The release by Hammer Films of a new version of Stoker's "Dracula" in 1958 is something of a landmark in the history of the horror film. To begin with more than eighty percent of the vampire films produced throughout the world have come after the Hammer *Dracula* as the financial success of this adaptation motivated a succession of similarly low-budget companies to exploit the vampire *genre*. As they did this with increasing profit, the list of vampire films grew; but more central to this study is a second consideration: the shift to emphatic and overt elements in these productions. *Dracula* (1958) is quite a change from the Universal version of less than thirty years earlier and its informal sequels which had dominated the market. Many things left implicit in the naive manner so endemic to Universal's product or diluted in order to satisfy the needs of censorship surfaced, and the psycho-sexual aspects of the vampire myth were explored to an unprecedented depth. Much of the integrity of the source work was, as a result, restored; and the world of the Hammer vampires was, from the first, one in which psychologists, legend-hunters, and devotees of Nineteenth-century literature alike could revel. The male vampire figure became a tall and virile demon (especially so when played by Christopher Lee) with none of the posturing or ludicrousness which touched some of his

---
[1]. Jones, "On the Nightmare."

predecessors, while the female vampires of his retinue became voluptuous and voracious succubi. "Desire" and "obsession" became the key words as Thanatos and Eros were intermingled in victim and oppressor, translating into dramatic terms Friedlander's observation that "the active impulse to die is based on a libidinal impulse."[2] The Lucy of the Hammer *Dracula* awaits her deadly leman in bed, breathless and eager. Even the quintessentially Victorian Mina has her repressions dissolved as Dracula bestows kisses and caresses on her before indulging his vampiric thirst. Jones's analysis of the vampire phenomenon is particularly relevent here:

> The explanation of these (vampiric) phantasies is surely not hard. A nightly visit from a beautiful or frightful being, who first exhausts the sleeper with passionate embraces and then withdraws from him a vital fluid: all this can point only to a natural and common process, namely to nocturnal emissions accompanied with dreams of a more or less erotic nature. In the unconscious mind blood is commonly an equivalent for semen, and it is not necessary to have recourse, as Hock does, to the possibility of . . . 'wounds inflicted on oneself by scratching during a voluptuous dream.'

It does not involve much extrapolation to appreciate that views such as this must have affected the creators at Hammer Studios.

Hammer's introduction of colour to the vampire film also had a specific effect. On the one hand, it increased the realism of the productions (something Hammer was to aim for continually): vampires with blood-streaked fangs and breasts and the richly coloured tones of the sets create a mood of unsettling actuality far different from the black and white, neo-Gothic expressionism of Universal. On the other hand, colour could suggest quite the opposite of realism, could enhance the sensual, dreamlike quality of the films, as in the blue moonbeams that float through the air on the balcony of Lucy's room when she awaits Dracula's fatal embrace or the vivid red—traditionally associated with the devil and eroticism—which becomes a colour motif for the title figure in many of the films, to the point where some of his close-ups are completely suffused with that colour. Ultimately this use of colour is most effective in amplifying the nightmare state of these films. While most black-and-white productions do achieve visual distortions in camera angle, lighting, and set construction which are suggestive of nightmare; while allegorical conflicts and terrifyingly surreal events still abound, colour is uniquely able to add a layer of ineluctable, visceral immediacy to the image.

Watching a horror film, an audience probes the periphery of its unconscious—propelled through suspension of its disbelief toward a

---

[2]. Kate Friedlander, "On the 'Longing to Die'," in "Death Interpretations."

At Lucy's tomb from DRACULA (1958)

moment when repressed desires and psychological struggles are clarified in symbolic terms and then just as suddenly distanced and forced to consider the "reality" of what is on the screen in terms of their own dreams and fantasies. What became the Hammer style and was imitated by other companies worldwide was an exploitation of a general audience's susceptibility to fantasy and horror and a stress on psychological realism, eroticism, and natural detail in both performance and decor. Michael Carreras, Jimmy Sangster, Terence Fisher, and Anthony Hinds were among the most important forces behind this development, with Fisher and Hinds as good examples of radically different contributions made to the synthesis of the Hammer style.

Fisher in *Dracula, Brides of Dracula* (1960) and *Dracula, Prince of Darkness* (1965) relies heavily—particularly in relation to other Hammer products—on understatement. By means of finely-drawn characters and a flexible visual style, Fisher employs shifting moods to elicit tension. Van Helsing's arduous, fascinating struggle with his arch-enemy is the vortex of Fisher's Dracula films: he is a cool, methodical man (incarnated by Peter Cushing, with certain mannerisms carried over from his Frankenstein portrayal for Fisher) using modern scientific instruments as proficiently as he uses garlic and the crucifix, and in that very close to the original conception. On the other hand, Anthony Hinds, writing under the pseudonym John Elder, has scripted films which are far more hysterical and deviate in plot, temperament, and characterisation. In works like *Kiss of the Vampire* (1963), *Dracula Has Risen from the Grave* (1968), *Taste the Blood of Dracula* (1969) and *Scars of Dracula* (1970), Hinds initiates an exploration of the classic dichotomies of vampire fiction. Living and dead, light and dark, bestial and human, chaotic and ordered, good and evil are but a few examples of these dichotomies. The allegory is simple and direct like that of a Medieval morality play. The vampire is a creature of the night, an accomplice of the devil who is finally, and often quite literally, defeated by the forces of light in the form of men with faith, knowledge, and good purpose. Hinds, however, goes beneath the surface of the myth and draws out the more obscure, psychological oppositions inscribed in it. In the process the conflict becomes more of a struggle between the ego and the unconscious. Not unlike the counter-impulses of "Lamia" or "La morte amoureuse," the contest in films like *Kiss of the Vampire* is between the "reasonableness" of repression—the Victorian temper itself—and libidinous irrationality.

Hinds, then, associates the vampire myth in his films with the same psychic material which Jones speaks of:

> The love motif can, however, especially when in a state of repression, regress to an earlier form of sexuality, particularly to the sadistic-masochistic phase of development. It was remarked above that the masochistic side of a personality tends to regard the idea of Death as an aggressive onslaught, and the same is even truer of the idea of a dead person. A dead person who loves will love forever and will never be weary of giving and receiving caresses.
>
> On the other hand the dead being allows everything, can offer no resistance, and the relationship has none of the inconvenient consequences that sexuality may bring in its train in life. The phantasy of loving such a being can therefore make a strong appeal to the sadistic side of the sexual instinct.
>
> It [vampirism] evidently signifies a reversion to the most primitive aspects of sadism, both of the oral and anal kind.

The cult in *Kiss of the Vampire*—headed by a handsomely gaunt roué named Ravna who, with the help of an incestuous son and daughter,

Noel Williams introduces Jennifer Daniel to the vampire cult in
KISS OF THE VAMPIRE

lures young men and women into their group of corrupt devotees—exemplifies the reversion which Jones isolates. Ravna's orgies and black rites, for all the manorial splendor which surrounds them, are primitive enactments. One of his victim/disciples, a daughter of the local innkeeper, typifies the cruel frenzy of one who has become a ravenous

Isobel Black prepares to vampirise Edward de Souza in KISS OF THE VAMPIRE

undead. The oral-sadistic complexes connected with her vampirism could hardly be more explicit than in the scene in the graveyard where she bites the hand of Professor Zimmer who has interrupted her in the midst of an orgasmic summoning of a corpse or the later languorous assault/seduction of Gerald. The pleasure these aggressive actions give her is entirely manifest and forms a strong contrast to the morose and self-mortifying (in both his physical self-abuse and his drunkenness) demeanour of the bearded, black-clad Zimmer. The loss of his own daughter to Ravna has made him a monomaniac concerned only with the destruction of the cult and driven to adopt the elaborate ritual means which turn the forces of evil upon themselves and accomplish his end.

Hinds's Dracula films introduce a severe reversal of traditional roles. In *Dracula Has Risen from the Grave*, one of the king-vampire's followers is a priest and his antagonist, an agnostic. But the film in which

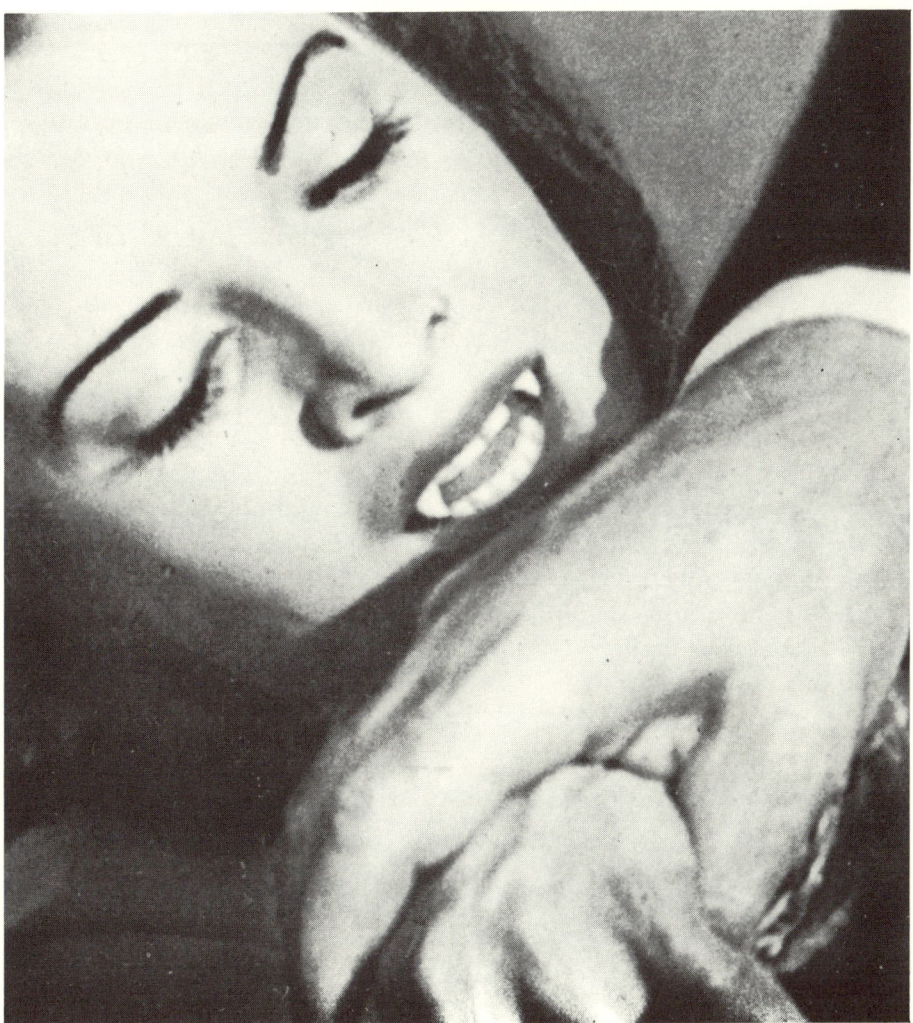

Isobel Black bites the hand of Clifford Evans in KISS OF THE VAMPIRE

Hinds seems most conscious of the underlying hypocrisy of moral postures is *Taste the Blood of Dracula*. Here, Hinds's vision of the Victorian-Edwardian family is focused on an overbearing father secretly indulging his sexual aberrations while restraining his children's natural desires. The Dracula figure is subsumed into this scheme as a catalyst, a ritual projection who leads the children to patricide and sexual fulfillment with him as their master.

In 1970 Hammer released the film adaptation of Le Fanu's "Carmilla" under the title of *The Vampire Lovers*, it perpetuated the studio tradition. Eroticism and attention to the period and intent of the original were, as with the male figure embodied in the *Dracula* series, a key to the psychology of the female vampire typified by Carmilla. While preying on men as well as women, the compulsive, carnivorous sexuality of the Hammer Carmilla in this film and *Lust for a Vampire* is tempered by her sentimental attachments to members of her own sex, which results in a double bind between affection for the love object and the need to consume it. *Twins of Evil* (1971 and written by Tudor Gates, who has worked on both *The Vampire Lovers* and *Lust for a Vampire*) contains a characterisation of a female undead who, as in Hinds's films, is the dramatic centre of a struggle between Puritanism and libido. Peter Cushing as the witchfinder Weil assimilates much of Hinds's Professor Zimmer, developing a portrait of a fanatic anti-Satanist who resembles a character from a Hawthorne tale.

Vampire Circus (1971) —a dense film containing sufficient personages to populate an expansive Victorian novel and consequently quite complex and difficult to follow—addresses the conflict of good and evil on a more obviously allegorical level than most Hammer productions. In a prologue, a young woman entices a child into the castle of her lover, the vampiric Count Mitterhouse. He is destroyed by a throng of frenzied villagers, and she is stripped and made to run the gamut. Like Weil, the vampire hunters are excessively Puritanical and sadistic,

From TWINS OF EVIL

Adrienne Corri supervises the diabolical rites in VAMPIRE CIRCUS

Robert Tayman is destroyed by a group of angry villagers in VAMPIRE CIRCUS

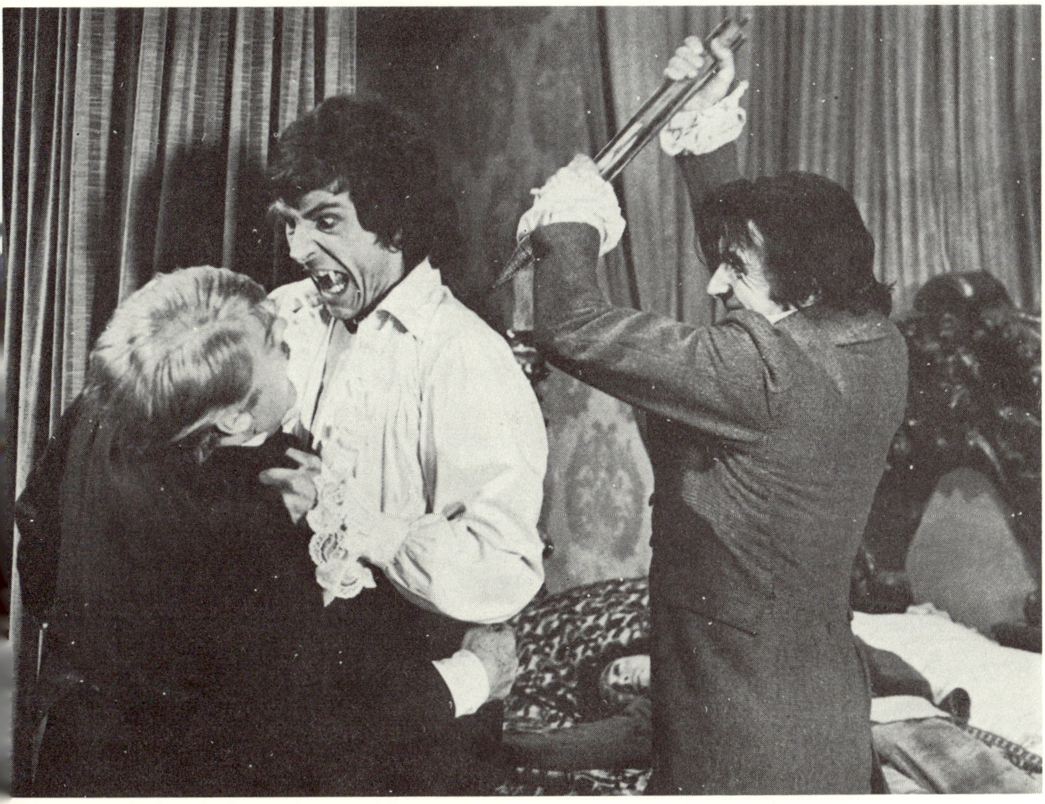

Baron Hartog defends himself from a pretty vampire in VAMPIRE LOVERS

villifying her as much for her adulterous love as for participation in the murder of the child and obviously taking pleasure in the beating which they administer as a group. The remainder of the film takes place fifteen years later in the midst of a plague which the more superstitious townspeople believe is the result of Mitterhouse's dying curse. After the local doctor (the voice of rationalism: "Old wives' tales. The vampire exists only in legend nowhere else") has left in search of serum, a circus arrives promising "a thousand delights" to which the distraught villagers willingly surrender. The ritual aspects of this seduction of the entire town are externalised in both the calliope-like score of the film and the tricks of the circus performers—tumblers turning into bats; a panther becoming a man; the "mirror of life" which acts like an extra-spatial passageway (reminiscent of Cocteau's *Orpheus*) —all contribute to a scheme of explicit non-real or symbolic events which haze the distinction between the material and the illusionary, a distortion which is exploited for suspense in later scenes when the vampires are pursued by the townsmen or for a more immediate, Lewtonesque *frisson* when a pair of jewelled boot buckles are taken for a pair of deadly animal eyes. Simultaneously, the stylised sexuality of the prologue (the beating or the image of a bat emerging from the eye of a skull) becomes more overt, containing implications of bestiality as the panther-man seduces the young daughter of the *burgermeister* and incest as the headmistress of the circus is revealed to be the woman of the prologue who now sets her undead twins (fathered presumably by Mitterhouse) on her mortal daughter.

Finally, *Countess Dracula* concentrates, as in Sasdy and Hinds's earlier *Taste the Blood of Dracula*, on the psychological cannibalism and latent incest of family life. Countess Elisabeth enters into her relationship with Imre Toth after having figuratively devoured and assimilated her offspring's personality. Constrained by the enactment of child murder and the fantasy of recaptured youth fulfilled, the Countess vacillates schizophrenically between the role of mother and jealous lover, alternatively cradling Toth to her breast or rocking him like an infant and reprimanding him for bringing a whore into the castle. H. F. Searles characterises such a relationship—which on a more general level is typical of the ambivalent response of a victim to a vampiric predator—in this way:

> We have records of the parent of the schizophrenic patient who behaved in an inordinately seductive way towards the child, thus fostering in the latter an intense conflict . . . between, on the one hand, his desire to mature and fulfill his own individuality, and, on the other hand, his regressive desire to remain in an infantile symbiosis with his parent, to remain there at the cost of investing even his sexual strivings . . . in that regressive relationship.[3]

II. MARIO BAVA AND THE BAROQUE IMAGE

>   What man that see the ever-whirling
>   wheel
>   Of Change, the which all mortall things
>   doth sway
>   But that thereby doth find, and plainly
>   feele,
>   How MUTABILITY on them doth play
>   Her cruell sports, to many mens decay?
>   Spenser, "The Faerie Queene,"
>   VII, i, 1-5

A carved sarcophagus reposes in a high-arched, tenebrous crypt. After a montage in which the corpse/woman within it has undergone a metamorphosis from the bony remains of necrosis to new-moving flesh, the camera has pulled back to medium long shot. From this vantage, the

---

3. Harold F. Searles, "The Effort to Drive the Other Person Crazy" in the *British Journal of Medical Psychiatry*.

Barbara Steele watches over her father's corpse in BLACK SUNDAY

Barbara Steele and John Richardson in BLACK SUNDAY

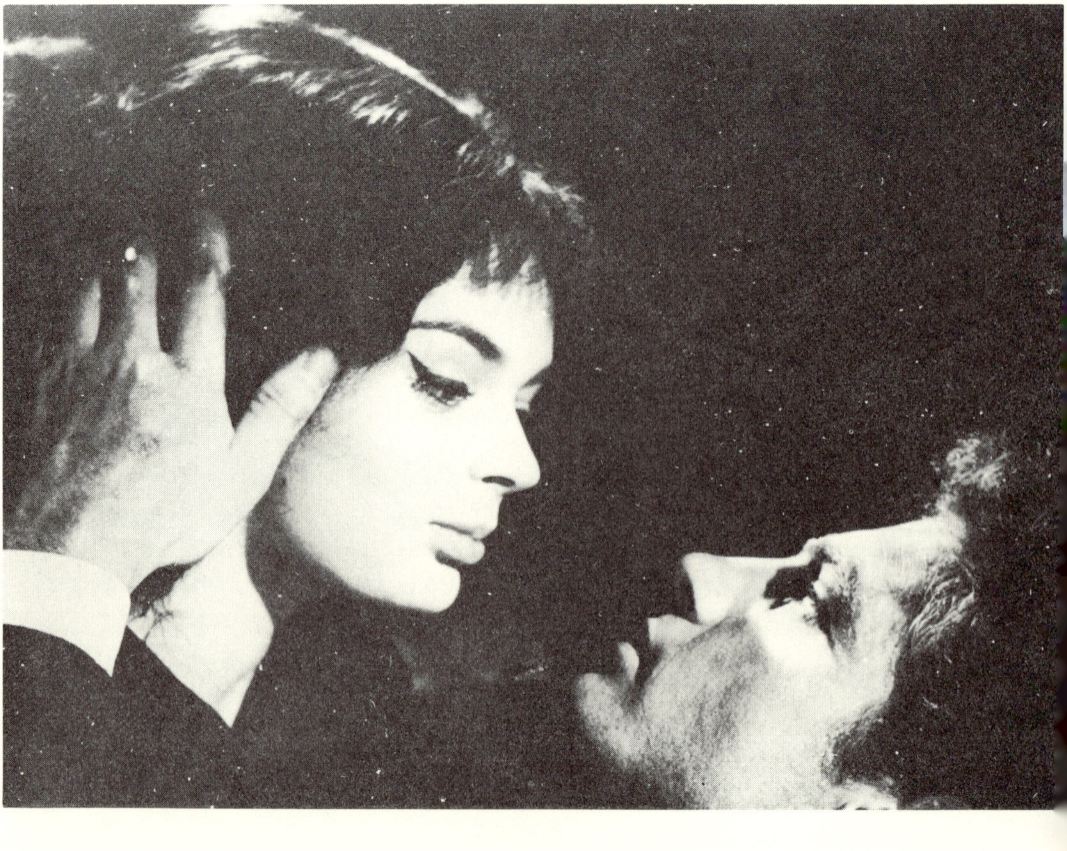

spectator familiar with the constructs of the genre may anticipate a hand stretching out painfully from the enclosure (cf. a similar resurrection in *Dracula—Prince of Darkness*). Instead, the virulent energy which has reformed the ashes into unnatural life is suffused into the cinerary stone itself. There is a crack; an explosion: granite fragments break away and crumble into heaps on the floor of the vault. The thin cloud of dust, newly disturbed after hundreds of years, settles again and reveals the body still lying, unmoved, on the catafalque.

This sequence from Mario Bava's Black Sunday *(La maschera del demonio,* 1960) illustrates some of the expressive power of Bava's *mise-en-scène,* suggests something of the scope and invention of his Baroque imagery which in turn defines his approach to the genre, an approach that, to borrow Coleridge's terms, "dissolves, diffuses, and dissipates . . . is essentially vital, even as all objects (as objects) are essentially fixed and dead."[4] Here the "fixed and dead objects" are the conventions of the vampire film (some overused to the point of stereotypification and cliché), which for many filmmakers become suffocating restrictions. Bava's tactic is a heavy reliance on visual expression which externalises the metaphysical implications of the subject matter. The unseen energy postulated by the intricate series of dissolves as the skull in *Black Sunday* begins to reacquire flesh in slow, barely perceptible stages, as each layer of skin reappears and the punctures left by the demon's mask close into fine circles and vanish, as the black, empty sockets gradually disclose the whites of eyes enraged by centuries of death, until finally the nostrils flare, the neck muscles constrict, and the whole body arches up under the sting of renewed life—that energy (and the expectations it engenders in the viewer) builds to the point where it can no longer be contained, where the stone itself must rupture and release it.

Coming as it does in the forefront of scores of vampire films which have been produced since 1960, compared to the relatively few made before that date, *Black Sunday* simultaneously recalls the seminal expressionism of Murnau in its iconography—the sophisticated optical devices which create the graphic reality of the vampire's revivification are differentiated from the earlier filmmaker's undercranking and negative images principally in terms of technological advances—and anticipates the psychological realism of many later films in its characterisations. More importantly, perhaps, all of Bava's films are staged with a consistency of viewpoint inapparent in other European productions. While a motion picture such as the German *Cave of the Living Dead (Der Fluch der grunen Augen,* 1963) may project shadows of a vampire onto

4. "Biographia Literaria," XIII.

From **PLANET OF THE VAMPIRES**

Two space "vampires" in PLANET OF THE VAMPIRES

white walls in a manner reminiscent of *Nosferatu*, the insertion of such highly stylised shots within the context of a modern setting causes an iconic confusion, a disintegration more appropriate to parody than straight dramatic treatment. While *The Last Man on Earth* (made in Italy in 1964) may adapt the science-fiction vampirism of Matheson's "I Am Legend," its final scenes of the killing in the church lapse into quasi-religious symbolism and deific myths, which are barred from Bava's *Planet of the Vampires* (*Terrore nello spazio*, 1965), being instead a more rigorous synthesis of the two *genres* which draws its novel and bizarre sense of horror from such juxtapositions as dead astronauts rising from their shallow, slab-covered graves to tear through their airless shrouds of transparent plastic. Most basically, the world which Bava conveys in his films is a mutable one, composed of shifting contrasts and colours, of complements and atonalities, a world which moves like Spenser's "ever-whirling wheel" from real to unreal and back again, from life to death and death to life in an unstable landscape of phantasmagorical sights and sounds. Bava's characters are often thrust into the mutable middle-ground between these two existential extremities, where figures glide through misty, opulently-decorated yet insubstantial and illusionary settings, a universe of semi-darkness where shadows and hallucinations are as graphically actualized as the personages, a spectral passageway linking the natural and supernatural where the way forward or back is uncertain. The oracle Medea in *Hercules in the Haunted World* (*Ercole al centro della terra*, 1961) typifies one stranded in this limbo. The masked form of the woman is merged with an eerie, laboured voice on the soundtrack, modulated as if she were calling up from a chamber deep below ground; she is separated by a curtain of glimmering beads from the camera's (real world's) plane of view and is caught in a flood of changing lights of green, blue, and gold which spin through the frame alternately striking her body and falling behind her to throw her into silhouette, while she sits swaying between intangible polarities.

While many of these expressions are rooted in a photographic style which Bava may have developed earlier in his career, as a cinematographer, the mood and quality of the images in his own films seem dictated by an underlying conception of life as an uncomfortable union of

Christopher Lee as Lichas in HERCULES IN THE HAUNTED WORLD

Barbara Steele as Katia in BLACK SUNDAY

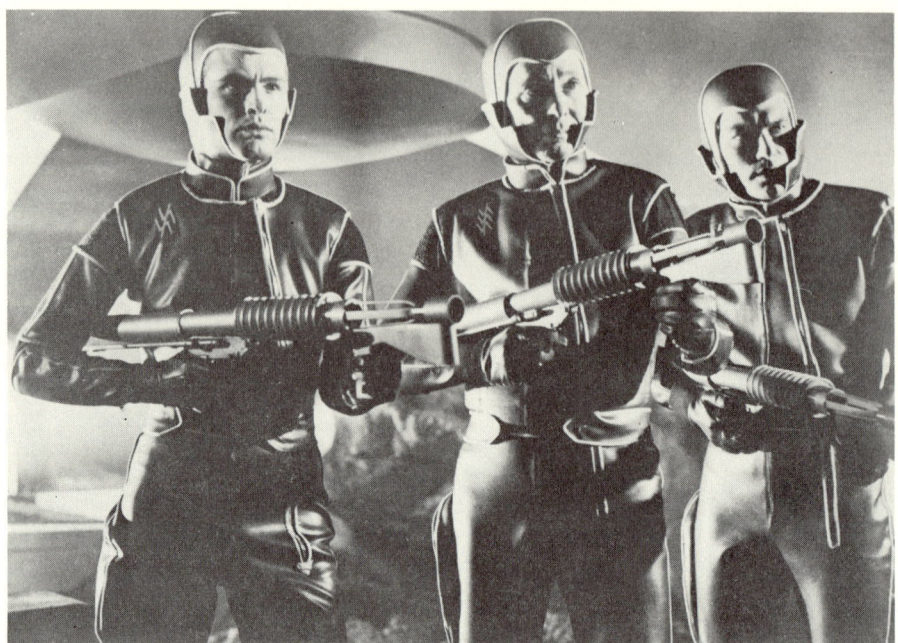

From PLANET OF THE VAMPIRES

illusion and reality and are fused into a dramatic conflict which is primarily psychological as his characters confront the dilemma of distinguishing between the two perceptions. In *Black Sunday,* the protagonist is faced with a choice between a seductive vampire and a virginal young woman who happen to be identical in appearance and who, to further confound his recognition of one or the other, can exchange souls; in the conclusion of *What!* (*La frusta e il corpo,* 1963) the heroine dies without resolving the ambiguity over whether she has genuinely been haunted by the ghost of a murdered former lover or simply conjured up his aspect out of her guilt-ridden subconscious; in *Hercules in the Haunted World,* the travellers to Hades are explicitly warned about the power of illusions by the Hesperides—"Do not believe in what you think you see"—which counsel is verified visually when Hercules and Theseus dive into a sea of flames to discover it is only water.

Just as Bava evokes the *genre* on a formal level—of stylistic resonances with both antecedent and subsequent films—he adds detail to it in his own motion pictures via a specific visual and figurative usage. The cold blue light which envelops the father returning from killing the Turkish vampire, and now undead himself, in the final episode of *Black Sabbath* (*I tre volti della paura,* 1963) makes it instantaneously clear that his family's and his own fear that he might become a *vourdalak* have been realised, that the pall of light which grips him is the equivalent of an aura of death. The apprehension of a character moving down a corridor in *Black Sunday* is transmitted by a shifting side-light, which strikes first one half of the face then the other in an equation of fear and curiosity driving the figure hesitatingly forward (an equation only partially complete in the black-and-white frame of *Black Sunday*, which Bava compounds by also changing from blue to red light with their respective connotations of cold and warmth in analogous sequences in later colour films). Equally informing is the red mist through which Hercules and his companions drift unconsciously, a visceral premonition of the rust-coloured tangled trees and crimson lakes of lava which await them in the underworld. Bava often recruits mythic and social codes as well as purely filmic conventions to instill a sense of anxiety in the viewer based on "misreading"—the two mastiffs which accompany the entry of Barbara Steele playing a dual role in *Black Sunday* hint incorrectly that in this instance she might be the vampire come back with two bestial familiars, who turn out to be mortal pets; or the plot twist at the end of *Planet of the Vampires* which indicates that the astronauts seen throughout the film have not been of the earthly origin which the audience supposed from their speech and human features.

Ultimately all these elements are united to maximise the chances of a positive, emotional response from all viewers—both the novice and the sophisticate in the *genre*—as, for example, in the dissolution of the female *revenant* in *Black Sunday* or in the last combat in *Hercules in the Haunted World* in which the mythic hero uproots a grove of petrified trees to dispatch a cohort of stone-men in garments that resemble cobwebs and overpowers the vampire, Lichas, who wields a knife formed from the fingers of a skeletal hand. When the witch returns to ashes in *Black Sunday*, when the figure of Lichas bursts into flames and falls to dust, neither the event nor its context are new—it is only the rendering, which in these cases and countless similar ones, in films by Bava and scores of others, can transmute both the particulars of narrative and the generalisations of *genre*, can make yet another recounting of the vampire myth as fresh as the oldest of its tellings.

Part Two
Filmography and Bibliography

Filmography

Since we have attempted in this study to confine ourselves to vampires of Eastern European tradition as described in the first section, this delimitation has been carried over into the filmography. Accordingly, many films which feature "vampire" in the title, hoax-vampire films, "non-human" vampire films, or *femme fatale* vampire films—to name but a few of the possible other categories—are not included. We have, however, made a few necessary exceptions: (1) historical or natural "vampires" of the type described in Chapter One; (2) *Terrore nello spazio* because of its relationship to other of Mario Bava's vampire films; (3) *Omega Man* because its source is the vampire novel "I Am Legend;" (4) *Queen of Blood* because its extra-terrestrial female vampire closely resembles the human type; and (5) *London after Midnight* and *Mark of the Vampire* because they are important in considering Browning and Lugosi.

We have listed the films by original title whenever possible and their year according to their release in their country of origin. Also whenever possible we have included the American distributor.

Key:
Prod. Co.—Production Company
Dist—Distributor
Prod—Producer
Dir—Director
Sc—Screenwriter
Ph—Photographer
Art Dir—Art Director
Ed—Editor
Real names are listed in [brackets] after pseudonyms

Bela Lugosi and Lou Costello in ABBOTT AND COSTELLO MEET FRANKENSTEIN

ABBOTT AND COSTELLO
  MEET FRANKENSTEIN (1948)
  U.S.A.
Prod. Co.: Universal
Dir.: Charles T. Barton
Sc.: Robert Lees, Frederic Rinaldo, John Grant
Ph.: Charles Van Enger
Art Dir.: Bernard Herzbrun, Hilyard Brown
Mus.: Frank Skinner
Ed.: Frank Gross
Bud Abbott, Lou Costello, Lon Chaney Jr. (*Lawrence Talbot*), Bela Lugosi (*Dracula*), Glenn Strange, Jane Randolph, Charles Bradstreet, Leonore Aubert, Frank Ferguson.
83 mins.

AHKEA KKOTS (THE BAD
  FLOWER) (1961) South Korea
Prod. Co.: Sunglim
Dir.: Yongmin Lee
Sc.: Based on Bram Stoker's "Dracula"

L'AMANTE DEL VAMPIRO
  (THE VAMPIRE'S LOVER,
  THE VAMPIRE AND THE
  BALLERINA) (1961) Italy
Prod. Co.: ACIF Consorzio
Dist.: United Artists
Dir.: Renato Polselli
Sc.: Renato Polselli, Ernesto Gastaldi,
Ph.: Angelo Baistrocchi
Walter Brandi, Maria Luisa Rolando, Tina Gloriani, Isarco Ravaioli, John Turner.

ANAK PONTIANAK (SON OF
  THE VAMPIRE, CURSE OF
  THE VAMPIRE) (1958) Malaya
Prod. Co.: Shaw
Dir.: Ramon Estella

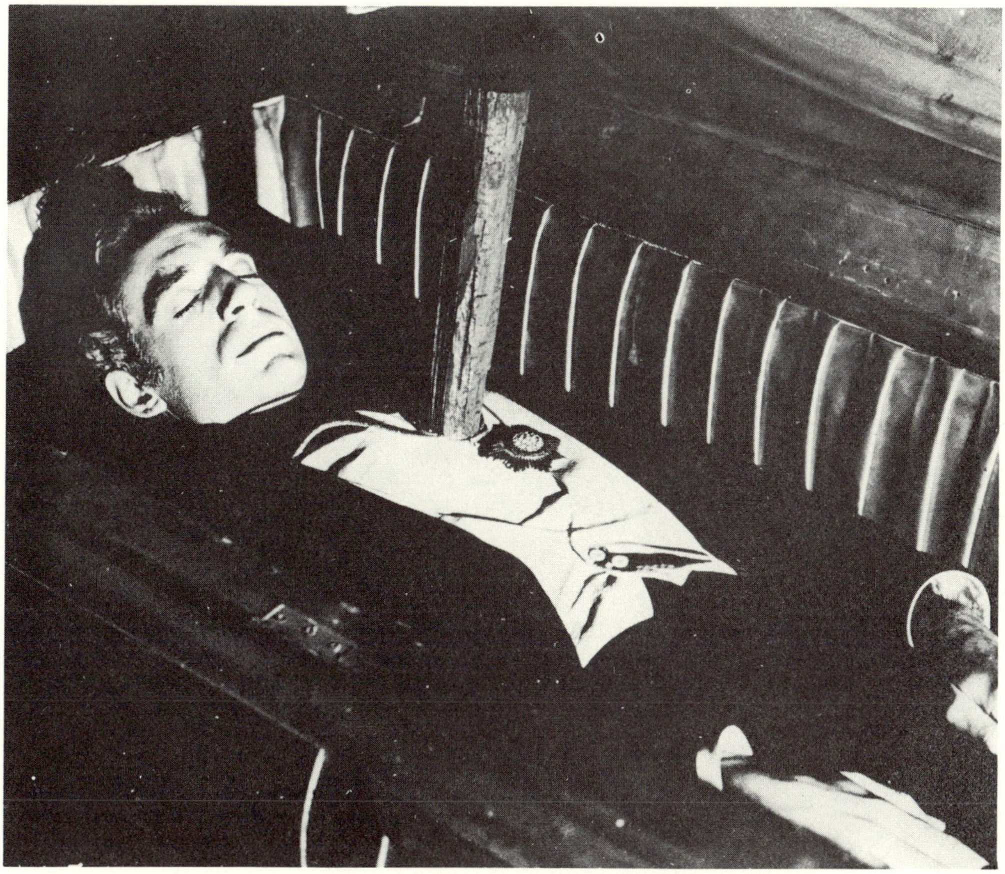

German Robles in EL ATAUD DEL VAMPIRO

From EL ATAUD DEL VAMPIRO

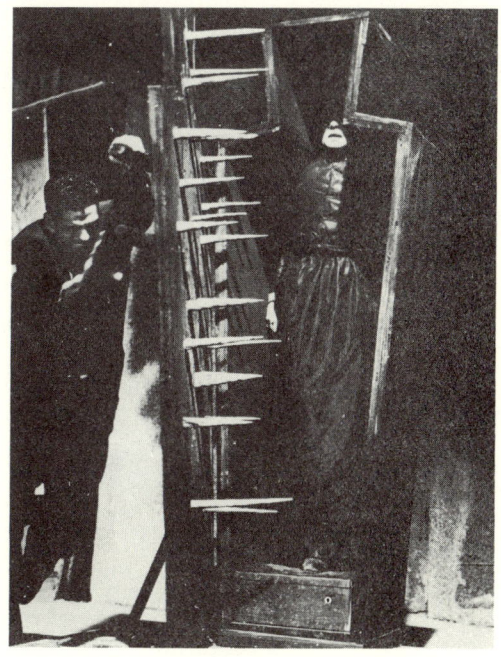

**EL ATAUD DEL VAMPIRO
(THE VAMPIRE'S COFFIN)**
(1957) Mexico
Prod. Co.: Abel Salazar/Cinematografica ABSA
Dir.: Fernando Mendez
Sc.: Ramon Obon, after an idea by Raul Zenteno. Dialogue by Javier Mateos
Ph.: Victor Herrera
Mus.: G.C. Carrion
German Robles (*Count Lavud/Duval*), Ariadna Welter, Abel Salazar, Yeire Beirute, Alicia Montoya, Guillermo Oraa, Carlos Ancira.

THE BAD FLOWER see AHKEA KKOTS

BEAST OF MOROCCO see THE HAND OF NIGHT

From Mario Bava's BLACK SABBATH

Boris Karloff carrying his grandson played by Massimo Righi in BLACK SABBATH

FILMOGRAPHY 149

The Witch Princess in BLACK SUNDAY

William Marshall in a revengeful mood

BEISS MICH, LIEBLING (BITE ME, DARLING) (1970) West Germany
Prod. Co.: Cinerama
Dir./Sc.: Helmut Foernbacher
Ph.: Igor Luther (Colour)
Eva Renzi, Patrick Jordan, Amadeus August.
102 mins.

BILLY THE KID VS. DRAUCLA (1966) U.S.A.
Prod. Co.: Avco-Embassy/Circle
Dir.: William Beaudine
Sc.: Karl Hittleman
Ph.: Lothrop Worth (Colour)
John Carradine (*Dracula*), Bing Russell, Roy Barcroft, Melinda Plowman, Harry Carey Jr., Charlita.
72 mins.

BITE ME, DARLING see BEISS MICH, LIEBLING

BLACK SABBATH see I TRE VOLTI DELLA PAURA

BLACK SUNDAY see LA MASCHERA DEL DEMONIO

BLACULA (1972) U.S.A.
Prod. Co.: American International
Prod.: Joseph T. Naar
Dir.: William Crain
Sc.: Joan Torres, Raymond Koenig
Ph.: John Stevens (Colour)
Art Dir.: Walter Herndon
Mus.: Gene Page
Ed.: Allan Jacobs
Sound: Charles Knight
William Marshall (*Mamuwalde/Blacula*), Denise Nicholas (*Michelle*), Vonetta McGee (*Tina*), Gordon Pinsent (*Lt. Peters*), Thalmus Rasulala (*Gordon Thomas*), Charles McCauley (*Dracula*), Emily Yancy, Lance Taylor, Ted Harris, Rick Metzler,

John Carradine in BILLY THE KID VS. DRACULA

Jitu Cumbuka, Logan Field, Ketty Lester, Elisha Cook, Eric Brotherson.
92 mins.

BLOOD AND ROSES see ET MOURIR DE PLAISER

BLOOD CEREMONY see CEREMONIA SANGRIENTA

THE BLOOD DEMON see DIE SCHLANGENGRUBE UND DAS PENDEL

THE BLOOD DRINKERS (1961)
Philippines
Pro. Co.: Hemisphere
Dir.: Gerardo de Leon
Sc.: Cesar Amigo, Rico Omagao
Ph.: F. Sacdalan (Colour)
Amelia Fuentes, Ronald Remy, Eddie Fernandez.
88 mins.

BLOOD FIEND see THEATRE OF BLOOD

BLOOD OF DRACULA (1957)
U.S.A.
Prod. Co.: Carmel
Dist.: American International
Prod.: Herman Cohen
Dir.: Herbert L. Strock
Sc.: Ralph Thornton
Ph.: Monroe Askins

Art Dir.: Leslie Thomas
Mus.: Paul Dunlap
Ed.: Robert Moore
Sandra Harrison (*Nancy Perkins*), Louise Lewis (*Miss Branding*), Gail Ganley (*Myra*), Jerry Blaine (*Tab*), Heather Ames (*Nola*), Malcolm Atterbury (*Lt. Dunlap*), Mary Adams (*Mrs. Thorndyke*), Thomas B. Henry, Don Devlin, Jeanne Dean, Richard Devon, Paul Maxwell, Carlyle Mitchell, Shirley de Lancey, Michael Hall.
70 mins.

BLOOD OF DRACULA'S CASTLE
  (1969) U.S.A.
Prod. Co.: A & E Film Corp.—
   Paragon
Dist.: Crown International
Dir.: Al Adamson, Jean Hewitt
Sc.: Rex Carlton
Ph.: Leslie (Laszlo) Kovacs
   (Colour)
John Carradine, Paula Raymond, Alex D'Arcy (*Dracula*), Robert Dix, Gene O'Shane.
82 mins.

BLOOD OF FRANKENSTEIN see DRACULA VS. FRANKENSTEIN

BLOOD OF NOSTRADAMUS see LA SANGRE DE NOSTRADAMUS

BLOOD OF THE VAMPIRE
  (1958) England
Prod. Co.: Universal/Eros
Dir.: Henry Cass
Sc.: Jimmy Sangster
Ph.: Geoffrey Seaholme
   (Colour)
Donald Wolfit, Vincent Ball, Barbara Shelley, Victor Maddern, John Le Mesurier, Milton Reid.

BLOOD OF THE VAMPIRE
  (Philippines) see CURSE OF THE VAMPIRES

From THE BLOOD DRINKERS

in her eyes...DESIRE! in her veins...the blood of a MONSTER!

BLOOD OF DRACULA
WILL GIVE YOU NIGHTMARES FOREVER

From Herbert L. Strock's BLOOD OF DRACULA

Sandra Harrison with a victim in BLOOD OF DRACULA

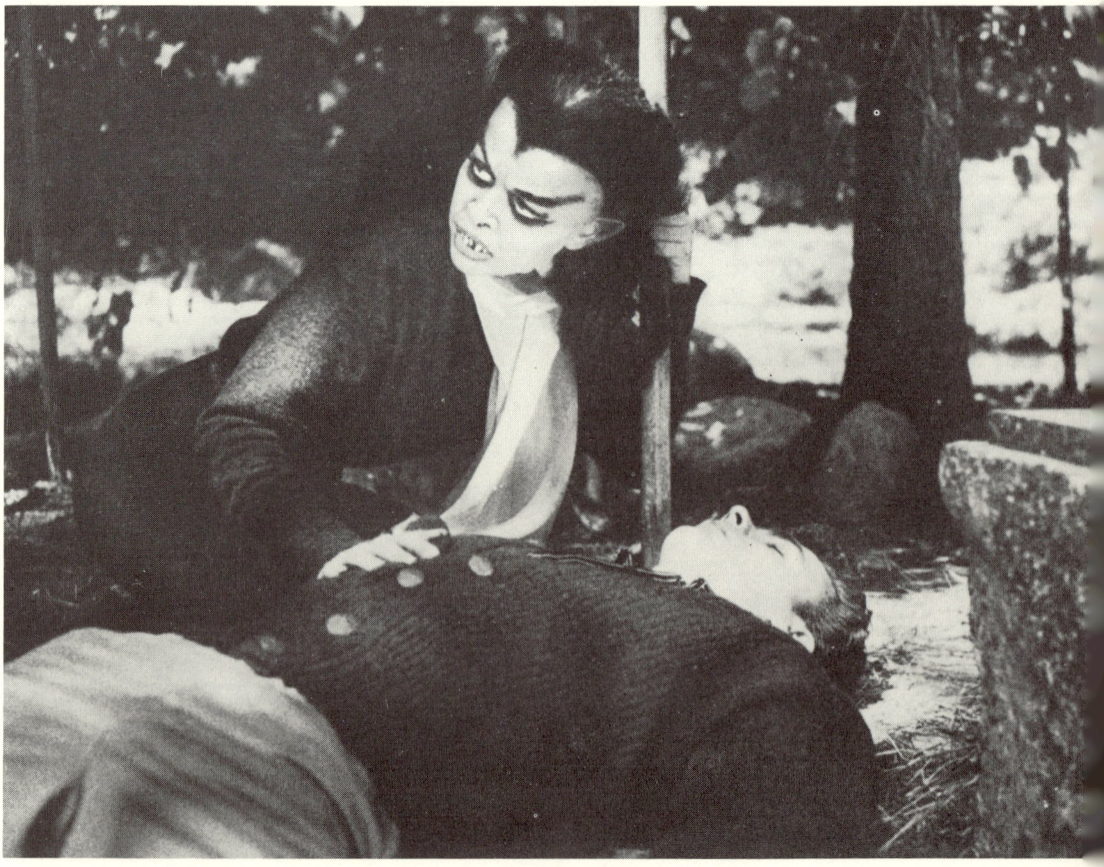

Victor Maddern, Vincent Ball and Donald Wolfit in BLOOD OF THE VAMPIRE

David Peel in BRIDES OF DRACULA

Peter Cushing with Yvonne Monlaur in BRIDES OF DRACULA

BLOODSUCKERS see INCENSE FOR THE DAMNED

BLOOD THIRST (1971)
Philippines
Prod. Co.: Chevron
Dir.: Newt Arnold
Sc.: N.I.P. Dennis
Ph.: Herme Santos (Colour)
Robert Winston [Adam Roarke], Katherine Henryk, Yvonne Nelson, Vic Diaz, Eddie Infante.

BLOOD THIRSTY EYES see CHI O SU ME

THE BLOODY VAMPIRE see EL VAMPIRO SANGRIENTO

THE BODY BENEATH (1970)
ENGLAND
Prod. Co.: Cinemedia
Dist.: Nova International
Dir./Sc./Ph.: Andy Milligan (Colour)
Gavin Read, Jackie Skarvellis, Susan Clark, Colin Gordon.
85 mins.

BRIDES OF DRACULA (1960)
England
Prod. Co.: Hammer
Dist.: Universal
Prod.: Anthony Hinds
Assoc. Prod.: Anthony Nelson-Keys
Dir.: Terence Fisher
Sc.: Jimmy Sangster, Peter Bryan, Edward Percy
Ph.: Jack Asher (Colour)
Art Dir.: Bernard Robinson, Thomas Goswell
Mus.: Malcolm Williamson
Ed.: Jim Needs, Alfred Cox
Peter Cushing (Van Helsing) Yvonne Monlaur (Marianne), Freda Jackson (Greta), David Peel (Baron Meinster), Martita Hunt (Baroness Meinster), Andrée Melly (Gina), Mona Washbourne (Frau Lang), Henry Oscar (Lang), Norman Pierce (Landlord), Vera Cook (Landlord's Wife), Fred Johnson (Curé), Miles Malleson (Dr. Tobler), Michael Mulcaster (Latour), Victor Brooks (Hans), Harold Scott (Severin), Marie Devereux (Village Girl).
85 mins.

BRING ME THE VAMPIRE see ECHENME AL VAMPIRO

THE CAKE OF BLOOD see PASTEL DE SANGRE

CAPURCITA Y PULGARCITO CONTRA LOS MONSTRUOS (TOM THUMB AND LITTLE RED RIDING HOOD VS. THE MONSTERS (1962)
Mexico
Prod. Co: Azteca (Colour)
Dir.: Roberto Rodriquez
Sc.: Roberto Rodriquez, Sergio Magaña, Fernando M. Ortiz, A. T. Portillo

CARRY ON SCREAMING (1966)
England
Prod. Co.: Sigma III/Anglo—Amalgamated/Warner—Pathe
Dir.: Gerald Thomas
Sc.: Talbot Rothwell
Ph.: Peter Rogers (Colour)
Kenneth Williams, Harry Corbett, Dennis Blake, Joan Sims, Jon Pertwee, Fenella Fielding (A Vampire)

EL CASTILLO DE LOS MONSTRUOS (1958) Mexico
Prod. Co.: Sotomayor
Dir.: Julian Soler
Sc.: Fernando Galiana, Carlos Orellana

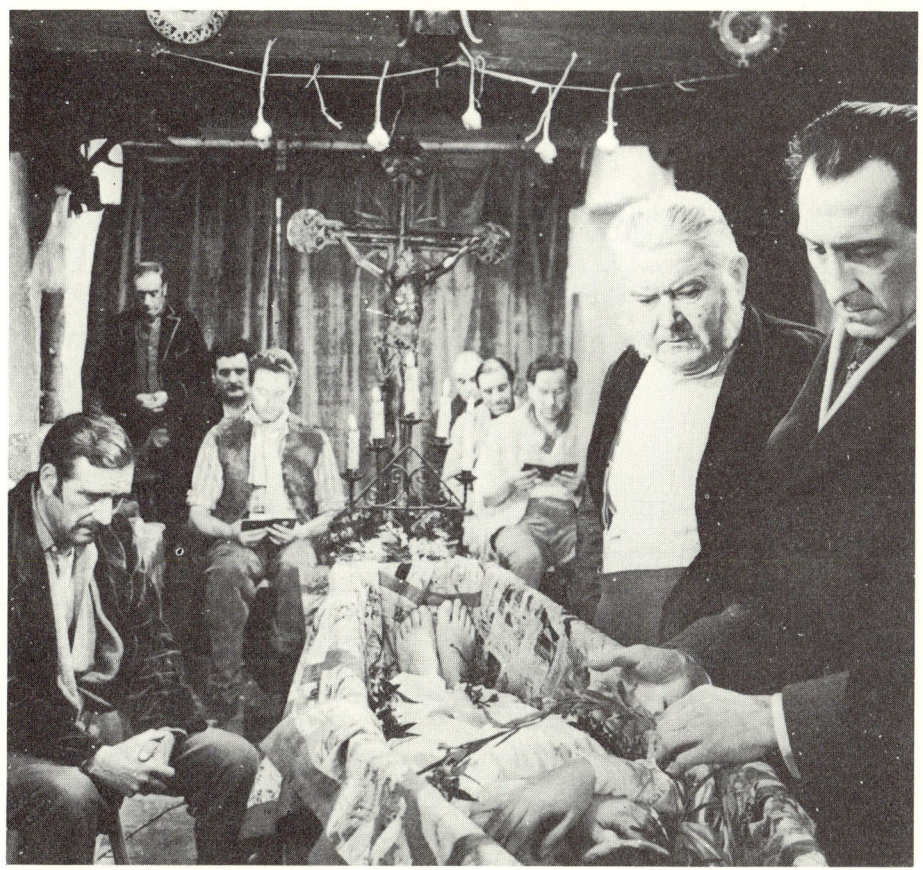
Van Helsing examines a corpse in BRIDES OF DRACULA

Ph.: Victor Herrera
German Robles (*Vampire*), Clavillazo, Evangelina Elizondo, Carlos Orellana.
85 mins.

CASTLE OF THE MONSTERS
see EL CASTILLO DE LOS MONSTRUOS

CAVE OF THE LIVING DEAD
see DER FLUCH DER GRUNEN AUGEN

CEREMONIA SANGRIENTA (BLOOD CEREMONY, RITUAL OF BLOOD) (1973)
Spain/Italy

Prod. Co.: X Films/Luis Films
Dir.: Jorge Grau
Sc.: Jorge Grau, Juan Tebar, Sandro Continenza
Ph.: Fernando Arribas
(Colour)
Lucia Bosé (*Erzebeth Bathory*), Karl Ziemmer, Ewa Aulin, Ana Farra, Silvano Zranquilli, Lola Gaos, Franca Grey, Angel Menendez.

CHANOC CONTRA EL TIGRE Y EL VAMPIRO (CHANOC [OR CHANO] VS. THE TIGER AND THE VAMPIRE) (1971)
Mexico
Prod. Co.: Azteca (Colour)
Dir.: Gilberto Martinez Solares

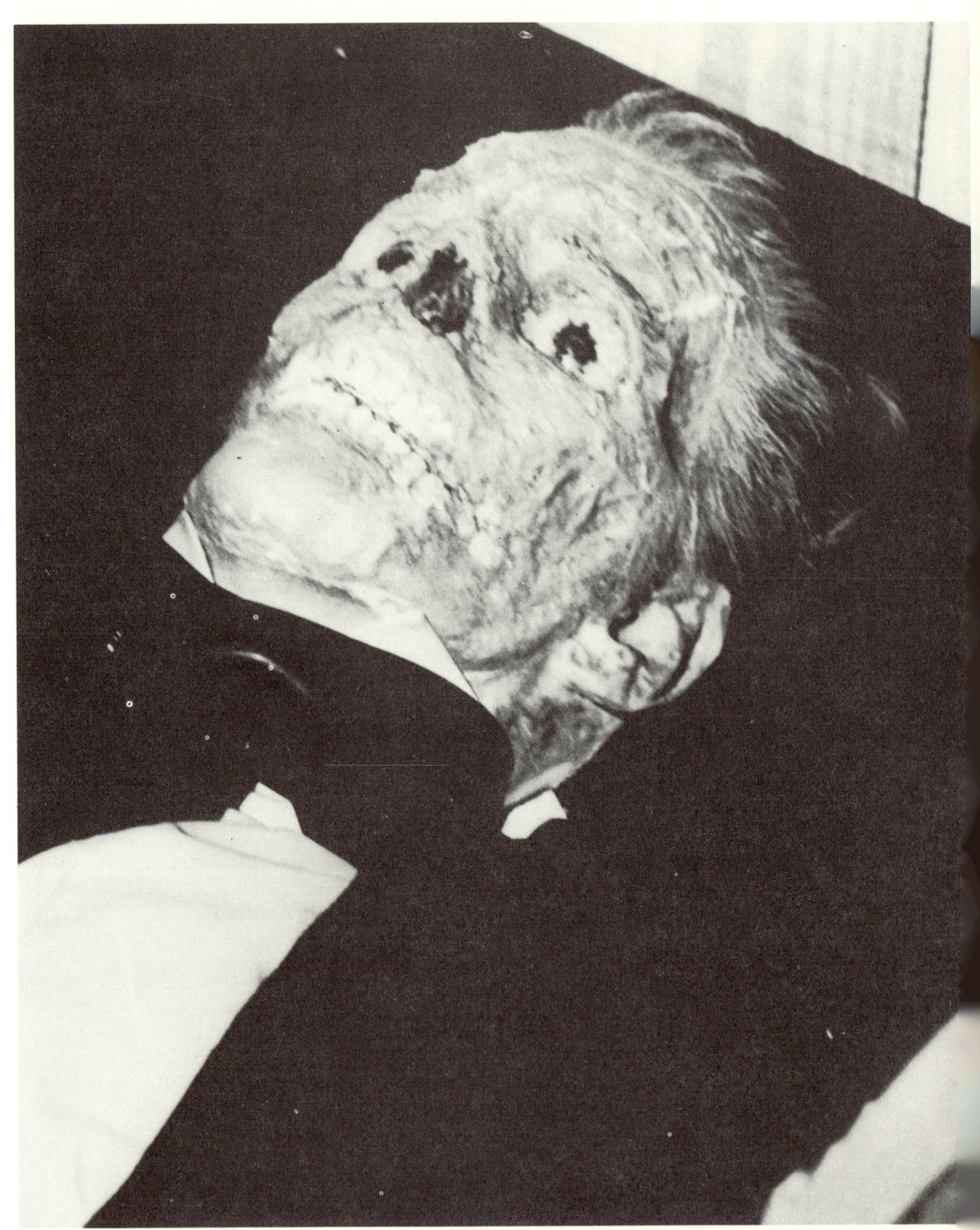

Count Dracula decomposing in EL CONDE DRACULA

Sc.: Raul Martinez Solares, Rafael Perez Grovas
Tin-Tan [German Valdes], Gregorio Casal, Aurora Cavel.

CHANOC VS. THE TIGER AND THE VAMPIRE see **CHANOC CONTRA EL TIGRE Y EL VAMPIRO**

CHAPPAQUA (1966) U.S.A.
Prod. Co.: Conrad Rooks Productions
Dir.: Conrad Rooks
Ph.: Robert Frank (Colour)
Jean-Louis Barrault, Conrad Rooks, William S. Burroughs, Allen Ginsberg.
A Dracula figure appears in one sequence.

EL CHARRO DE LAS CALAVERAS (THE RIDER OF THE SKULLS) (1967) Mexico
Prod. Co.: Azteca
Dir.: Alfredo Salazar
Dagoberto Rodriguez, David Silva, Alicia Caro.

LES CHEMINS DE LA VIOLENCE (LIPS OF BLOOD) (1972) France
Prod. Co.: Les Films de L'Epee
Dist.: Gemini
Prod.: Michel Grimaud
Dir.: Ken Ruder
Ph.: Raymond Heil (Colour)
Michel Flynn, Richard Vitz, Georges Rigaud, Jacques Bernard, Catherine Frank, Sandra Reeves.
71 mins.

CHI O SU ME (LAKE OF DRACULA, DRACULA'S LUST FOR BLOOD, BLOODTHIRSTY EYES) (1971) Japan
Prod. Co.: Toho International
Dir.: Michio Yamanoto
Sc.: Ei Ogawa
Ph.: Rokuro Nishigaki
(Colour; Tohoscope)
Mori Kishida, Midori Fujita, Osahide Takahasri, Sanae Emi, Kaku Taskashina.
82 mins.

EL CONDE DRACULA (COUNT DRACULA) (1971) Spain/Italy/Germany
Prod. Co.: Towers of London-C.C. Fenix Films-Filmar Cinematografica-Korona Film
Prod.: Harry Alan Towers
Dir.: Jess [Jesus] Franco
Sc.: Jesus Franco, Augusto Finochi.
Adapted by Carlo Fadda, M.G. Cuccia, Peter Welbeck [Harry Alan Towers], from the novel "Dracula" by Bram Stoker.
Ph.: Manuel Merino (Colour)
Art Dir.: Karl Schneider
Mus.: Bruno Nicolai
Cost.: Jose Marilli
Christopher Lee (*Count Dracula*), Herbert Lom (*Van Helsing*), Klaus Kinski (*Renfield*), Frederick Williams (*Jonathan Harker*), Maria Rohm (*Mina Harker*), Soledad Miranda (*Lucy*), Jack Taylor (*Dr. Seward*), Paul Muller (*Quincy Morris*), Teresa Gimpera.
98 mins.

CONDEMNED TO LIVE (1935) U.S.A.
Prod. Co.: Maury M. Cohen Productions
Dist.: Invincible
Dir.: Frank Strayer
Sc.: Karen De Wolf
Ph.: M.A. Andersen
Ed.: Roland D. Reed
Ralph Morgan, Maxine Doyle, Russell Gleason, Mischa Auer, Lucy

Christopher Lee in **EL CONDE DRACULA**

Christopher Lee dines with Frederick Williams in **EL CONDE DRACULA**

From EL CONDE DRACULA

Beaumont, Carl Stockade.
67 mins.

COUNT DRACULA see EL CONDE DRACULA

COUNT EROTICA, VAMPIRE
(1971) U.S.A.
Prod. Co.: Lobo
Dir.: Tony Teresi
Sc.: Antonio Teritoni, Hans Klepper
Ph.: Ron Pitts (Colour)
John Peters, Mary Simon.

COUNT YORGA, VAMPIRE
(1970) U.S.A.
Prod. Co.: American International
Prod.: Michael Macready
Dir.: Bob Kelljan
Sc.: Bob Kelljan
Narr. by: George Macready
Ph.: Arch Archambault (Colour)
Mus.: William Marx
Ed.: Tony De Zarraga
Robert Quarry *(Count Yorga)*
Roger Perry *(Dr. Hayes)*, Michael Murphy *(Paul)*, Michael Macready *(Michael)*, Donna Anders *(Donna)*, Judith Lang *(Erica)*, Edward Walsh

 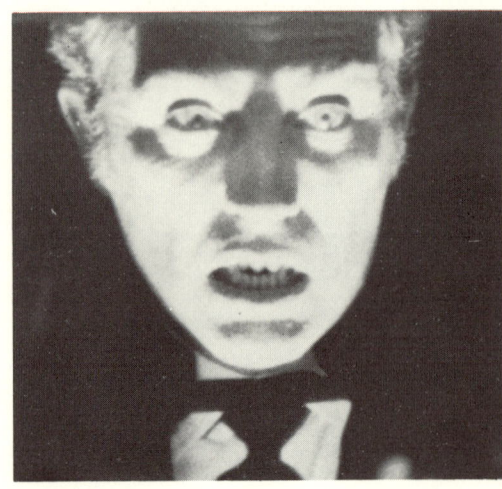

Robert Quarry as Count Yorga chasing a victim in RETURN OF COUNT YORGA

Count Yorga peering through a window

A seance in COUNT YORGA, VAMPIRE

(*Brudah*) Julie Conners, Paul Hansen, Sybil Scotford, Marsha Jordan, Deborah Darnell, Erica Macready.
90 mins.

COUNTESS DRACULA (1971)
England
Prod. Co.: Hammer
Prod.: Alexander Paul
Dir.: Peter Sasdy
Sc.: Jeremy Paul, from a story by Sasdy, Alexander Paul and Gabriel Ronay
Ph.: Ken Talbot (Colour)
Art Dir.: Philip Harrison
Mus.: Harry Robinson
Cost.: Raymond Hughes
Ed.: Henry Richardson
Chore.: Mia Nardi
Ingrid Pitt *(Countess Elisabeth Nadasdy)*, Nigel Green *(Captain Dobi)*, Sandor Eles *(Imre Toth)*, Maurice Denham *(Master Fabio)*, Patience Collier *(Julia)*, Peter Jeffrey *(Captain Balogh)*, Lesley-Anne Down *(Ilona)*, Leon Lissek *(Sergeant of Bailiffs)*, Jessie Evans *(Rosa)*, Andrea Lawrence *(Ziza)*, Susan Brodrick *(Teri)*, Ian Trigger *(Clown)*, Nike Arrighi *(Gypsy Girl)*, Peter May *(Janco)*, John Moore *(Priest)*, Joan Haythorne *(Second Cook)*, Marianne Stone *(Kitchen Maid)*, Charles Farrell *(The Seller)*, Sally Adcock *(Bertha)*, Anne Stallybrass *(Pregnant Woman)*.
93 mins.

CREATURES OF THE PREHISTORIC PLANET (1969)
[Released in 1971 with added footage and re-editing as HORROR OF THE BLOOD MONSTERS. On television: VAMPIRE MEN OF THE LOST PLANET] U.S.A.
Prod. Co.: Independent International (Colour)

Ingrid Pitt reproaches her young lover Sandor Eles in COUNTESS DRACULA

Prod/Dir.: Al Adamson
Sc.: Sue McNair
John Carradine, Robert Dix, Vicki Volante.

LA CRIPTA E L'INCUBO see LA MALDICION DE LOS KARNSTEINS

THE CRYPT OF HORROR see LA MALDICION DE LOS KARNSTEINS

CURSE OF DRACULA see THE RETURN OF DRACULA

CURSE OF NOSTRADAMUS see LA MALDICION DE NOSTRADAMUS

CURSE OF THE BLOOD GHOULS see LA STRAGE DEI VAMPIRI

THE CURSE OF THE KARENSTEINS see LA MALDICION DE LOS KARNSTEINS

CURSE OF THE UNDEAD (1959) U.S.A.
Prod. Co.: Universal
Prod.: Joseph Gershenson
Dir.: Edward Dein
Sc.: Edward Dein, Mildred Dein
Ph.: Ellis Carter
Art Dir.: Alexander Golitzen, Robert Clatworthy
Mus.: Irving Gertz, Milton Rosen
Sound: Leslie Carey, Joe Lapis
Cost.: Bill Thomas
Eric Fleming (*Preacher Dan Young*), Kathleen Crowley (*Dolores Carter*), Michael Pate (*Drake Robey*), John Hoyt (*Dr. John Carter*), Bruce Gordon (*Buffer*), Jimmy Murphy (*Tim Carter*), Helen Kleeb (*Dora*), Ed Binns, Edwin Parker, Jay Adler, John Truax.
79 mins.

CURSE OF THE VAMPIRE (Malaya) see ANAK PONTIANAK

CURSE OF THE VAMPIRES (BLOOD OF THE VAMPIRES) (1970) Philippines
Prod. Co.: Hemisphere
Dir.: Gerardo de Leon
Sc.: B. Feleo, Pierre L. Salas
Ph.: Mike Accion (Colour)
Amelia Fuentes, Eddie Garcia, Romeo Vasquez.

DANCE OF THE VAMPIRES (THE FEARLESS VAMPIRE KILLERS OR PARDON ME, BUT YOUR TEETH ARE IN MY NECK) (1967) England
Prod. Co.: Martin Ransohoff-Roman Polanski Production/Cadre Films/Filmways
Dist: MGM
Prod.: Gene Gutowski
Dir.: Roman Polanski
Sc.: Roman Polanski, Gerard Brach
Ph.: Douglas Slocombe (Colour)
Art Dir.: Fred Carter
Prod. Des.: Wilfrid Shingleton
Mus.: Krzysztof Komeda
Ed.: Alistair McIntyre
Cost.: Sophie Devine
Sound: George Stephenson
Jack MacGowran (*Professor Abronsius*), Sharon Tate (*Sarah*), Alfie Bass (*Yoine Shagal*), Ferdy Mayne (*Count Krolock*), Terry Downes (*Koukol*), Roman Polanski (*Alfred*), Jessie Robbins (*Rebecca*), Fiona Lewis (*Magda*), Iain Quarrier (*Herbert*), Ronald Lacey (*Village Idiot*), Sydney Bromley (*Sleigh Driver*).
98 mins. Original British version

At the vampire ball – from DANCE OF THE VAMPIRES

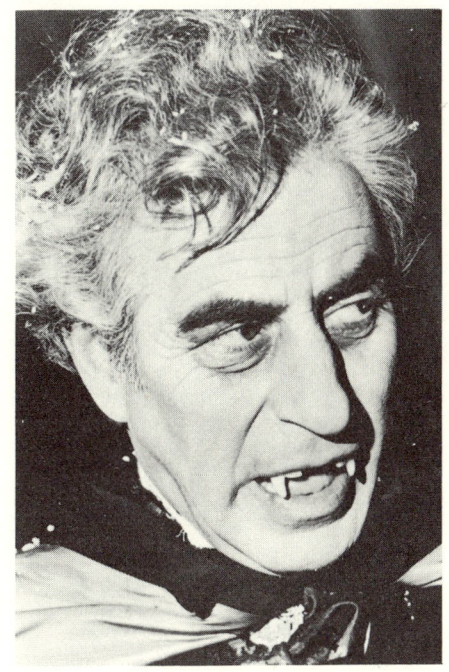

Ferdy Mayne as Count Krolock in the DANCE OF THE VAMPIRES

was 118 minutes. Martin Ransohoff recut, redubbed, and altered sound effects and music on the 98 mins. version. He also added a cartoon at the beginning.

DAMN YANKEES (1958) U.S.A.
Prod. Co.: George Abbott-Stanley Donen Production
Dist.: Warner Bros.
Dir.: Stanley Donen, George Abbott
Sc.: George Abbott, from the play "Damn Yankees" by Abbott and Douglass Wallopp
Ph.: Harold Lipstein (Colour)

Tab Hunter, Gwen Verdon, Ray Walston, Jean Stapleton.
There is a short sequence during one of Walston's songs in which a vampire is shown.

FILMOGRAPHY

DAUGHTERS OF DARKNESS
see LE ROUGE AUX LEVRES

DEAD MEN WALK (1942) U.S.A.
Prod. Co.: PRC/Pathe
Dir.: Sam Newfield
Sc.: Fred Myton
Ph.: Jack Greenhalgh
George Zucco, Mary Carlisle, Ned Young, Dwight Frye, Fern Emmett, Robert Strange.
64 mins.

THE DEATHMASTER (1972) U.S.A.
Prod. Co.: American International
Prod.: Fred Sadoff
Assoc. Prod.:
   Robert Quarry
Dir.: Ray Danton
Sc.: R.L. Grove
Ph.: Wilmer C. Butler
   (Colour)
Ed.: Harold Lime
Mus.: Bill Marx
Robert Quarry (*Khorda*), Bill Ewing (*Pico*), Brenda Dickson (*Rona*), John Fiedler (*Pop*), Betty Anne Rees (*Esslin*), William Jordan (*Monk*), Le Sesne Hilton (*Barbado*), John Lasell (*Detective*), Freda T. Vanterpool (*Dancer*), Tari Tabakins (*Mavis*).
88 mins.

THE DEMON PLANET see TERRORE NELLO SPAZIO

DENDAM PONTIANAK (REVENGE OF THE VAMPIRE) (1957) Malaya
Prod. Co.: Keris
Dir.: B.N. Rao
Maria Menado (*Vampire*), M. Maarof.

DEVILS OF DARKNESS (1965) England
Prod. Co.: Planet
Dist.: 20th Century-Fox
Dir.: Lance Comfort
Sc.: Lyn Fairhurst
William Sylvester, Hubert Noel, Tracy Reed, Carole Gray, Diana Decker, Rona Anderson, Victor Brooks.

DR. TERROR'S GALLERY OF HORRORS (RETURN FROM THE PAST, THE BLOOD DRINKERS, THE BLOOD SUCKERS) (1967) U.S.A.
Prod. Co.: American General
Dir.: David L. Hewitt
Sc.: Gary Heacock, David Prentiss, Russ Jones
Ph.: Austin McKinney
   (Colour)
Lon Chaney, John Carradine, Rochelle Hudson, Roger Gentry, Mitch Evans, Russ Jones.
82 mins. There are five stories, two deal with vampires.

DR. TERROR'S HOUSE OF HORRORS (1964) England
Prod. Co.: Amicus
Dist.: Paramount
Prod.: Milton Subotsky, Max J. Rosenberg
Dir.: Freddie Francis
Sc.: Milton Subotsky
Ph.: Alan Hume, (Colour, Techniscope)
Peter Cushing (*Dr. Schreck*) 1. *Werewolf*: Neil McCallum, Ursula Howells, Peter Madden. 2. *Creeping Vine*: Alan Freeman, Ann Bell, Bernard Lee. 3. *Voodoo*: Roy Castle, Kenny Lynch, Harold Lang. 4. *Crawling Hand*: Christopher Lee, Michael Gough, Isla Blair, Judy Cornwell. 5. *Vampire*: Donald Sutherland, Max

Robert Quarry in THE DEATHMASTER

Adrian, Jennifer Jayne, Irene Richmond, Frank Barry.
98 mins. Only the final episode deals with a vampire.

DRACULA (1931) U.S.A.
Prod. Co.: Universal
Prod.: Carl Laemmle Jr.
Dir.: Tod Browning
Sc.: Garrett Fort, Dudley Murphy, from the play by John Balderston and Hamilton Deane adapted from the novel by Bram Stoker
Ph.: Karl Freund
Art Dir.: Charles D. Hall
Mus.: Tchaikovsky, Wagner
Ed.: Milton Carruth
Bela Lugosi (*Count Dracula*), David Manners (*John Harker*), Helen Chandler (*Mina Seward*), Dwight Frye (*Renfield*), Edward Van Sloan (*Van Helsing*), Herbert Bunston (*Dr. Seward*), Charles Gerrard (*Martin*), Frances Dade (*Lucy Weston*), Joan Standing (*Briggs*), Michael Visaroff (*Innkeeper*), Moon Carroll (*Maid*), Josephine Velez (*English Nurse*), Donald Murphy (*Man in Coach*).
75 mins.
At the same time a Spanish version of *Dracula* was made at Universal. Dir.: George Melford. With Carlos Villarias, Lupita Tovar, Barry Norton.

DRACULA (HORROR OF DRACULA) (1958) England
Prod. Co.: Hammer
Dist.: Universal
Prod.: Anthony Hinds
Dir.: Terence Fisher
Sc.: Jimmy Sangster, from the novel by Bram Stoker
Ph.: Jack Asher (Colour)
Art Dir:. Bernard Robinson
Mus.: James Bernard
Ed.: James Needs, Bill Lenny

Peter Cushing (*Dr. Van Helsing*), Christopher Lee (*Count Dracula*), Michael Gough (*Arthur*), Melissa Stribling (*Mina*), Carol Marsh (*Lucy*), Olga Dickie (*Gerda*), John Van Eyssen (*Jonathan*), Valerie Gaunt (*Vampire Woman*).
82 mins.

DRACULA (1974) U.S.A.
Prod. Co.: Dan Curtis Productions
Dir.: Dan Curtis
Sc.: Richard Matheson based on the novel by Bram Stoker
Ph.: Oswald Morris (Colour)
Ed.: Richard A. Harris
Mus.: Robert Cobert
Jack Palance (*Count Dracula*), Nigel Davenport (*Van Helsing*), Simon Ward (*Arthur Holmwood*), Fiona Lewis (*Lucy Westenra*), Penelope Horner (*Mina Murray*), Murray Brown (*Jonathan Harker*), Pamela Brown (*Mrs. Westenra*).
100 mins.

From DRACULA (1958)

From Terence Fisher's HORROR OF DRACULA

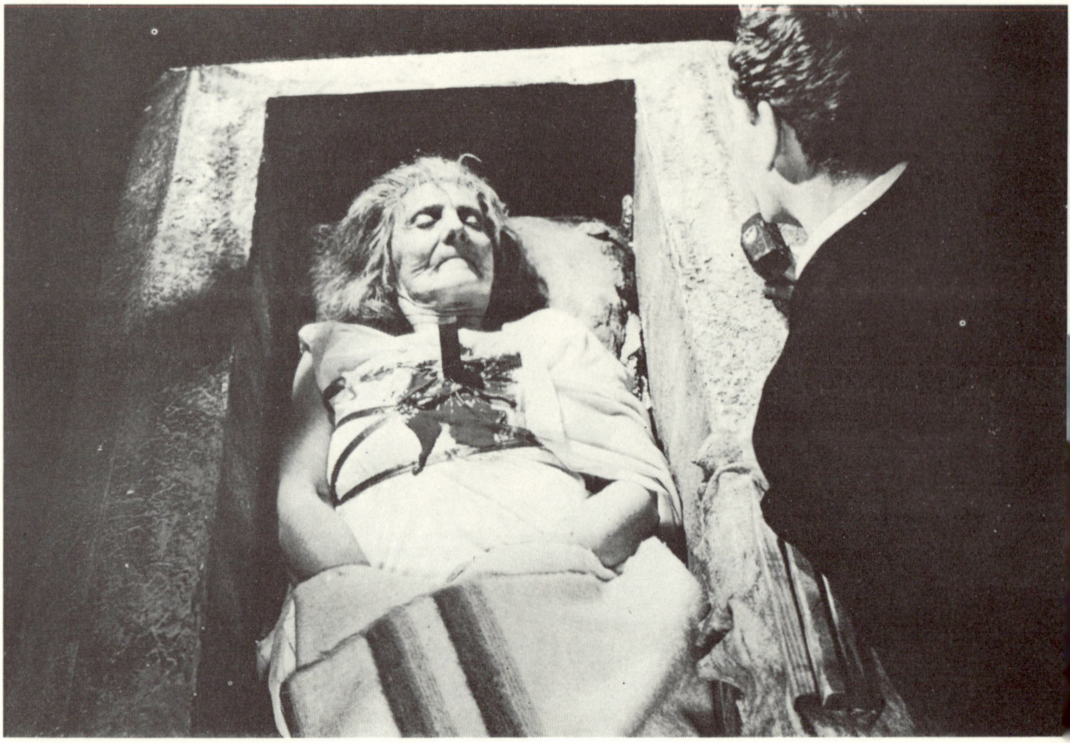

John Van Eyssen stakes Dracula's mistress played by Valerie Gaunt in DRACULA (1958)

Dracula decomposing in DRACULA (1958)

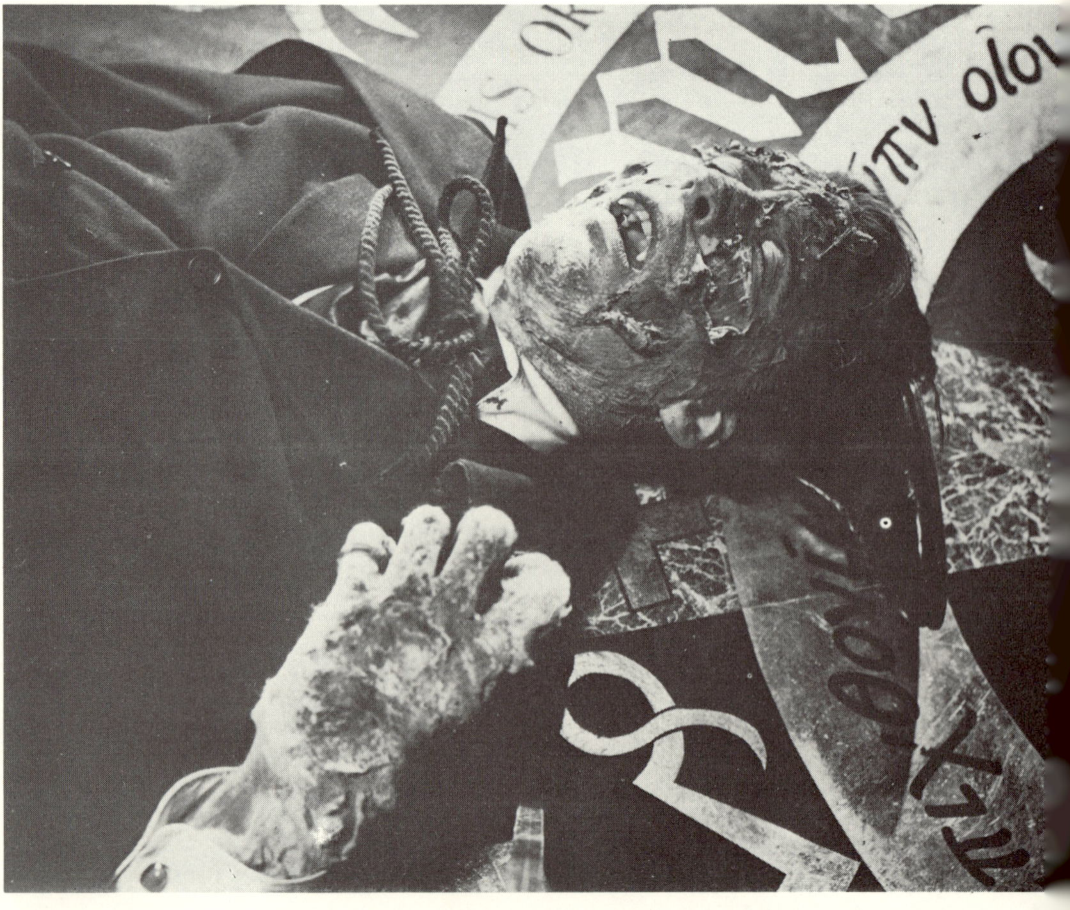

FILMOGRAPHY 169

Peter Cushing as Van Helsing in DRACULA A.D. 1972

DRACULA A.D. 1972 (1972)
England
Prod Co.: Hammer/Warner Bros.
Dist.: Columbia/Warner
Exec. Prod.: Michael Carreras
Prod.: Josephine Douglas
Prod. Sup.: Roy Skeggs
Dir.: Alan Gibson
Sc.: Don Houghton
Ph.: Richard Bush (Colour)
Art Dir.: Don Mingaye
Sp. Ef.: Les Bowie
Mus.: Michael Vickers
Ed.: James Needs
Sound: A. W. Lumkin

Christopher Lee (*Count Dracula*), Peter Cushing (*Prof. Van Helsing*), Stephanie Beacham (*Jessica Van Helsing*), Michael Coles (*Inspector Murray*), Christopher Neame (*Johnny Alucard*), William Elis (*Joe Mitchum*), Marsha Hunt (*Gaynor*), Philip Miller (*Bob*), Michael Kitchen (*Greg*), David Andrews (*Sergeant Pearson*), Caroline Munro (*Laura*), Janet Key (*Anna*), Lally Bowers (*Matron*).
95 mins.

Above and below:
Christopher Lee as Dracula in DRACULA A.D. 1972

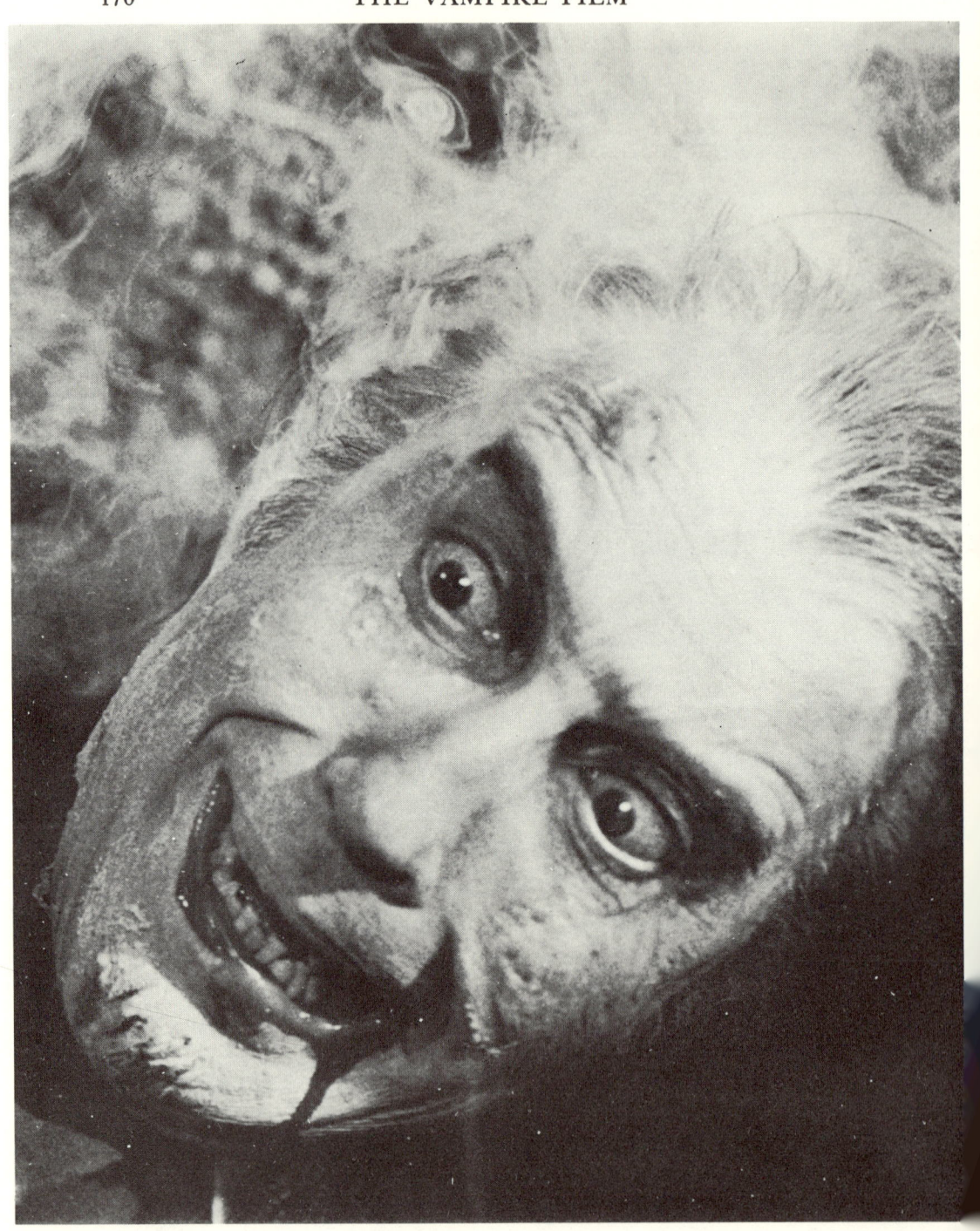

From DRACULA A.D. 1972

From DRACULA HAS RISEN FROM THE GRAVE

DRACULA HAS RISEN FROM THE GRAVE (1968) England
Prod. Co.: Hammer
Dist.: Warner
Prod.: Aida Young
Dir.: Freddie Francis
Sc.: John Elder [Anthony Hinds]
Ph.: Arthur Grant (Colour)
Art Dir.: Bernard Robinson
Mus.: James Bernard
Ed.: Spencer Reeve
Ed. Sup.: James Needs
Sp. Ef.: Frank George
Sound: Wilfred Thompson
Christopher Lee (Count Dracula), Rupert Davies (Monsignor), Veronica Carlson (Maria), Barbara Ewing (Zena), Barry Andrews (Paul), Ewan Hooper (Priest), Marion Mathie (Anna), Michael Ripper (Max), John D. Collins (Student), George A. Cooper (Landlord), Chris Cunningham (Farmer), Norman Bacon (Boy).
92 mins.

DRACULA HUNTS FRANKENSTEIN see EL HOMBRE QUE VINO DE UMMO

From DRACULA HAS RISEN FROM THE GRAVE

From DRACULA HAS RISEN FROM THE GRAVE

DRACULA IN ISTANBUL (1952) Turkey
Dir.: Mehmet Muhtar
Sc.: Umit Deniz from Ali Riza Seyfi's "The Impaling Viovode" and Stoker's "Dracula"
Atif Kaptan (*Dracula*)

Dracula with Diana in DRACULA—PRINCE OF DARKNESS

DRACULA—PRINCE OF DARKNESS (1965) England
Prod. Co.: Hammer
Dist.: Warner
Prod.: Anthony Nelson Keys
Dir.: Terence Fisher
Sc.: John Sansom, from an idea by John Elder [Anthony Hinds]
Ph.: Michael Reed (Technicolor, Techniscope)
Art Dir.: Don Mingaye, Bernard Robinson
Mus.: James Bernard
Ed.: Chris Barnes

Christopher Lee (*Dracula*), Barbara Shelley (*Helen*), Andrew Keir (*Father Sandor*), Francis Matthews (*Charles*), Suzan Farmer (*Diana*), Charles Tingwell (*Alan*), Thorley Walters (*Ludwig*), Philip Latham (*Klove*), Walter Brown (*Brother Mark*), George Woodbridge (*Landlord*), Jack Lambert (*Brother Peter*), Philip Ray (*Priest*), Joyce Hemson (*Mother*), John Maxim (*Coach Driver*).
90 mins.

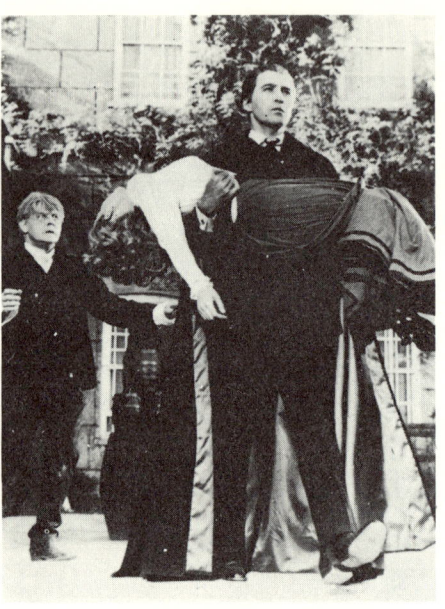

From DRACULA—PRINCE OF DARKNESS

DRACULA, THE DIRTY OLD MAN (1969) U.S.A.
Prod.: Whit Boyd
Dir/Sc.: William Edwards
Ph.: William Troiam (Colour)
Vince Kelly, Ann Hollis.

DRACULA VS. FRANKENSTEIN (also BLOOD OF FRANKENSTEIN) (1971) U.S.A.
Prod. Co.: Independent International
Prod.: Al Adamson and Samuel M. Sherman
Dir.: Al Adamson

FILMOGRAPHY

Christopher Lee meets his end in the ice in DRACULA—PRINCE OF DARKNESS

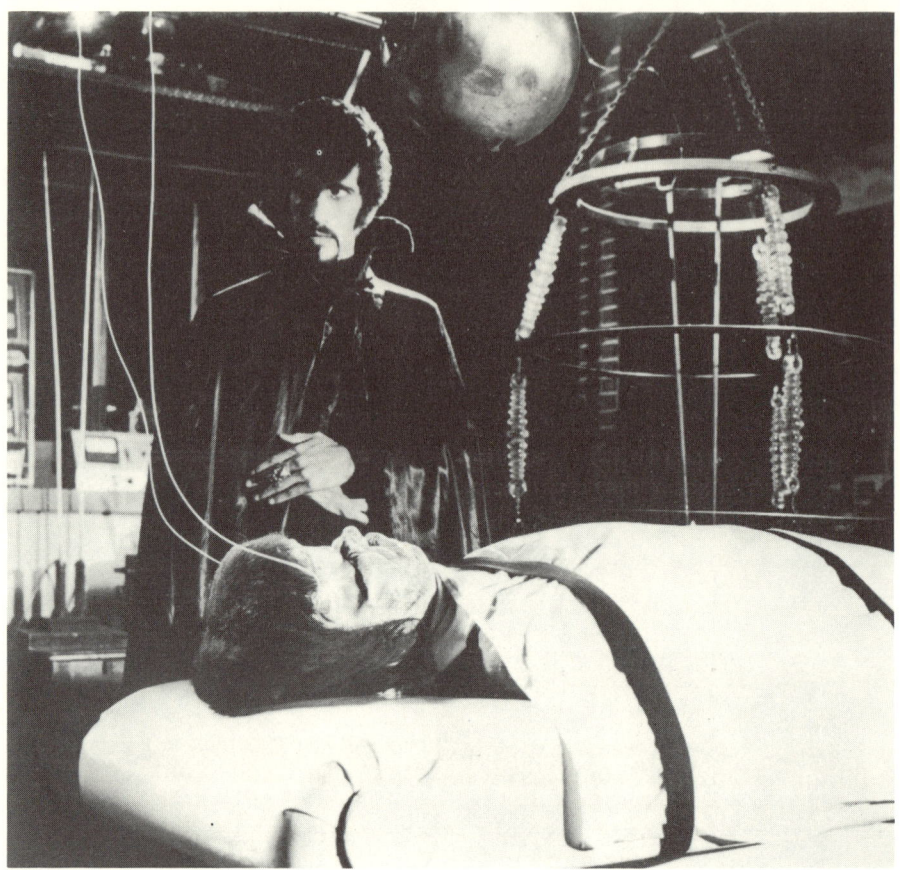

From DRACULA VS. FRANKENSTEIN

Sc.: William Pugsley, Sam M. Sherman
Ph.: Gary Graver, Paul Glickman (Colour)
Sp. Ph.: Rod Bristow

J. Carrol Naish (*Dr. Frankenstein*), Lon Chaney Jr. (*Groton, the Zombie*), Zandor Vorkov (*Count Dracula*), Russ Tamblyn, Jim Davis, Anthony Eisley, Regina Carrol, John Bloom, Shelly Weiss.
90 mins.

DRACULA VS. FRANKENSTEIN (Spain/West Germany/Italy) see EL HOMBRE QUE VINO DE UMMO

DRACULA'S DAUGHTER (1936) U.S.A.
Prod. Co.: Universal
Prod.: E.M. Asher
Dir.: Lambert Hillyer
Sc.: Garrett Fort, John Balderston, suggested by Oliver Jeffries, based on Bram Stoker's "Dracula's Guest."
Ph.: George Robinson
Art Dir.: Albert D'Agostino
Ed.: Milton Carruth
Mus.: Heinz Roemheld

Otto Kruger (*Dr. Jeffrey Garth*), Gloria Holden (*Countess Marya*

Otto Kruger confronts Gloria Holden and Irving Pichel in DRACULA'S DAUGHTER

Otto Kruger examines Nan Grey in DRACULA'S DAUGHTER

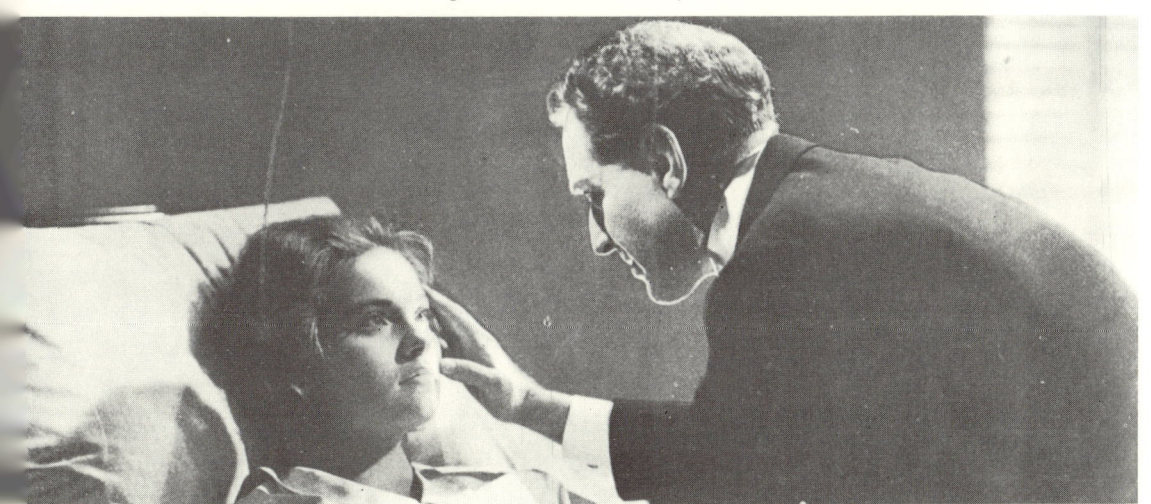

Zaleska/Countess Dracula), Edward Van Sloan (Van or Von Helsing), Marguerite Churchill (Janet Blake), Irving Pichel (Sandor), Gilbert Emery (Sir Basil), Hedda Hopper (Lady Hammond), Nan Grey (The Model), Claude Allister (Aubrey Vail), E.E. Clive (Sergeant Wilkes), Halliwell Hobbes (Constable Hawkins), Billy Bevan (Albert), Gordon Hart (Host), Douglas Wood (Doctor Townsend), Joseph E. Tozer (Dr. Graham), Lily Malyon (Miss Peabody), Fred Walton (Dr. Bemish), Edgar Norton (Hobbs).
69 mins.

DRACULA'S LUST FOR BLOOD
see CHI O SU ME

DRACULA'S LUSTERNE VAMPIRE (DRACULA'S VAMPIRE LUST) (1970) Switzerland
Prod. Co.: Monarex
Dir.: Mario D'Alcala
Des Roberts.

DRACULA'S VAMPIRE LUST
see DRACULA'S LUSTERNE VAMPIRE

A DREAM OF VAMPIRES
see UM SONHO DE VAMPIROS

ECHENME AL VAMPIRO (THROW ME TO THE VAMPIRE, BRING ME THE VAMPIRE) (1964) Mexico
Prod. Co.: Clasa-Mohme
Dir.: A.E. Crevenna
Sc.: Alfredo Ruanova, from a story by Mario Garcia Camberos
Ph.: F. Colin
Carlos Riquelme, Hector Godoy, Mantequilla, Borolas.

THE EMPIRE OF DRACULA
see EL IMPERIO DE DRACULA

ERCOLE AL CENTRO DELLA TERRA (HERCULES IN THE CENTER OF THE EARTH, HERCULES IN THE HAUNTED WORLD) (1961) Italy
Prod. Co.: SPA Cinematografica
Prod.: Achille Piazzi
Dir.: Mario Bava
Sc.: Alessandro Continenza, Mario Bava, Giorgio Prosperi, Duccio Tessari
Ph.: Mario Bava, Ubaldo Terzano (Colour, Totalscope)
Art Dir.: Franco Lolli
Mus.: Armando Trovajoli
Ed.: Mario Serandrei
Cost.: Mario Giorsi
Sound: Luigi Puri
Reg Park (Hercules), Leonora Ruffo (Deianira), Christopher Lee (Lichas), Giorgio Ardisson (Theseus), Ida Galli, Ely Draco, Marisa Belli.
77 mins.

EVERY HOME SHOULD HAVE ONE (1970) England
Prod. Co.: Example
Dir.: Jim Clark
Sc.: Marty Feldman, Barry Took, Denis Norden
Ph.: Ken Hodges (Colour)
Marty Feldman, Barry Took, Julie Ege.
There is a short vampire sequence.

THE FEARLESS VAMPIRE KILLERS, OR PARDON ME, BUT YOUR TEETH ARE IN MY NECK see DANCE OF THE VAMPIRES

LES FEMMES VAMPIRES see LE VIOL DU VAMPIRE

From HERCULES IN THE HAUNTED WORLD

FIRST MAN INTO SPACE
  (1959) England
Prod. Co.: MGM/Amalgamated
Dir.:   Robert Day
Sc.:   John C. Cooper, Lance Z. Hargreaves
Ph.:   Geoffrey Faithfull
Marshall Thompson, Marla Landi, Bill Edwards, Robert Ayres.

DER FLUCH DER GRUNEN AUGEN (THE CURSE OF GREEN EYES, NIGHT OF THE VAMPIRES, CAVE OF THE LIVING DEAD) (1963) West Germany/Yugoslavia
Prod. Co.: Objectiv-Triglav-Film
Dir.:   Akosvon Rathony
Sc.:   C.V. Rock, from an idea by Rathony
Ph.:   Saric Hrvoj
Ed.:   Klaus Dudenhofer
Adrian Hoven, Erika Remberg, Carl Mohner, Wolfgang Preiss, Karin Field, Emmerich Schrenk, John Kitzmiller.
85 mins.

FRANKENSTEIN, EL VAMPIRO Y CIA (FRANKENSTEIN, THE VAMPIRE, AND CO.) (1961) Mexico
Prod. Co.: Calderon
Dir.: Benito Alazraki
Sc.: Alfredo Salazar
Manuel Valdes, Jose Jasso, Nora Vetran, Arturo Castro.

FRANKENSTEIN, THE VAMPIRE, AND CO. see **FRANKENSTEIN, EL VAMPIRE, Y CIA**

FRANKENSTEIN'S BLOODY TERROR see **LA MARCA DEL HOMBRE LOBO**

LE FRISSON DES VAMPIRES (VAMPIRE THRILLS, SHUDDER OF THE VAMPIRE) (1970) France
Prod. Co.: Les Films Modernes
Dir./Sc.: Jean Rollin
Ph.: Jean-Jacques Renon (Colour)
Art Dir.: Michel Delesalle
Mus.: Groupe Acanthus
Sandra Jul[l]ien, Jean-Marie Durand, Michel Delahaye, Jacques Robiolles, Marie-Pierre, Kuelan Herca, Dominique.
95 mins.

GARU THE MAD MONK (1970) England
Prod. Co.: Maipix
Dir.: Andy Milligan
Sc.: Andy Milligan, based on a story by M. A. Isaacs
Ph.: Andy Milligan (Colour)
Neil Flanagan, Jacqueline Webb, Judith Isral, Julia Willis.

GENIE OF DARKNESS see **NOSTRADAMUS Y EL GENIO DE LAS TINIEBLAS**

GOLIATH AND THE VAMPIRES see **MACISTE CONTRO IL VAMPIRO**

GRAVE OF THE VAMPIRE (1974) U.S.A.
Prod. Co.: Entertainment Pyramid/Millenium
Prod.: Daniel Cady
Dir.: John Hayes
Sc.: David Chase
Ph.: Paul Hipp (Colour)
William Smith, Mike Pataki, Lynn Peters, Dianne Holden, Jay Adler, Kitty Vallacher, Jay Scott, Lieux Dressler, William Guhl, Inga Neilsen, Lindus Guiness.

GUESS WHAT HAPPENED TO COUNT DRACULA? (1971) U.S.A.
Prod. Co.: Merrick International
Dir.: Laurence Merrick
Sc.: Laurence Merrick (Colour)
Des Roberts, Claudia Barron, John Landon.

THE HAND OF NIGHT (BEAST OF MOROCCO) (1965) England
Prod.: Schoenfield/Associated British-Pathe
Dir.: Frederick Goode
Sc.: Bruce Stewart
Ph.: William Jordan (Colour)
William Sylvester, Diane Clare, Edward Underdown, Terence de Marney, Alizia Gur.
72 mins.

HAPPENING DER VAMPIRE (THE VAMPIRE HAPPENING) (1971) West Germany
Prod. Co.: Aquila
Dir.: Freddie Francis
Sc.: August Rieger
Ph.: Gerard Vandenberg (Colour, Scope)
Ferdy Mayne (*Dracula*), Pia Degermark, Yvor Murillo.

From Giacomo Gentilomo's GOLIATH AND THE VAMPIRES

HARD TIMES FOR VAMPIRES
see TEMPI DURI PER I VAMPIRI

HERCULES IN THE CENTER OF THE EARTH see ERCOLE AL CENTRO DELLA TERRA

HERCULES IN THE HAUNTED WORLD see ERCOLE AL CENTRO DELLA TERRA

EL HOMBRE QUE VINO DE UMMO (DRACULA VS. FRANKENSTEIN, DRACULA HUNTS FRANKENSTEIN) (1969) Spain/West Germany/Italy.
Prod. Co.: Producciones Jaime Prades-Juan Ramon Jimenez-Eichberg Film-International Jaguar
Dir.: Tulio Demicheli (and Hugo Fregonese)
Sc.: Jacinto Molina Alvarez
Ph.: Godofredo Pacheco (Colour, 70mm)
Michael Rennie, Karin Dor, Craig Hill, Patty Shepard, Paul Naschy, Angel del Pozo.
81 mins.

THE VAMPIRE FILM

HORROR OF DRACULA see
  DRACULA (1958)

HOUSE OF DARK SHADOWS
  (1970) U.S.A.
Prod. Co.: Dan Curtis Productions
Dist.:   MGM
Prod./Dir.: Dan Curtis
Sc.:   Sam Hall, Gordon Russell
Ph.:   Arthur Ornitz (Colour)
Art Dir.: Trevor Williams, Ken
             Fitzpatrick
Mus.:   Robert Cobert
Ed.:   Arline Garson
Jonathan Frid (*Barnabas Collins*),
Grayson Hall (*Dr. Julia Hoffman*),
Kathryn Leigh Scott (*Maggie Evans*),
Roger Davis (*Jeff Clark*), Nancy

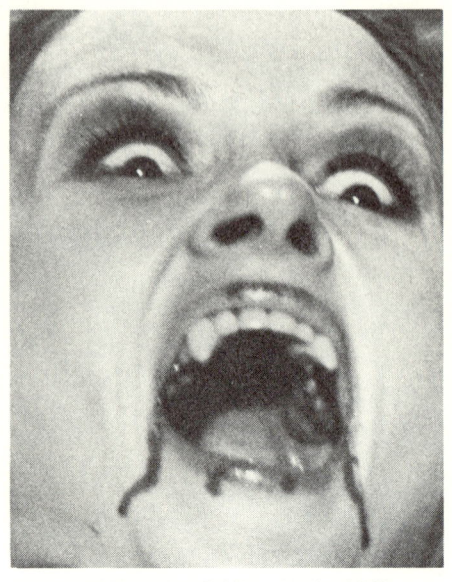

From HOUSE OF DARK SHADOWS

Jonathan Frid and his vampire bride in HOUSE OF DARK SHADOWS

Jonathan Frid as Barnabus Collins in HOUSE OF DARK SHADOWS

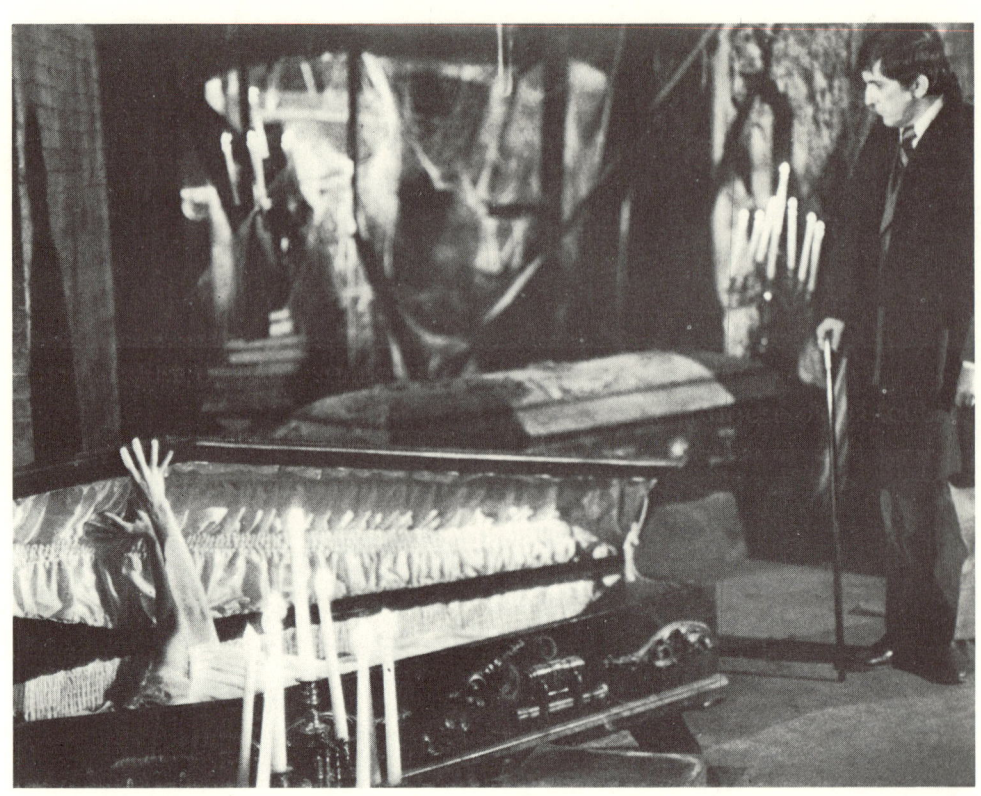

From HOUSE OF DARK SHADOWS

John Carradine in HOUSE OF DRACULA

FILMOGRAPHY

Barrett (*Carolyn Stoddard*), John Karlen (*Willie Loomis*), Thayer David (*Prof. T. Eliot Stokes*), Louis Edmonds (*Roger Collins*), Donald Briscoe (*Todd Jennings*), Joan Bennett (*Elizabeth Stoddard*).
97 mins.

HOUSE OF DRACULA (1945) U.S.A.

Prod. Co.: Universal
Prod.: Paul Malvern
Dir.: Erle C. Kenton
Sc.: Edward T. Lowe
Ph.: George Robinson
Art Dir.: John B. Goodman, Martin Obzina
Mus.: Edgar Fairchild
Ed.: Russell Schoengarth

John Carradine (*Count Dracula/Baron Latoes*), Lon Chaney Jr. (*Lawrence Talbot*), Onslow Stevens (*Dr. Edelman*), Martha O'Driscoll (*Miliza*), Lionel Atwill (*Inspector*), Glenn Strange (*The Monster*), Jane Adams (*Nina*), Skelton Knaggs (*Steinmuhl*), Joseph E. Bernard (*Brahms*), Dick Dickinson (*Villager*), Fred Cordova (*Gendarme*), Gregory Muradian (*Johannes*).
67 mins.

HOUSE OF FRANKENSTEIN (1944) U.S.A.

Prod. Co.: Universal
Prod.: Paul Malvern
Dir.: Erle C. Kenton
Sc.: Edward T. Lowe, from a story by Curt Siodmak
Ph.: George Robinson
Art Dir.: John B. Goodman, Martin Obzina
Mus.: H. J. Salter
Ed.: Philip Cahn

Boris Karloff (*Dr. Niemann*), J. Carrol Naish (*Daniel*), Lon Chaney Jr. (*Larry Talbot*), John Carradine (*Count Dracula*), Glenn Strange (*The Monster*), Anne Gwynne (*Rita*), Peter Coe (*Carl Hussman*), Lionel Atwill (*Arnz*), George Zucco (*Lampini*), Elena Verdugo (*Ilonka*), Sig Rumann (*Hussman*), William Edmunds (*Fejos*), Philip Van Zandt (*Muller*), Julius Tannen (*Hertz*), Michael Mark (*Strauss*), Frank Reicher (*Ullman*).
70 mins.

THE HOUSE THAT DRIPPED BLOOD (1970) England

Prod. Co.: Amicus
Dist.: Cinerama
Prod.: Max J. Rosenberg, Milton Subotsky
Dir.: Peter Duffell
Sc.: Robert Bloch
Ph.: Ray Parslow (Colour)
Art Dir.: Tony Curtis
Mus.: Michael Dress
Ed.: Peter Tanner
Sound: Nolan Roberts, Ken Ritchie, Michael Redbourn

1. *Method for Murder*: Denholm Elliott, Joanna Dunham, Tom Adams, Robert Lang.
2. *Waxworks*: Peter Cushing, Joss Ackland, Wolfe Morris.
3. *Sweets to the Sweet*: Christopher Lee, Nyree Dawn Porter, Chloe Franks.
4. *The Cloak*: Jon Pertwee (*Paul Henderson*), Ingrid Pitt (*Carla*).

102 mins.
The fourth episode is a vampire tale.

LA HUELLA MACABRA (THE MACABRE MASK) (1963) Mexico

Prod. Co.: Azteca
Dir.: Alfredo B. Crevenna

Guillermo Murray, Rosa Carmina, Carmen Molina, Jamie Fernandez.

Onslow Stevens and John Carradine in HOUSE OF DRACULA

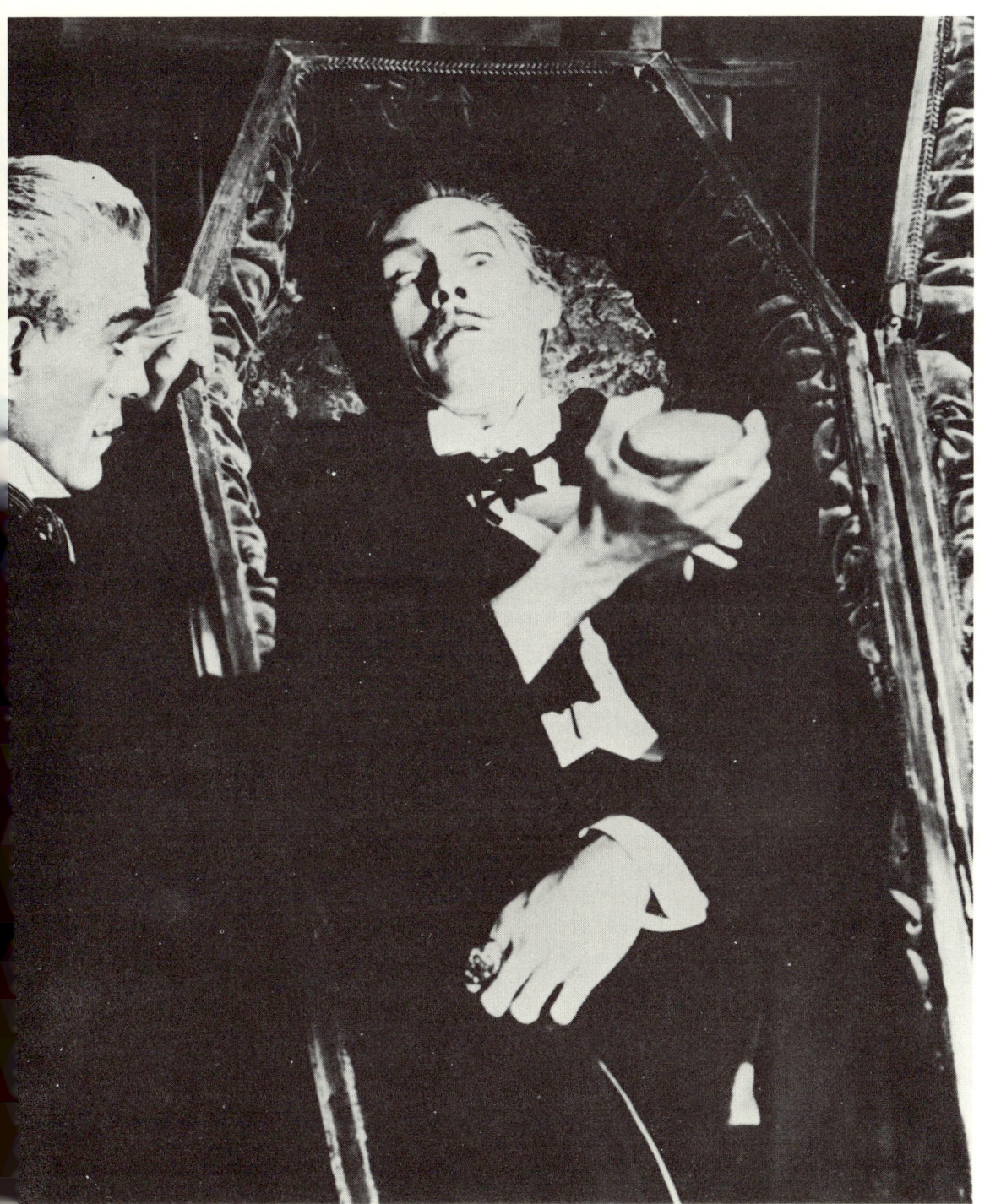

Boris Karloff resurrects Dracula in HOUSE OF FRANKENSTEIN

Jon Pertwee and Ingrid Pitt in THE HOUSE THAT DRIPPED BLOOD

From INCENSE FOR THE DAMNED

EL IMPERIO DE DRACULA
   (THE EMPIRE OF DRACULA,
   LAS MUJERES DE DRACULA)
   (1967) Mexico
Prod. Co.: Vergara
Dir.:   Federico Curiel
Sc.:   Ramon Obon
Ph.:   Alfredo Uribe (Colour)
Ethel Carrillo, Eric del Castillo, Cesar del Campo, Lucha Villa.

INCENSE FOR THE DAMMED
   (BLOODSUCKERS) (1970)
   England
Prod.:   Chevron-Paragon/
           Lucinda-Titan
Dir.:   Michael Burrowes
           (Robert Hartford-
           Davis)
Sc.:   Julian More, from
           "Doctors Wear Scarlet"
           by Simon Raven
Ph.:   Desmond Dickinson
           (Colour)
Peter Cushing, Patrick Macnee, Patrick Mower, Alex Davion.
87 mins.

LA INVASION DE LOS MUERTOS
   (THE INVASION OF THE
   DEAD) (1972) Mexico
Prod. Co.: Azteca
Dir.:   Rene Cardona
The Blue Demon, Jorge Mistral, Cesar Silva, C. Linder.

LA INVASION DE LOS VAM-
   PIROS (INVASION OF THE
   VAMPIRES) (1962) Mexico
Prod. Co.: Tele-Talia
Dir./Sc.: Miguel Morayta
Ph.:   Raul M. Solares
Carlos Agosti (*The Vampire, Count Frankenhausen*), Bertha Moss, Rafael Etienne, Tito Junco, David Reynoso, "Mantequilla."
78 mins.

Isobel Black confronts Clifford Evans in KISS OF THE VAMPIRE

THE INVASION OF THE DEAD
see LA INVASION DE LOS
MUERTOS

INVASION OF THE VAMPIRES
see LA INVASION DE LOS
VAMPIROS

JONATHAN (1970) West Germany
Prod. Co.: Iduna Films
Dist.: New Yorker Films
Dir./Sc.: Hans W. Geissendorfer
Ph.: Robby Muller (Colour)
Art Dir.: Hans Gailling
Mus.: Roland Kovac
Ed.: Wolfgang Hedinger
Jurgen Jung (*Jonathan*), Hans Dieter Jendreyko (*Josef*), Paul Albert Krumm (*The Count*), Thomas Astan (*Thomas*), Ilse Kunkele (*Lena's Mother*), Oskar von Schaab (*Professor*).
103 mins.

KISS ME QUICK (1964) U.S.A.
Prod. Co.: Fantasy Films
Dir.: Russ Meyer
Jackie DeWitt, Althea Currier, Frank Coe.

KISS OF THE VAMPIRE (1963)
England
Prod. Co.: Hammer
Dist.: Universal
Prod.: Anthony Hinds
Dir.: Don Sharp
Sc:. John Elder [Anthony Hinds]
Ph.: Alan Hume (Colour)

Above and below: from **KISS OF THE VAMPIRE**

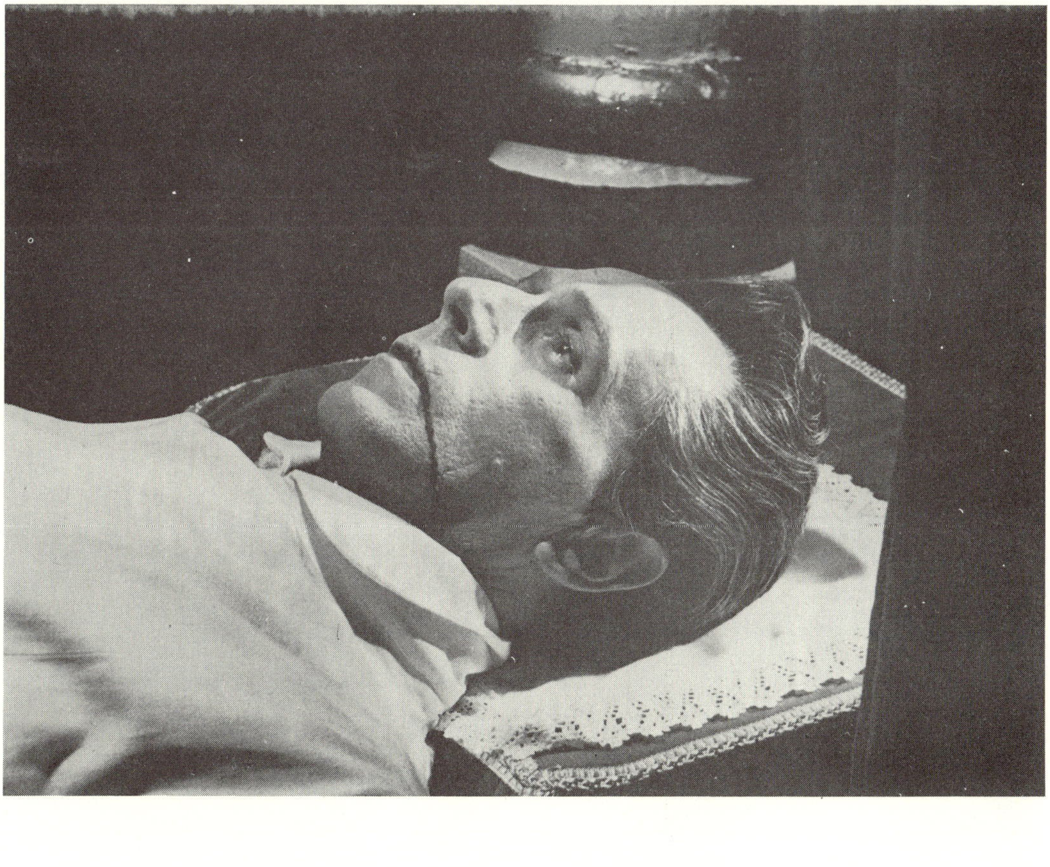

Art Dir.: Don Mingaye, Bernard Robinson
Sp. Ef.: Les Bowie
Mus.: James Bernard
Ed.: James Needs
Clifford Evans (*Prof. Zimmer*), Noel Willman (*Ravna*), Edward de Souza (*Gerald Harcourt*), Jennifer Daniel (*Marianne*), Barry Warren (*Carl*), Jaquie Wallis (*Sabena*), Isobel Black (*Tania*), Peter Madden (*Bruno*), Vera Cook (*Anna*), Noel Howlett (*Fr. Xavier*), Brian Oulton (*1st Disciple*), John Harvey (*Police Sergeant*), Stan Simmons (*Servant*), Olga Dickie (*Woman in Graveyard*), Margaret Reed, Elizabeth Valentine.
87 mins.

Edward de Souza and Jennifer Daniel in KISS OF THE VAMPIRE

KURONEKO (1968) Japan
Prod. Co.: Toho
Dir./Sc.: Kaneto Shindo
Ph.: Kiyomi Kuroda (Tohoscope)
Mus.: Hikaru Hayashi
Kichiemon Nakamura, Nobuko Otowa, Kiwako Taichi, Kei Sato, Taiji Tonoyama.
99 mins.

LAKE OF DRACULA
see CHI O SU ME

THE LAST MAN ON EARTH (1964) Italy/U.S.A.
Prod. Co.: Associated Producers, Inc./Produzioni La Regina
Dist.: American International
Prod.: Robert L. Lippert
Dir.: Sidney Salkow
Sc.: Logan Swanson, William P. Leicester from the novel "I Am Legend" by Richard Matheson
Ph.: Franco Delli Colli
Art Dir.: Giorgio Giovannini
Mus.: Paul Sawtell, Bert Shefter
Ed.: Gene Ruggiero
Vincent Price (*Robert Morgan*), Franca Bettoia (*Ruth*), Emma Danieli (*Virginia*), Giacomo Rossi-Stuart (*Ben Cortman*), Umberto Rau, Christi Courtland, Tony Corevi, Hector Ribotta.
86 mins.

THE LEGEND OF THE SEVEN GOLDEN VAMPIRES (1974) England/Hong Kong
Prod. Co.: Hammer/Shaw Brothers
Prod./Sc: Don Houghton
Dir.: Roy Ward Baker
Peter Cushing, Julie Ege, Robin Stewart.

THE LEMON GROVE KIDS MEET THE MONSTERS (1966) U.S.A.
Prod. Co.: Morgan—Steckler (Colour)
Dir.: Ray Steckler
Sc.: Jim Harmon, Ron Haydock

LIPS OF BLOOD see
LES CHEMINS DE LA VIOLENCE

LONDON AFTER MIDNIGHT (1927) U.S.A.
Prod. Co.: MGM
Prod.: Tod Browning
Dir.: Tod Browning
Sc.: Waldemar Young, from a story by Browning
Ph.: Merritt B. Gerstad

Lon Chaney, Henry B. Walthall, Marceline Day, Conrad Nagel, Polly Moran.

LUST FOR A VAMPIRE (1971) England
Prod.: Hammer
Dist.: MGM/EMI
Prod.: Harry Fine
Dir.: Jimmy Sangster
Sc.: Tudor Gates based on J. Sheridan Le Fanu's "Carmilla"
Ph.: David Muir (Colour)
Art Dir.: Don Mingaye
Mus.: Harry Robinson, Frank Godwin
Choreog.: Babbie McManus
Ed.: Spencer Reeve
Sound: Terry Poulton, Ron Barron, Len Abbott

Ralph Bates (*Giles Barton*), Barbara Jefford (*Countess*), Suzanna Leigh (*Janet*), Michael Johnson (*Richard Lestrange*), Yutte Stensgaard (*Mircalla*), Mike Raven (*Count Karnstein*), Helen Christie (*Miss Simpson*), David Healy (*Pelley*), Michael Brennan (*Landlord*), Pippa Steele (*Susan*), Luan Peters (*Trudi*), Christopher Cunningham (*Coachman*), Judy Matheson (*Amanda*), Caryl Little (*Isabel*), Jack Melford (*Bishop*), Erik Chitty (*Professor Hertz*), Chirstopher Neame (*Hans*), Harvey Hall (*Heinrich*).
95 mins.

THE MACABRE MARK see LA HUELLA MACABRE

MACISTE CONTRO IL VAMPIRO (MACISTE VS. THE VAMPIRE, GOLIATH AND THE VAMPIRES) (1961) Italy
Prod. Co.: Ambrosiana Cinematografica
Exec. Prod.: Dino De Laurentiis
Prod.: Paolo Moffa
Dir.: Giacomo Genilomo, Sergio Corbucci
Sc.: Sergio Corbucci, Duccio Tessari
Ph.: Alvaro Maniori (Colour, Totalscope)
Ed.: Eraldo Da Roma

Gordon Scott (*Maciste* or *Goliath* in English version), Gianna Maria Canale (*Astra*), Leonora Ruffo (*Giulia*), Annabella Incontrera (*Magda*), Rocco Vitolazzi, Jacques Sernas.
92 mins.

MACISTE VS. THE VAMPIRE see MACISTE CONTRO IL VAMPIRO

MAD MONSTER PARTY (1967) England
Prod. Co.: English Videocraft International
Dist.: Embassy
Dir.: Jules Bass
Sc.: Len Korobkin, Harvey Kurtzman
(in Animagic and Color)

Animated puppets with the voices of Boris Karloff, Phyllis Diller and others.

THE MAGIC CHRISTIAN (1969) England
Prod. Co.: Grand
Dir.: Joseph McGrath
Sc.: Terry Southern, Peter Sellers, Joseph McGrath, from the book by Southern

Ph.: Geoffrey Unsworth (Colour)
Christopher Lee (*Ship's Vampire*), Peter Sellers, Ringo Starr, Raquel Welch.

LA MALDICION DE LOS KARNSTEINS (LA CRIPTA E L'INCUBO, THE CRYPT OF HORROR, TERROR IN THE CRYPT, THE CURSE OF THE KARNSTEINS) (1963) Italy/Spain

Prod. Co.: Hispamer/Mec
Prod.: William Mulligan
Dir.: Thomas Miller [Camillo Mastrocinque]
Sc.: Julian Berry [Ernesto Gastaldi], Robert Bohr [Bruno Valeri], Jose L. Monter, Maria del Carmen Martinex Roman, from J. Sheridan Le Fanu's "Carmilla."
Ph.: Giuseppe Aquari, Julio Ortas
Mus.: Carlo Savina

Christopher Lee (*Count Karnstein*), Audr[e]y Amber [Adriana Ambesi] (*Laura*), Ursula Davis (*Lyuba*), Jose Campos, Vera Valmont, Nela Conjiu, Jose Villasante, Angela Minervini, Carla Calo, Benito Carif, Ignazio Balsamo.
84 mins.

LA MALDICION DE NOSTRADAMUS (THE CURSE OF NOSTRADAMUS) (1960) Mexico

Prod. Co.: Bosas Priego
Dir.: Federico Curiel
Sc.: Carlos Taboada, Alfredo Ruanova
Ph.: Fernando Colin

German Robles (*Nostradamus*), Domingo Soler, Julio Aleman.
78 mins.

THE MALE VAMPIRE see ONNA KYUKETSUI

LA MARCA DEL HOMBRE LOBO (MARK OF THE WOLFMAN, FRANKENSTEIN'S BLOODY TERROR) (1969) Spain

Prod. Co.: Maxper
Dir.: Enrique L. Eguiluz
Sc.: Jacinto Molina
Ph.: Emilio Foriscot (Colour, 3-D, 70mm)

Paul Naschy, Dianik Zurakowska, Manuel Manzaneque, Rosanna Yanni, Julian Ugate.
133 minutes.

MARK OF THE VAMPIRE (1935) U.S.A.

Prod. Co.: MGM
Prod.: E.J. Mannix
Dir.: Tod Browning
Sc.: Guy Endore, Bernard Schubert, from the story by Browning
Ph.: James Wong Howe
Ed.: Ben Lewis

Bela Lugosi, Lionel Barrymore, Elizabeth Allan, Lionel Atwill, Jean Hersholt, Henry Wadsworth, Donald Meek, Jessie Ralph, Carole Borland (*Luna*).
62 minutes.
A remake of LONDON AFTER MIDNIGHT.

MARK OF THE WOLFMAN see LA MARCA DEL HOMBRE LOBO

Bela Lugosi as Count Mora

From MARK OF THE VAMPIRE

LA MASCHERA DEL DEMONIO
(BLACK SUNDAY) (1960)
Italy
Prod. Co.: Galatea-Jolly
Dist.: American International
Dir.: Mario Bava
Sc.: Mario Bava, Ennio de Conci, Mario Serandrei, from the story "The Viy" by Nikolai Gogol
Ph.: Mario Bava
Art Dir.: Giorgio Giovannini
Mus.: Roberto Nicolosi (in Italy) Les Baxter (in English version)
Ed.: Mario Serandrei
Barbara Steele (*The Witch Princess and Katia*), John Richardson (*Dr. Gorobec*), Ivo Garrani (*Katia's Father*), Andrea Checchi (*Dr. Choma*), Arturo Dominici (*Javutich*), Enrico Olivieri (*Katia's Brother*), Clara Bindi (*Innkeeper*), Germana Dominici (*Innkeeper's Daughter*), Mario Passante (*Nikita*), Tino Bianchi (*Ivan*).
84 mins.

Katia and her lover Gorobec in BLACK SUNDAY

THE MONSTERS DEMOLISHER
see NOSTRADAMUS Y EL
DESTRUCTOR DE
MONSTRUOS

MEN OF ACTION MEET
WOMEN OF DRACULA
(1969) Philippines
Prod. Co.: Villanueva
Dir.: Artemio Marquez
Dante Varona Eddie Torrente, Ruben Obligacion.

ET MOURIR DE PLAISIR
(BLOOD AND ROSES) (1960)
France/Italy
Prod. Co.: E.G.E. Films/Documento Films
Dist.: Paramount
Prod.: Raymond Eger
Dir.: Roger Vadim
Sc.: Roger Vadim, Roger Vailland,
adapted from J. Sheridan Le Fanu's *Carmilla* by Claude Brule, C. Martin
Ph.: Claude Renoir
(Technirama, Colour)
Art Dir.: Jean Andre
Mus.: Podromines
Ed.: Victoria Mercanton
Sound: Robert Bieart
Cost.: Marcel Escoffier
Mel Ferrer (*Leopoldo De Karnstein*), Elsa Martinelli (*Georgia Monteverdi*), Annette Vadim (*Carmilla Von Karnstein*), Jacques-René Chauffard (*Dr. Verari*), Marc Allegret (*Judge Monteverdi*), Alberto Bonucci (*Carlo Ruggieri*), Serge Marquand (*Giuseppe*), Gabriella Farinon (*Lisa*), Renato Speziali (*Guido Naldi*), Edythe Peters (*The Cook*), Gianni De Benedetto (*Police Marshal*), Carmilla Stroyberg (*Marthe*), Nathalie Le Foret (*Marie*).
87 mins. original, later cut to 74 mins.

LAS MUJERES DE DRACULA
see EL IMPERIO DE DRACULA

EL MUNDO DE LOS
VAMPIROS (THE WORLD
OF THE VAMPIRES) (1960)
Mexico
Prod. Co.: Cinematografica ABSA
Dir.: Alfonso Corona Blake
Sc.: Javier Torya, Ramon Obon, from a story by Raul Zenteno
Ph.: Jack Draper
Mauricio Garces, Silvia Fournier, Erna Martha Bauman, Jose Baviera.

MUNSTER, GO HOME (1966)
U.S.A.
Prod. Co.: Universal
Dir.: Earl Bellamy
Sc.: G. Tibbles, Joe Connelly, Bob Mosher
Ph.: Benjamin Kline
(Colour)
John Carradine, Yvonne De Carlo, Al Lewis, Butch Patrick, Debbie Watson, Hermione Gingold, Cliff Norton, Fred Gwynne.

THE NAKED VAMPIRE see
LA VAMPIRE NUE

NIGHT OF THE VAMPIRE
see DER FLUCH DER
GRUNEN AUGEN

THE NIGHT STALKER (1972)
U.S.A.
Prod. Co.: Dan Curtis Films/ABC
Prod.: Dan Curtis
Dir.: John L. Moxey
Sc.: Richard Matheson
Ph.: Michael Hugo
Mus.: Robert Colbert
Ed.: Desmond Marquette
Darren McGavin (*Carl Kolchak*), Carol Lynley (*Gail Foster*), Simon Oakland (*Vincenzo*), Ralph Meeker (*Bernie Jenks*), Claude Akins (*Sheriff Butcher*), Charles McGraw

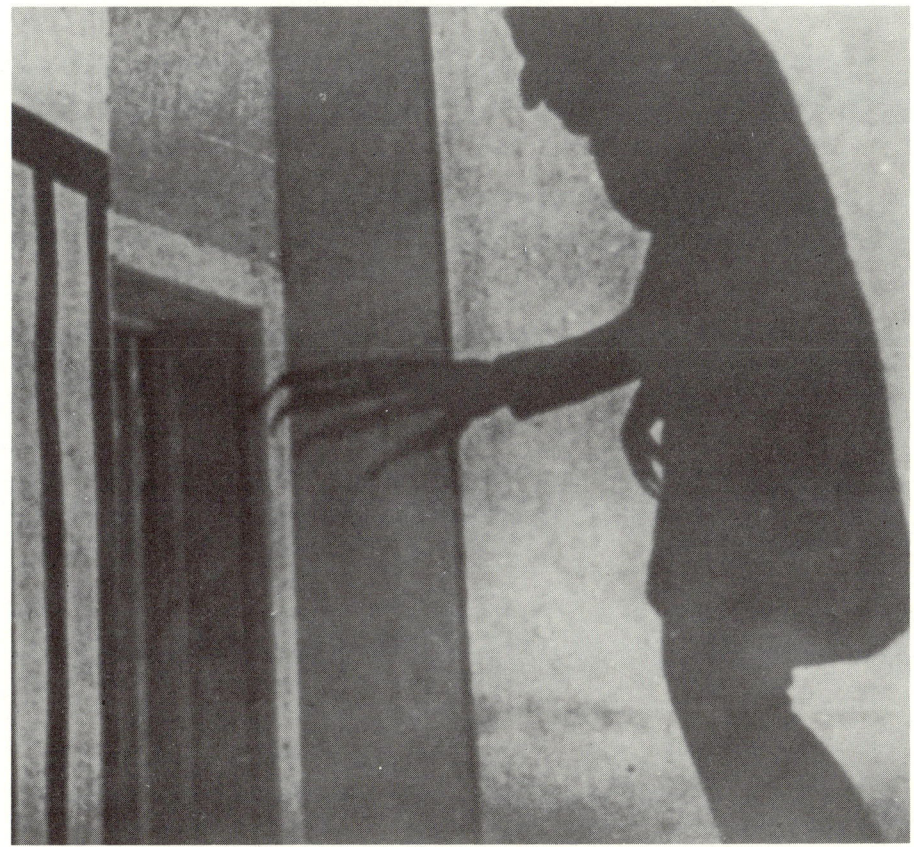

The vampire on the stairs outside Nina's room in NOSFERATU

(*Chief Masterson*), Kent Smith (*D.A. Paine*), Barry Atwater (*Janos Skorzeny*).
75 mins.

LA NOCHE DE WALPURGIS (THE NIGHT OF WALPURGIS, THE WEREWOLF VS. THE VAMPIRE WOMAN) (1972)
Spain/West Germany
Prod. Co.: Plata Films/Hi-Fi Stereo
Dist.: Western International/ Ellman Enterprises
Dir.: Leon Klimovsky
Sc.: Jacinto Molina, Hans Munkell
Ph.: Leopoldo Villasenor (Colour)
Paul Naschy, Gaby Fuchs, Barbara Capell, Yelena Samarina, Andres Resino, Patty Shepard.
88 mins.

NOSFERATU, EINE SYMPHONIE DES GRAUENS — A SYMPHONY OF HORRORS (1922) Germany
Prod. Co.: Prana Film G.m.b.H.
Dir.: F.W. Murnau
Sc.: Henrik Galeen, from Bram Stoker's "Dracula"
Ph.: Fritz Arno Wagner
Art Dir.: Albin Grau

The procession of the dead in NOSFERATU

Negative image of Orlof's carriage in NOSFERATU

Max Schreck (*Graf Orlof/Nosferatu*), Alexander Granach (*Knock, an estate agent*), Gustav von Wangenheim (*Hutter, his assistant*), Great Schroeder (*Ellen, Hutter's wife*), G.H. Schnell (*Harding, a shipbuilder*), Ruth Landshoff (*Annie, his wife*), John Gottowt (*Professor Bulwer*), Gustav Botz (*Professor Sievers*), Max Nemetz (*Sea Captain*), Wolfgang Heinz (*First Sailor*), Albert Venchr (*Second Sailor*), Herzfeld (*Innkeeper*), Hardy von Francois (*Hospital Doctor*), Heinrich Witte.
65 mins.

NOSTRADAMUS AND THE DESTROYER OF MONSTERS see NOSTRADAMUS Y EL DESTRUCTOR DE MONSTRUOS

NOSTRADAMUS AND THE GENIE OF DARKNESS see NOSTRADAMUS Y EL GENIO DE LAS TINIEBLAS

NOSTRADAMUS Y EL DESTRUCTOR DE MONSTRUOS (NOSTRADAMUS AND THE DESTROYER OF MONSTERS, THE MONSTERS DEMOLISHER) (1962) Mexico
Prod. Co.: Bosas Priego
Dir.: Federico Curiel
Sc.: Alfredo Ruanova, Carlos Taboada
Ph.: F. Colin
German Robles (*Nostradamus*), Julio Aleman, Domingo Soler, Aurora Alvarado.

NOSTRADAMUS Y EL GENIO DE LAS TINIEBLAS (NOSTRADAMUS AND THE GENIE OF DARKNESS, GENIE OF DARKNESS) (1960) Mexico

Prod. Co.: Bosas Priego
Dir.: Federico Curiel
Sc.: Carlos Taboada, Alfredo Ruanova
Ph.: Fernando Colin
German Robles (*Nostradamus*), Domingo Soler.
77 mins.

THE NUDE VAMPIRE see LA VAMPIRE NUE

OMEGA MAN (1970) U.S.A.
Prod. Co.: Walter Seltzer Production
Dist.: Warner Bros.
Dir.: Boris Sagal
Sc.: John William Corrington, Joyce H. Corrington, from the novel "I Am Legend" by Richard Matheson.
Ph.: Russell Metty (Colour)
Charlton Heston, Anthony Zerbe, Rosalind Cash, Paul Koslo, Lincoln Kilpatrick.

ONE MORE TIME (1969) England
Prod. Co.: United Artists/Chrislaw/Trace-Mark
Dir.: Jerry Lewis
Sc.: Michael Pertwee
Ph.: Ernest W. Steward (Colour)
Sammy Davis Jr., Peter Lawford, Percy Herbert, Christopher Lee (*Dracula*), Peter Cushing (*Dr. Frankenstein*).
Both Lee and Cushing have cameos.

ONNA KYUKETSUI (MALE VAMPIRE, VAMPIRE MAN) (1959) Japan
Prod. Co.: Shin Toho
Dir.: Nobuo Nakagawa
Sc.: Shin Nakazawa, Katsuyoshi Nakatsu
Ph.: Yoshimi Hirano (Shin Toho Scope)
Shigeru Amachi, Yoko Mihara,

Keinosuke Wada, Junko Ikeuchi.
78 mins.

PARIS WHEN IT SIZZLES
  (1964) U.S.A.
Prod. Co.: Paramount
Dir.: Richard Quine
Sc.: George Axelrod
Ph.: Charles Lang Jr.
        (Colour)
William Holden, Audrey Hepburn, Tony Curtis, Noël Coward.
There is a short vampire scene.

PASTEL DE SHANGRE (CAKE OF BLOOD) (1972) Spain
Prod. Co.: P.C. Tiede
Dir.: Jose Maria Valles, Emilio Martinez Lazaro, Francisco Bellmunt, Jaime Chavarri
        (4 episodes)
Sc.: Jose Maria Valles, Emilio Martinez Lazaro, Francisco Bellmunt, Jaime Chavarri.
Ph.: Luis Cuadrado (Colour, Techniscope)
Marta May, Charo Lopez, Marisa Paredes, Romy, Julian Ugarte, Carolos Otero, Luis Ciges, Eusebio Poncela, Jaime Chavarri.
89 mins.

PONTIANAK (THE VAMPIRE)
  (1957) Malaya
Prod. Co.: Keris
Maria Menado.

PONTIANAK GUA MUSANG (THE VAMPIRE OF THE CAVE) (1964) Malaya
Prod. Co.: Keris
Dir.: B.N. Rao
Suraya Haron.

PONTIANAK KEMBALI (THE VAMPIRE RETURNS) (1963) Malaya
Prod. Co.: Keris
Dir.: R. Estellia
Maria Menado.

PREHISTORIC PLANET see QUEEN OF BLOOD

THE PROMISE OF RED LIPS see LE ROUGE AUX LEVRES

PLAN NINE FROM OUTER SPACE (1956) U.S.A.
Prod. Co.: Criswell
Dir.: Edward D. Wood Jr.
Bela Lugosi, Vampira.

Vampira in PLAN 9 FROM OUTER SPACE

From PLAN 9 FROM OUTER SPACE

PLANET OF BLOOD see
  QUEEN OF BLOOD

PLANET OF THE VAMPIRES
  (Italy) see TERRORE NELLO
  SPAZIO

PLANET OF VAMPIRES
  (U.S.A.) see QUEEN OF BLOOD

PLAYGIRLS AND THE
  VAMPIRE see L'ULTIMA
  PREDA DEL VAMPIRO

QUEEN OF BLOOD (PLANET
  OF BLOOD, PLANET OF
  VAMPIRES, PREHISTORIC
  PLANET) (1966) U.S.A.
Prod. Co.: American International
Dir.:   Curtis Harrington
Sc.:   Curtis Harrington from

the story "The Veiled Woman"
Ph.: Vilis Lapenieks (Colour)
Basil Rathbone, Florence Marly, Judi Meredith, John Saxon, Dennis Hopper, Forrest J. Ackerman, Terry Lee.
79 mins.

QUEEN OF THE VAMPIRES see LE VIOL DU VAMPIRE

RAPE OF THE VAMPIRE see LE VIOL DU VAMPIRE

LA REINE DES VAMPIRE see LE VIOL DU VAMPIRE

RETURN OF COUNT YORGA (1971) U.S.A.
Prod. Co.: American International
Prod.: Michael Macready
Dir.: Bob Kelljan
Sc.: Bob Kelljan, Yvonne Wilder
Ph.: Bill Butler (Colour)
Art Dir.: Vince Cresceman
Mus.: Bill Marx
Ed.: Fabien Todjmann
Robert Quarry (*Count Yorga*), Mariette Hartley (*Cynthia*), Roger Perry (*David*), Yvonne Wilder (*Jennifer*), Tom Toner (*Rev. Thomas*), Rudy Deluca, Craig Nelson (*Policemen*), Philip Frame (*Tommy*), George Macready (*Professor*), Walter Brooke (*Bill Nelson*).
96 mins.

RETURN OF DRACULA (CURSE OF DRACULA) (1958) U.S.A.
Prod. Co.: Levy-Gardner Production
Dist.: United Artists
Dir.: Paul Landres
Sc.: Pat Fielder
Ph.: Jack MacKenzie
Art Dir.: James Vance
Ed.: Sherman Rose

Mus.: Gerald Fried
Francis Lederer (*Dracula/Bellac*), Norma Eberhardt (*Rachel Mayberry*), Ray Stricklyn (*Tim*), Jimmie Baird (*Mickey Mayberry*), Greta Granstedt (*Cora Mayberry*), Virginia Vincent (*Jenny*), John Wengraf (*Merriman*), Gage Clark (*The Reverend*), Norbert Schiller, Charles Tannen, John MacNamara, Hope Summers, Robert Lynn, Harry Harvey, Mel Allen.
77 mins.

THE RETURN OF THE VAMPIRE (1943) U.S.A.
Prod. Co.: Columbia
Prod.: Sam White
Dir.: Lew Landers
Sc.: Griffin Jay, from an idea by Kurt Neumann
Add. Dia.: Randall Faye
Ph.: John Stumar, L.W. O'Connell
Ed.: Paul Borofsky
Bela Lugosi (*Armand Tesla*), Frieda Inescort (*Lady Jane Ainsley*), Nina Foch (*Nicki Saunders*), Roland Varno (*John Ainsley*), Miles Mander (*Sir Frederick Fleet*), Matt Willis (*Andreas Obry*), Gilbert Emery (*Professor Saunders*), Ottola Nesmith (*Elsa*), Leslie Dennison (*Lynch*), William C.P. Austin (*Gannet*).
69 mins.

REVENGE OF THE VAMPIRE see DENDAM PONTIANAK

THE RIDER OF THE SKULLS see EL CHARRO DE LAS CALAVERAS

RITUAL OF BLOOD see CEREMONIA SANGRIENTA

LE ROUGE AUX LEVRES (THE PROMISE OF RED LIPS, DAUGHTERS OF

Bela Lugosi in coffin and Matt Willis, the Werewolf, in THE RETURN OF THE VAMPIRE

DARKNESS) (1970) Belgium/
France/West Germany/Spain
Prod. Co.: Showking/Cine Vog,
 Maya, Roxy Films, and
 Mediterranea Films
Dist.: Gemini Releasing/
 Maron Films
Prod.: Paul Collet, Alain C.
 Guilleaume
Dir.: Harry Kumel
Sc.: Pierre Drouot, Harry
 Kumel, J.J. Amiel
Ph.: Edward van der Enden
 (Colour)
Mus.: François de Roubaix
Ed.: Gust Verschueren,
 Denis Bonan
Art Dir.: Françoise Hardy
Delphine Seyrig (*Countess Elisabeth Bathory*), Danièle Ouimet (*Valerie*), John Karlen (*Stefan*), Andrea Rau (*Ilona*), Paul Esser (*Porter*), George Jamin (*The Man*), Joris Collet (*The Butler*), Fons Rademakers (*Mother*).
96 mins.

SAMSON VS. THE VAMPIRE
 WOMEN see SANTO CONTRA
 LAS MUJERES VAMPIRAS

LA SANGRE DE
 NOSTRADAMUS (BLOOD OF
 NOSTRADAMUS) (1960)
 Mexico
Prod. Co.: Producciones Bosas
 Priego
Dir.: F. Curiel
Sc.: C. Taboada, Alfredo
 Ruanova
Ph.: F. Colin
German Robles (*Nostradamus*), Julio Aleman, Domingo Soler.
98 mins.

SANGRE DE VIRGENES
 (BLOOD OF THE VIRGINS)
 (1968) Mexico
Prod. Co.: Azteca (Colour)
Dir.: Emilio Vieyra
 (Colour)
Gloria Prat, Ricardo Bauleo, Rolo Puente, Susana Beltran.

SANTO AGAINST BARON
 BRAKOLA see EL SANTO
 CONTRA EL BARON
 BRAKOLA

SANTO AND DRACULA'S
 TREASURE see EL VAMPIRE
 Y EL SEXO

SANTO AND THE BLUE
 DEMON VS. DRACULA AND
 THE WOLF MAN see SANTO
 Y EL BLUE DEMON
 CONTRA DRACULA Y EL
 HOMBRE LOBO

SANTO AND THE BLUE
 DEMON VS. THE MONSTERS
 see SANTO Y EL BLUE
 DEMON CONTRA LOS
 MONSTRUOS

EL SANTO CONTRA EL BARON
 BRAKOLA (SANTO AGAINST
 BARON BRAKOLA) (1965)
 Mexico
Prod. Co.: Vergara
Dir.: Jose Diaz Morales
Santo, Fernando Oses, Susana Robles.

SANTO CONTRA LAS
 MUJERES VAMPIRAS
 (SANTO VS. THE VAMPIRE
 WOMEN, SAMSON VS. THE
 VAMPIRE WOMEN) (1962)
 Mexico
Prod. Co.: Tele-Cine-Radio
Dir.: Alfonso Corona Blake
Sc.: A.C. Blake, from a story
 by A. Orellana, F. Osses,
 and R.G. Travesi
Santo, Lorena Velazquez, Maria Duval, Jaime Fernandez, Augusto Benedico, Ofelia Montesco.

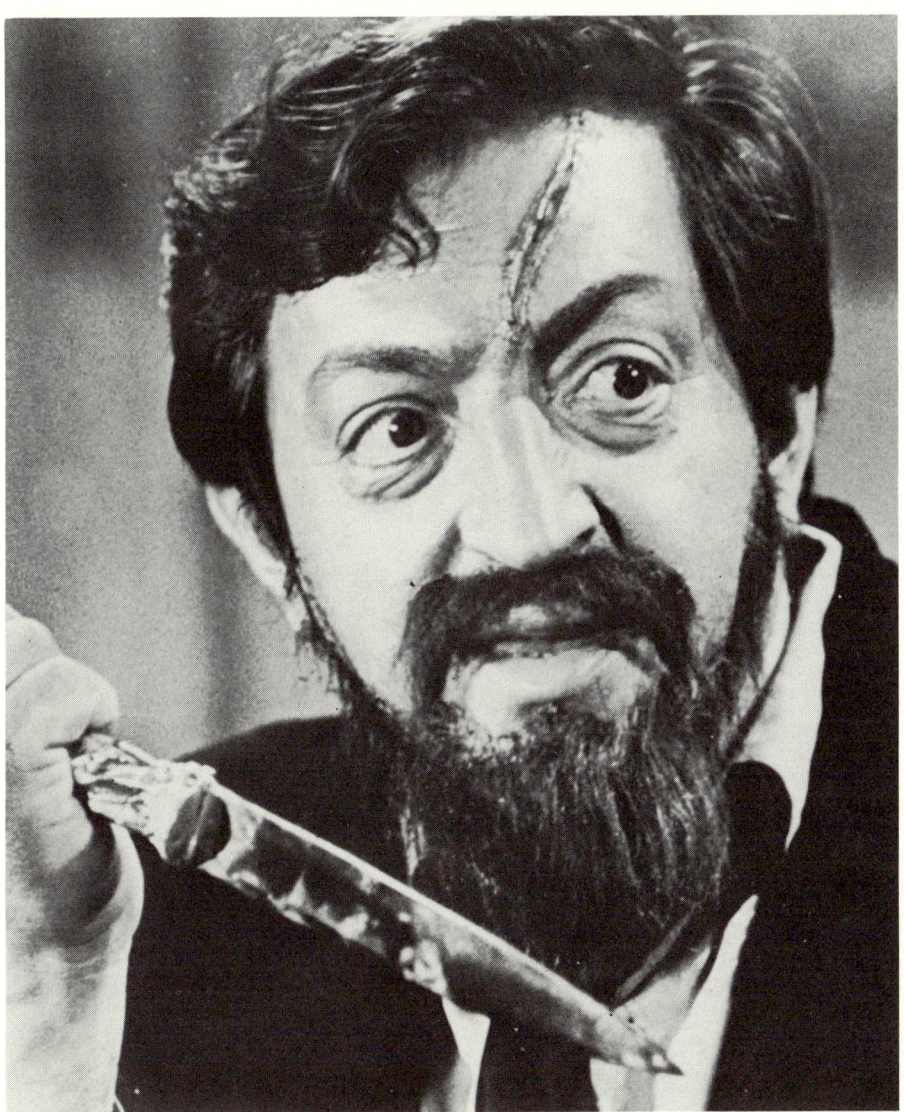

From SANTO Y BLUE DEMON CONTRA DRACULA Y EL HOMBRE LOBO

SANTO VS. THE VAMPIRE WOMEN see SANTO CONTRA LAS MUJERES VAMPIRAS

SANTO Y BLUE DEMON CONTRA DRACULA Y EL HOMBRE LOBO (SANTO AND THE BLUE DEMON VS. DRACULA AND THE WOLFMAN) (1973) Mexico
Prod. Co.: Cinematografica Calderon (Colour)
Santo, Aldo Monti, Agustin Martinez Solares.

From SANTO Y BLUE DEMON CONTRA DRACULA Y EL HOMBRE LOBO

 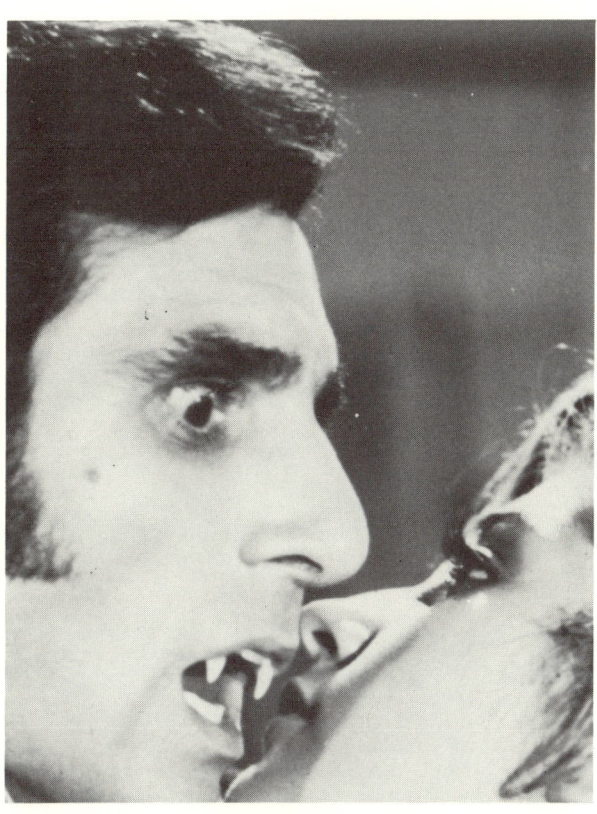

From SANTO Y BLUE DEMON CONTRA DRACULA Y EL HOMBRE LOBO

From SANTO Y BLUE DEMON CONTRA DRACULA Y EL HOMBRE LOBO

Santo in trouble again in SANTO Y BLUE DEMON CONTRA DRACULA Y EL HOMBRE LOBO

EL SANTO Y BLUE DEMON CONTRA LOS MONSTRUOS (SANTO AND THE BLUE DEMON VS. THE MONSTERS) (1969) Mexico
Prod. Co.: Sotomayor (Colour)
Dir.: Gilberto Martinez Solares
Santo, Resortes, Heydi Blue.

SATANIC RITES OF DRACULA (1974) Great Britain
Prod. Co.: Columbia-Warner
Prod.: Roy Skeggs
Dir.: Alan Gibson
Sc.: Don Houghton
Ph.: Brian Probyn (Colour)
Ed.: Chris Barnes
Mus.: John Cacavas
Christopher Lee (*Dracula*), Peter Cushing (*Van Helsing*), Michael Coles, William Franklyn, Freddie Jones, Joanna Lumley, Richard Vernon.
87 mins.

SCARS OF DRACULA (1970) England
Prod. Co.: Hammer/EMI
Dist.: MGM/EMI
Prod.: Aida Young
Dir.: Roy Ward Baker
Sc.: John Elder [Anthony Hinds]
Ph.: Moray Grant (Colour)
Art Dir.: Scott MacGregor
Mus.: James Bernard
Ed.: James Needs
Sound: Philip Martell, Roy Hyde, Ron Barron
Christopher Lee (*Count Dracula*), Dennis Waterman (*Simon*), Jenny Hanley (*Sarah Framsen*), Christopher Matthews (*Paul*), Patrick Troughton (*Klove*), Michael Gwynn (*Priest*), Wendy Hamilton (*Julie*), Anoushka Hempel (*Tania*), Delia Lindsay (*Alice*), Bob Todd (*Burgomaster*), Toke Townley (*Elderly Waggoner*).
96 mins.

DIE SCHLANGENGRUBE UND DAS PENDEL (THE SNAKE PIT AND THE PENDULUM, THE BLOOD DEMON) (1967) West Germany
Prod. Co.: Constantin
Dir.: Harald Reinl
Sc.: Manfred R. Kohler
Ph.: Ernst W. Kalinke (Colour)
Christopher Lee, Lex Barker, Karin Dor, Carl Lange.

SCREAM AND SCREAM AGAIN (1970) England
Prod. Co.: American International
Prod.: Max J. Rosenberg and Milton Subotsky
Dir.: Gordon Hessler
Sc.: Christopher Wicking, from the novel by Paul Saxon
Ph.: John Coquillon (Colour)
Art Dir.: Bill Constable
Mus.: Dave Whittaker
Ed.: Peter Elliot
Vincent Price (*Dr. Browning*), Christopher Lee (*Freemont*), Peter Cushing (*Benedek*), Judy Huxtable (*Sylvia*), Alfred Marks (*Supt. Bellaver*), Michael Gothard (*Keith*), Anthony Newlands (*Ludwig*), Marshall Jones (*Konratz*), Peter Sallis (*Schweitz*).
94 mins.

SCREAM, BLACULA, SCREAM (1973) U.S.A.
Prod. Co.: Joseph T. Naar Production
Dist.: American International
Dir.: Bob Kelljan
Sc.: Joan Torres, Raymond Koenig, Maurice Jules, from a story by Torres

Ph.: Isidore Mankofsky
(Colour)
Art. Dir.: Alfeo Boccicchio
Mus.: Bill Marx
Ed.: Fabien Tordjmann
William Marshall (*Mamuwalde/Blacula*), Don Mitchell (*Justin*), Pam Grier (*Lisa*), Michael Conrad (*Sheriff Dunlop*), Richard Lawson (*Willis*), Lynn Moody (*Denny*), Janee Michelle (*Gloria*), Barbara Rhoades (*Elaine*), Bernie Hamilton (*Ragman*), Arnold Williams, Van Kirksey, Bob Minor, Al Jones, Eric Mason.
95 mins.

SEX AND THE VAMPIRE see LE VIOL DU VAMPIRE

SEXY PROIBITISSIMO
  (FORBIDDEN FEMININITY, SEXY-SUPER INTERDIT, SEXY INTERDIT) (1963)
  Italy
Prod. Co.: Gino Nordini Produzioni
Dir./Sc.: Marcello Martinelli
Ph.: Adalberto Albertini
(Colour)
87 mins.
One of the sketches is a vampire tale.

SHUDDER OF THE VAMPIRE see LE FRISSON DES VAMPIRES

SLAUGHTER OF THE VAMPIRES see LA STRAGE DEI VAMPIRI

THE SNAKE PIT AND THE PENDULUM see DIE SCHLANGENGRUBE UND DAS PENDEL

SON OF DRACULA (1943)
  U.S.A.
Prod. Co.: Universal
Prod.: Ford Beebe

Dir.: Robert Siodmak
Sc.: Eric Taylor, from a story by Curt Siodmak
Ph.: George Robinson
Art Dir.: John B. Goodman, Martin Obzina
Mus.: Hans J. Salter
Ed.: Saul Goodkind
Spe. Eff.: John P. Fulton
Lon Chaney Jr. (*Count Alucard/Dracula*), Louise Allbritton (*Katherine Caldwell*), George Irving (*Colonel Caldwell*), Robert Paige (*Frank Stanley*), Frank Craven (*Dr. Brewster*), J. Edward Bromberg (*Professor Lazlo*), Evelyn Ankers (*Claire Caldwell*), Samuel S. Hinds (*Judge Simmons*), Patrick Moriarity (*Sheriff Dawes*), Adeline Reynolds (*Queen Zimba*).
78 mins.

SON OF THE VAMPIRE see ANAK PONTIANAK

UM SONHO DE VAMPIROS
  (A DREAM OF VAMPIRES, A VAMPIRE'S DREAM)
  (1968) Brazil
Prod. Co.: Servicine-Servicos Cinematograficos Ltda./U.C.B.-Uniao Cinematografica Brasileira S.A./R.P.I. Filmes Brasileiros em Distribuicao Ltda.
Dir./Sc.: Ibere Cavalcanti
Ph.: Renato Neumann
(Colour)
Ankito, Irma Alvarez, Janet Chermont, Sonelio Costa, Augusto Maia Filho, Janira Santiago, Zuza Curi.
80 mins.

LA STRAGE DEI VAMPIRI
  (SLAUGHTER OF THE VAMPIRES, VAMPIRE, HOMME OU FEMME?;

CURSE OF THE BLOOD GHOULS) (1962) Italy
Prod. Co.: Dino Sant'Ambrogio
Dist.: Mercury/Pacemaker
Dir./Sc.: Roberto Mauri
Ph.: Ugo Brunelli
Art Dir.: Giuseppe Ranieri
Ed.: Jenner Menghi
Mus.: Aldo Piga
Walter Brandi, Graziella Granata, Dieter Eppler, Alfredo Rizzo, Paolo Solvay.
84 mins.

Graziella Granata plays the piano for her guests in LA STRAGE DEI VAMPIRI

Walter Brandi as the vampire rises from his tomb in LA STRAGE DEI VAMPIRI

FILMOGRAPHY 213

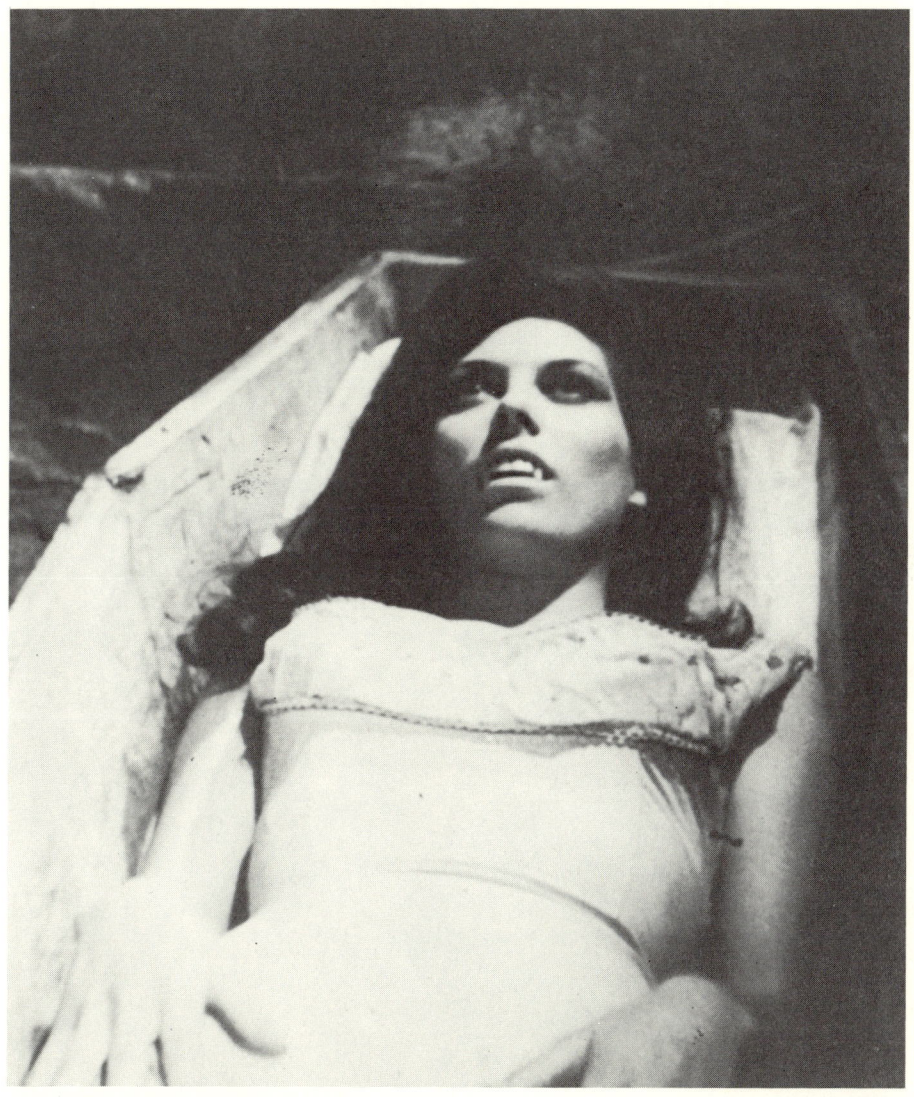

From LA STRAGE DEI VAMPIRI

SUMPAH PONTIANAK (THE VAMPIRE'S CURSE) (1958) Malaya
Prod. Co.: Keris

A TASTE OF BLOOD (1967) U.S.A.
Prod. Co.: Creative Film Enterprises
Dir.: Herschell G. Lewis
Sc.: Donald Stanford
Ph.: Andy Romanoff (Colour)
Bill Rogers, Elizabeth Wilkinson, Thomas Wood, Otto Schlesinger, Eleanor Vaill, Lawrence Tobin, Ted Schell.
120 mins.

TASTE THE BLOOD OF DRACULA (1969) England
Prod. Co.: Hammer

Dist.: Warner
Prod.: Aida Young
Dir.: Peter Sasdy
Sc.: John Elder [Anthony Hinds]
Ph.: Arthur Grant (Colour)
Art Dir.: Scott MacGregor
Mus.: James Bernard
Ed.: Chris Barnes

Christopher Lee (*Dracula*), Geoffrey Keen (*William Hargood*), Gwen Watford (*Martha Hargood*), Linda Hayden (*Alice Hargood*), Peter Sallis (*Samuel Paxton*), Anthony Corlan (*Paul Paxton*), Isla Blair (*Lucy Paxton*), John Carson (*Jonathan Secker*), Martin Jarvis (*Jeremy Secker*), Ralph Bates (*Lord Courtley*), Roy Kinnear (*Weller*), Michael Ripper (*Cobb*), Russell Hunter (*Felix*), Shirley Jaffe (*Hargood's maid*), Keith Marsh (*Father*), Peter May (*Son*), Reginald Barratt (*Vicar*), Maddy Smith (*Dolly*), Lai Ling (*Chinese Girl*), Malaika Martin (*Snake Girl*).
95 mins.

From TASTE THE BLOOD OF DRACULA

Linda Hayden and Isla Blair in TASTE THE BLOOD OF DRACULA

Linda Hayden as Alice Hargood lies on the tomb of her master Dracula in TASTE THE BLOOD OF DRACULA

FILMOGRAPHY

TEMPI DURI PER I VAMPIRI (HARD TIMES FOR VAMPIRES, UNCLE WAS A VAMPIRE) (1959) Italy
Prod. Co.: Maxima—Cei Incom-Montflour Film
Dist.: Embassy
Dir.: Stefano Steno
Sc.: Alessandro Continenza, Dino Verde, Anton
Ph.: Marco Scarpelli (Colour)
Art Dir.: Andrea Tomassi
Renato Rascel (*Osvaldo Lambertenghi*), Sylva Koscina (*Carla*), Christopher Lee (*The Vampire*), Lia Zoppelli (*Letizia*), Kay Fisher, Susanna Loret, Carl Wery.

TERROR IN OUTER SPACE see TERRORE NELLO SPAZIO

TERROR IN THE CRYPT see LA MALDICION DE LOS KARNSTEINS

TERRORE NELLO SPAZIO (TERROR IN OUTER SPACE, PLANET OF THE VAMPIRES, THE DEMON PLANET) (1965) Italy/Spain
Prod. Co.: Italian International Film/Castilla Cooperativa Cinematografica
Dir.: Mario Bava
Sc.: Mario Bava, Ib Melchior, Louis Heyward, Alberto Bevilacqua, R. Salvia, A. Roman, C. Cosulich, Pestriniero
Ph.: Antonio Rinaldi (Colour)
Barry Sullivan, Norma Bengell, Angel Aranda, Evi Marandi. 87 mins.

From TASTE THE BLOOD OF DRACULA

THEATRE OF DEATH (BLOOD FIEND) (1966) England
Prod. Co.: Hemisphere/Pennea
Dir.: Samuel Gallu
Sc.: Ellis Kadison, Roger Marshall
Ph.: Gilbert Taylor (Colour, Scope)
Christopher Lee, Julian Glover, L. Goldoni, Jenny Till, Ivor Dean.

THE THREE FACES OF FEAR see I TRE VOLTI DELLA PAURA

THROW ME TO THE VAMPIRE see ECHENME AL VAMPIRO

TOM THUMB AND LITTLE RED RIDING HOOD VS. THE MONSTERS see CAPURCITA Y PULCARCITO CONTRA LOS MONSTRUOS

I TRE VOLTI DELLA PAURA (THE THREE FACES OF FEAR, BLACK SABBATH) (1963) Italy
Prod. Co.: Galatea/Emmepi Cinematografica/Lyre Cinematografica
Dist.: American International
Dir.: Mario Bava
Sc.: Mario Bava, Marcello Fondato, Alberto Bevilacqua and Martini and Guerra based on stories by (respectively) Chekhov, F.G. Snyder, and Alexis Tolstoy.
Ph.: Ubaldo Terzano (Colour)
Art Dir.: Giorgio Giovannini
Mus.: Roberto Nicolosi (Italian version) Les Baxter (English version)

Ed.: Mario Serandrei
Cost.: Tini Grani
Sound: Titra Sound Corp.
Prod. Mgr.: Paolo Mercuri

1. *The Drop of Water:* Jacqueline Pierreux (*Helen*), Miny Monti (*The Maid*).
2. *The Telephone*: Michèle Mercier (*Rosy*), Lidia Alfonsi (*Mary*).
3. *The Wurdalak* based on Tolstoy's story "The Family of a Vourdalak"): Boris Karloff (*Gorca*), Susy Andersen (*Sdenka*), Mark Damon (*Vladimir*), Glauco Onorato (*Giorio*), Rika Dialina (*Giorgio's Wife*), Massimo Righi (*Pietro*).

All three episodes are introduced by Boris Karloff.
99 mins.
The final tale is a vampire story.

TWINS OF EVIL (1971) England
Prod. Co.: Hammer
Dist.: Universal
Prod.: Harry Fine, Michael Style
Dir.: John Hough
Sc.: Tudor Gates, based on characters in J. Sheridan Le Fanu's "Carmilla"
Ph.: Dick Bush (Colour) and 2nd Unit: Jack Mills
Art Dir.: Roy Stannard
Mus.: Harry Robinson
Ed.: Spencer Reeve
Sp. Eff.: Bert Luxford

Madeleine Collinson (*Frieda Gelhorn*), Mary Collinson (*Maria Gelhorn*), Peter Cushing (*Gustav Weil*), Kathleen Byron (*Katy Weil*), Dennis Price (*Dietrich*), Harvey Hall (*Franz*), Isobel Black (*Ingrid Hoffer*), Damien

The evil Count Karnstein indulges in black magic rites with his mistress in TWINS OF EVIL

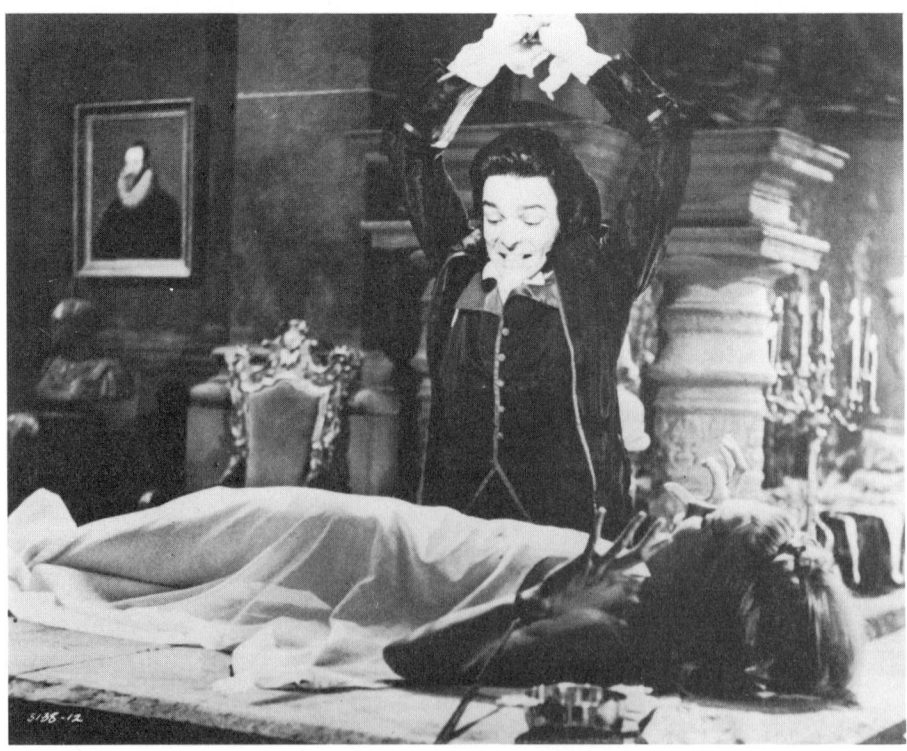

The woodman's daughter being burned at the stake, from TWINS OF EVIL

David Warbeck is restrained by fanatical witch hunters in TWINS OF EVIL

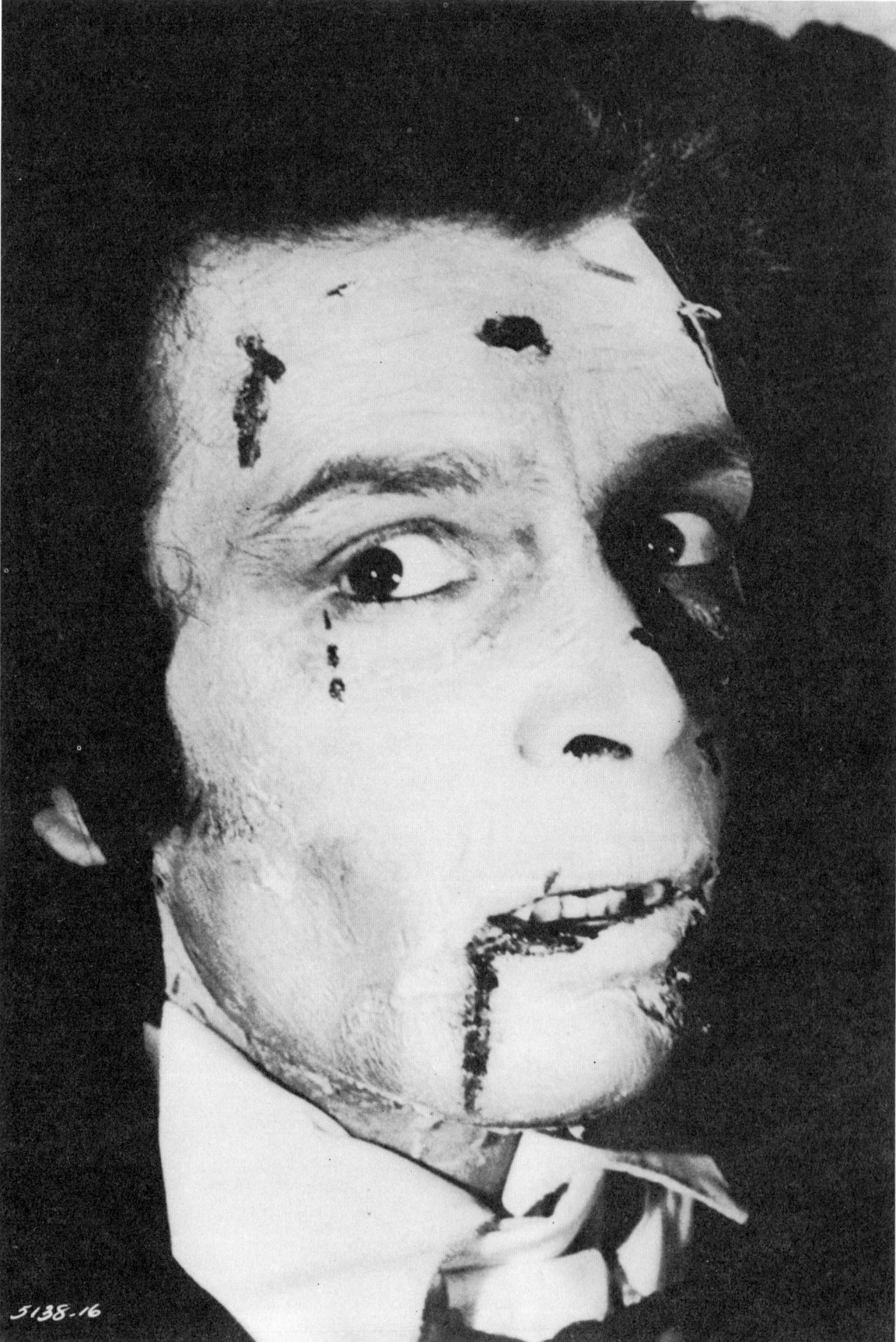

Thomas (*Count Karnstein*), David Warbeck (*Anton Hoffer*), Alex Scott (*Herman*), Katya Keith (*Countess Mircalla*), Roy Stewart (*Joachim*), Maggie Wright (*Girl on Tomb*), Luan Peters (*Gerta*), Inigo Jackson (*Woodman*), Judy Matheson (*Woodman's Daughter*), Sheelah Wilcox (*Lady in Coach*), Kirsten Lindholm (*Girl at Stake*), Peter Thompson (*Jailer*).
87 mins.

L'ULTIMA PREDA DEL VAMPIRO (THE PLAYGIRLS AND THE VAMPIRE) (1960) Italy
Prod. Co.: Tiziano Longo
Dir./Sc.: Piero Regnoli
Ph.: Ugo Brunelli
Lyla Rocco, Walter Brandi, Alfredo Rizzo, Maria Giovannini.

UNCLE WAS A VAMPIRE see TEMPI DURI PER I VAMPIRI

VALERIE A TYDEN DIVU (VALERIE AND THE WEEK OF WONDERS) (1969) Czechoslovakia
Prod. Co.: Barrandov
Dir.: Jaromil Jires

VALERIE AND THE WEEK OF WONDERS see VALERIE A TYDEN DIVU

LAS VAMPIRAS (THE VAMPIRE GIRLS) (1967) Mexico
Prod. Co.: Azteca (Colour)
Dir: Federico Curiel
John Carradine, Mil Mascaras, Pedro Armendariz, Martha Romeo, Maria Duval.

Count Karnstein from TWINS OF EVIL

THE VAMPIRE (Mexico) see EL VAMPIRO

THE VAMPIRE (Malaya) see PONTIANAK

THE VAMPIRE (1957) U.S.A.
Prod. Co.: United Artists/Gardner-Levy
Prod.: Jules Levy, Arthur Gardner
Dir.: Paul Landres
Sc.: Pat Fielder
Ph.: Jack McKenzie
Art Dir.: James Vance
Mus.: Gerald Fried
Ed.: Johnny Faure
John Beal (*Dr. Paul Beecher*), Coleen Gray (*Carol Butler*), Kenneth Tobey (*Buck*), Lydia Reed (*Betsy Beecher*), Dabbs Greer (*Dr. William Beaumont*), Herb Vigran (*George Ryan*), Ann Staunton (*Marion Wilkins*), James Griffith (*Henry Winston*).
75 mins.

THE VAMPIRE AND SEX see EL VAMPIRO Y EL SEXO

THE VAMPIRE AND THE BALLERINA see L'AMANTE DEL VAMPIRO

VAMPIRE CIRCUS (1971) England
Prod. Co.: Hammer
Prod.: Wilbur Stark
Dir.: Robert Young
Sc.: Judson Kinberg from a story by George Baxt and Wilbur Stark
Ph.: Moray Grant (Colour)
Art Dir.: Scott MacGregor
Mus.: David Whittaker
Ed.: Peter Musgrave
Sound: Claude Hitchcock
Adrienne Corri (*Gypsy Woman*), Laurence Payne (*Mueller*), Thorley

From Paul Landres's THE VAMPIRE

Walters (*Burgomaster*), John Moulder Brown (*Anton Kersh*), Lynne Frederick (*Dora Mueller*), Elizabeth Seal (*Gerta Hauser*), Anthony Corlan (*Emil*), Richard Owens (*Dr. Kersh*), Domini Blythe (*Anna Mueller*), Robin Hunter (*Hauser*), Robert Tayman (*Count Mitterhouse*), Mary Wimbush (*Elvira*), Lalla Ward (*Helga*), Robin Sachs (*Heinrich*), Dave Prowse (*Strongman*), Roderick Shaw (*Jon Hauser*), Barnaby Shaw (*Gustav Hauser*), Christine Paul (*Rosa*), Jane Darby (*Jenny*), Skip Martin (*Michael*), Milovan and Serena (*The Webbers*), John Brown (*Schilt*), Sibylla Kay (*Mrs. Schilt*), Dorothy Frere (*Grandma Schilt*), Jason James (*Foreman*), Arnold Locke (*Old Villager*), Bradford and Amoro (*Helga and Heinrich's Doubles*).
87 mins.

LE VAMPIRE DE DUSSELDORF
(1964) France/Italy/Spain
Prod. Co.: Rome-Paris-Films/B. Perojo/Manoletti

Dir.: Robert Hossein
Sc.: Robert Hossein, Claude Desailly, George and André Tabet
Ph.: Alain Levent

Robert Hossein, (*Peter Kurten*), Marie-France Pisier, Roger Dutoit, Annie Andersson, Paloma Valdes, Danick Patisson, Michel Dacquin.
86 mins.

A VAMPIRE FOR TWO see UN VAMPIRO PARA DOS

THE VAMPIRE GIRLS see LAS VAMPIRAS

THE VAMPIRE HAPPENING see HAPPENING DER VAMPIRE

VAMPIRE, HOMME OU FEMME? see LA STRAGE DEI VAMPIRI

THE VAMPIRE LOVERS (1970)
England
Prod. Co.: Hammer
Dist.: American International
Prod.: Harry Fine, Michael Style
Dir.: Roy Ward Baker
Sc.: Tudor Gates, from the novella "Carmilla" by J. Sheridan Le Fanu
Ph.: Moray Grant (Colour)
Art Dir.: Scott MacGregor
Mus.: Harry Robinson
Cost.: Brian Cox
Ed.: James Needs

Ingrid Pitt (*Carmilla Karnstein*), Madeline Smith (*Emma Morton*), Peter Cushing (*The General*), Pippa Steele (*Laura*), George Cole (*Mr. Morton*), Dawn Addams (*The Countess*), Kate O'Mara (*the Governess, Mme. Perrodon*), Douglas Wilmer (*Baron Hartog*), Jon Finch (*Carl*), Kirsten Betts (*First Vampire*), Harvey Hall (*Renton*), Janet Key (*Gretchen*), Charles Farrell (*Landlord*), Ferdy Mayne (*The Doctor*).
90 mins.

VAMPIRE MAN see ONNA KYUKETSUI

VAMPIRE MEN OF THE LOST PLANET see CREATURES OF THE PREHISTORIC PLANET

LA VAMPIRE NUE (THE NAKED VAMPIRE, THE NUDE VAMPIRE) (1969)
France
Prod. Co.: ABC Films
Dir.: Jean Rollin
Sc.: Jean Rollin, S. H. Moati
Ph.: Jean-Jacques Renon (Colour)
Art Dir.: Jio Berk
Mus.: Yvon Geraud, Francois Tusques

Christine François, Olivier Martin, Maurice Lemaitre, Ly Letrong, Bernard Musson, Jean Aron, Ursule Pauly.
90 mins.

THE VAMPIRE OF CASTLE FRANKSTEIN see EL VAMPIRO DE LA AUTOPISTA

THE VAMPIRE OF THE CAVE see PONTIANAK GUA MUSANG

THE VAMPIRE OF THE HIGHWAY see EL VAMPIRO DE LA AUTOPISTA

THE VAMPIRE OF THE OPERA see IL VAMPIRO DELL'OPERA

THE VAMPIRE RETURNS see PONTIANAK KEMBALI

VAMPIRE THRILLS see LE FRISSON DES VAMPIRES

THE VAMPIRE'S COFFIN see EL ATAUD DEL VAMPIRO

From EL ATAUD DEL VAMPIRO

THE VAMPIRE'S CURSE see SUMPAH PONTIANAK

A VAMPIRE'S DREAM see UM SONHO DE VAMPIROS

THE VAMPIRE'S GHOST (1945) U.S.A.
Prod. Co.: Republic
Prod.: Rudy Abel
Dir.: Lesley Selander
Sc.: Leigh Brackett, John K. Butler
Ph.: Robert Pittack, Ellis Thackeray
Art Dir.: Russell Kimball
Mus.: Richard Cherwin
Ed.: Tony Martinelli
John Abbott (*Webb Fallon*), Peggy Stewart (*Julie Vance*), Grant Withers (*Father Gilchrist*), Charles Gordon (*Roy Hendrick*), Adela Mara (*Lisa*), Emmet Vogan (*Thomas Vance*), Roy Barcroft (*Jim*), Martin Wilkins (*Simon Peter*), Zack Williams, Frank Jaquet, Floyd Shadelford, George Carlton, Fred Howard.
59 mins.

THE VAMPIRE'S LOVER see L'AMANTE DEL VAMPIRO

EL VAMPIRO (THE VAMPIRE) (1956) Mexico
Prod. Co.: Abel Salazar/ Cinematografica ABSA
Dir.: Fernando Mendez
Sc.: H. Rodriquez, Ramon Obon
Ph.: Rosario Solano
Art Dir.: Gunther Gerzo
Mus.: Gustavo C. Carrion
German Robles (*The Vampire/ Count Lavud/Duval*), Ariadna Welter, Abel Salazar, Jose Luiz Jiminez, July Danery, Joseph Chavez, Amado Zumaya, Mercedes Soler, Dick Barker.

EL VAMPIRO DE LA AUTOPISTA (THE VAMPIRE OF THE HIGHWAY, THE VAMPIRE OF CASTLE FRANKENSTEIN (1969) Spain
Prod. Co.: Cinefilms
Dir./Sc.: Jose Luis Madrid
Ph.: Francisco Madurga (Colour, Techniscope)
Valdemar Wohlfahrt, Patricia Loran, Luis Induni, Barta Barry, Adele Tauler, Anastasio Campoy.
91 mins.

IL VAMPIRO DELL'OPERA (THE VAMPIRE OF THE OPERA) (1961) Italy
Prod. Co.: NIF
Dir.: Renato Polselli
Vittoria Prada, Marc Maryn, Giuseppe Addobati.

UN VAMPIRO PARA DOS (A VAMPIRE FOR TWO) (1965) Spain
Prod. Co.: Belmar P.C.-Bravo Murillo
Dir.: Pedro Lazaga
Sc.: Jose Maria Palacio, Pedro Lazaga
Ph.: Eloy Mella
Gracita Morales, Jose Luis Lopez

John Abbott as Webb Fallon in THE VAMPIRE'S GHOST

Vazquez, Fernando Fernan Gomez, Trini Alonso.
85 mins.

EL VAMPIRO SANGRIENTO
(THE BLOODY VAMPIRE)
(1962) Mexico
Prod. Co.: Tele-Talia
Dir.:   Miguel Morayta
Sc.:   Miguel Morayta
Ph.:   Raul M. Solares
Carlos Agosti (*Count Frankenhausen*), Begona Palacios, Antonio Raxell, Erna Martha Bauman.
110 mins.

EL VAMPIRO Y EL SEXO (THE VAMPIRE AND SEX, SANTO AND DRACULA'S TREASURE)
(1969) Mexico
Prod. Co.: Cinematografica Calderon (Colour)
Dir.:   Rene Cardona
Sc.:   Alfredo Salazar
Santo, Aldo Monti, Noelia Noel, Carlos Agosti, Alberto Rojas.

VAMPYR (1932) Germany/France
Prod. Co.: Tobis-Klangfilm
Prod.:   Carl Dreyer, Nicholas de Gunzburg
Dir.:   Carl Dreyer
Sc.:   Carl Dreyer, Christen Jul, from the novella "Carmilla" by J. Sheridan Le Fanu

The Vampire in the mill from VAMPYR

A man at the ferry in VAMPYR

Ph.:	Rudolph Maté, Louis Née
Art Dir.:	Hermann Warm, Hans Bittmann, Cesare Silvani
Mus.:	Wolfgang Zeller

Julian West/Baron Nicolas de Gunzburg (*David Gray*), Maurice Schutz (*Lord of the Manor*), Sybille Schmitz (*Léone*), Rena Mandel (*Giséle*), Henriette Gérard (*Marguerite Chopin*), Jan Hieronimko (*The Doctor*), Albert Bras (*The Servant*), A. Babanini (*His Wife*), Jane Mora (*The Sick Girl*).
65 mins.

VAULT OF HORROR. (1973)
England
Prod. Co.: Metromedia-Amicus
Prod.: Max J. Rosenberg, Milton Subotsky
Exec. Prod.: Charles W. Fries
Dir.: Roy Ward Baker
Sc.: Milton Subotsky, based on tales from William Gaines's comic books

Daniel Massey, Anna Massey, Michael Craig, Curt Jurgens, Dawn Addams, Terry-Thomas, Glynis Johns, Tom Baker, Denholm Elliott.
93 mins.
Only the first of the five tales is a vampire story.

VIERGES ET VAMPIRES (VIRGINS AND VAMPIRES)
(1972) France
Prod. Co.: ABC Films
Prod.: Sam Selsky
Dir/Sc.: Jean Rollin
Ph.: Renan Pooes

Marie Pierre Castel, Mireille D'Argent, Philippe Gaste, Dominique, Michel De le Salle, Olivier François, Louise Dhour.

Daniel Massey finds himself "on tap" at very eerie restaurant in
VAULT OF HORROR

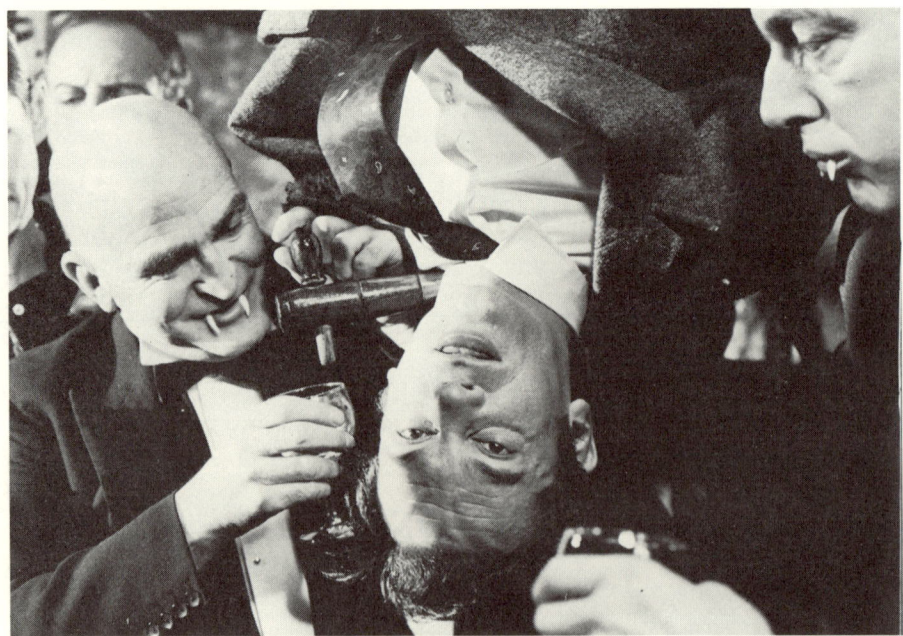

Anna Massey turns up at the restaurant thirsty for blood in VAULT OF HORROR

LE VIOL DU VAMPIRE (THE RAPE OF THE VAMPIRE, LES FEMMES VAMPIRES, SEX AND THE VAMPIRE, LA REINE DES VAMPIRES, QUEEN OF THE VAMPIRES) (1967) France
Prod. Co.: ABC Films
Prod.: Sam Selsky
Dir./Sc.: Jean Rollin
Ph.: Guy Leblond, Antoine Harispe
Mus.: Yvon Geraud, Francois Tusques
Bernard Letrou, Solange Pradel, Ursule Pauly, Nicole Romain, Jacqueline Sieger.
100 mins.

VIRGINS AND VAMPIRES see VIERGES ET VAMPIRES

WALPURGIS NIGHT see LA NOCHE DE WALPURGIS

THE WEREWOLF VS. THE VAMPIRE WOMAN see LA NOCHE DE WALPURGIS

THE WORLD OF THE VAMPIRES see EL MUNDO DE LOS VAMPIROS

Bibliography

BOOKS

Adkinson, Robert; Eyles, Allen; Fry, Nicholas. "The House of Horror." London: Lorrimer Publishing, 1973.

Aylesworth, Thomas G. "Monsters from the Movies." New York: J.B. Lippincott, 1972.

Baxter, John. "Hollywood in the Thirties." New York: A.S. Barnes/London: Tantivy, 1968.

Belmans, Jacques. "Roman Polanski." Paris: Seghers, 1971.

Buckley, J.H. "The Victorian Temper." New York: Vintage, 1964.

Butler, Ivan. "The Cinema of Roman Polanski." New York: A.S. Barnes/London: Tantivy, 1970.

Butler, Ivan. "Horror in the Cinema." New York: A.S. Barnes/London: Tantivy, 1967.

Clarens, Carlos. "An Illustrated History of the Horror Film." New York: G.P. Putnam's Sons, 1967.

Copper, Basil. "The Vampire in Legend, Fact and Art." London: Robert Hale, 1972.

Coulteray, George De. "Sadism in the Movies." New York: Medical Press, 1965. Translator: Steve Hult.

Dillard, R.H.W. "Even a Man Who is Pure at Heart: Poetry and Danger in the Horror Film" in "Man and the Movies." Louisiana: Louisiana State University Press, 1967.

Douglas, Drake. "Horror!" Toronto: Collier-Macmillan Co., 1969.

Durgnat, Raymond. "Films and Feelings." Massachusetts: M.I.T. Press, 1967.

Durgnat, Raymond. "A Mirror for England." New York: Praeger Publishers, 1971.

Edelson, Ed. "Great Monsters of the Movies." New York: Doubleday and Co., 1973.

Eisner, Lotte. "The Haunted Screen." Berkeley: University of California Press, 1969. Translator: Roger Greaves.

Eisner, Lotte. "Murnau." Berkeley: University of California Press, 1973.

Faivre, Tony. "Les Vampires." Paris: Le Terrain Vague, 1971.

Florescu, Radu and McNally, Raymond T. "Dracula: A Historical Biography of the Impaler." New York: Hawthorn Books, 1973.

Florescu, Radu and McNally, Raymond T. "In Search of Dracula." New York: New York Graphic Society, 1972.

Garden, Nancy. "Vampires." New York: J.B. Lippincott, 1973.

Gifford, Denis. "A Pictorial History of Horror Movies." New York: Hamlyn, 1973.

Glut, Donald. "True Vampires of History." New York: HC Publishers, 1971.

Greenberg, Joel and Higham, Charles. "Hollywood in the Forties." New York: A.S. Barnes, 1968./London: Tantivy.

Hays, H.R. "The Dangerous Sex." New York: Pocket Books, 1972.

Hurwood, Bernhardt J. "Vampires, Werewolves, and Ghouls." New York: Ace Books, 1968.

Huss, Roy and Ross, T.J. (Eds.). "Focus on the Horror Film." New Jersey: Prentice-Hall, 1972. (includes various articles on the horror film).

Jones, Ernest. "On the Nightmare." New York: Liveright, 1971.

Kracauer, Siegfried. "From Caligari to Hitler." London: Princeton University Press, 1947.

Krafft-Ebing, Richard Von. "Psychopathia Sexualis." New York: G.P. Putnam's Sons, 1965.

Kyrou, Ado. "Le surrealisme au cinema." Paris: Le Terrain Vague, 1963.

Laing, R.D. "Sanity, Madness, and the Family." London: Tavistock Publications, 1964.

Laing, R.D. "Self and Others." Middlesex: Penguin Books, 1971.

Lenne, Gérard "Le Cinema Fantastique et ses Mythologies." Paris: Editions du Cert, 1970.

Lennig, Arthur. "Classics of the Film." Wisconsin: Wisconsin Film Society Press, 1965.

Lovecraft, H.P. "Supernatural Horror in Literature." in "Dagon." New York: Panther, 1969.

Manchel, Frank. "Terrors of the Screen." New York: Prentice-Hall, 1970.

Masters, Anthony. "The Natural History of the Vampire." New York: G.P. Putnam's Sons, 1972.

Masters, R.E.L. and Lea, Eduard. "Sex Crimes in History." New York: Julian, 1963.

Mayo, H. "On the Truths contained in Popular Superstition." London: William Blackwood and Sons, 1851.

Milne, Tom. "The Cinema of Carl Dreyer." New York: A.S. Barnes, 1971./London: Tantivy.

Perrin, Claude. "Carl Dreyer." Paris: Seghers, 1969.

Pirie, David. "A Heritage of Horror." London: Gordon Fraser, 1973.

Predal, Rene. "Le Cinéma fantastique." Paris: Seghers, 1970.

Reed, Donald. "The Vampire on the Screen." Inglewood: Wagon and Star Publishers, 1965.

Ronay, Gabriel. "The Truth about Dracula." London: Stein and Day, 1973.

Rudorff, Raymond. "The Dracula Archives." New York: Arbor House, 1971.

Ruitenbeek, Hendrik M. (ed.) "Death: Interpretations." New York: Dell Publishing, 1969.

Rycaut, Paul. "The Present State of the Greek and Armenian Churches." London: John Starkey, 1678.

Searles, Harold F. "The Nonhuman Environment." New York: International Universities Press, 1960.

Stedman, Raymond W. "The Serials." Oklahoma: University of Oklahoma Press, 1971.

Steiger, Brad. "Monsters, Maidens, and Mayhem." New York: Cameraarts Publishing, 1965.

Summers, Montague. "The Vampire: His Kith and Kin." London: Routledge, Kegan Paul, 1928.

Summers, Montague. "The Vampire in Europe." London: Kegan Paul, Trench, Trubner, and Co., 1929.

Volta, Ornella. "Frankenstein and Company." Milan: Sugar Editore, 1966.

Volta, Ornella. "Le Vampire." Paris: Jean-Jacques Pauvert, Editeur, 1962.

Walker, Alexander. "The Celluloid Sacrifice." New York: Hawthorn Books, 1967.

Wright, Dudley. "Vampires and Vampirism." London: William Rider and Son, 1924.

PERIODICALS

Alpert, Hollis and Beaumont, Charles. "The Horror of It All." Playboy. March, 1959. p. 68.

Amis, Kingsley. "Son of Horror Film." Los Angeles Times West Magazine. October 26, 1969.

Armstrong, Michael. "Some Like It Chilled—Part 3—Theme—The Undead." Films and Filming. April, 1971. p. 37.

Bean, Robin. "Dracula and the Mad Monk." Films and Filming. August, 1965. p. 55.

Bizarre. "Cinéma Fantastique—L'Epouvante." with articles and filmographies on Tod Browning and Bela Lugosi. Nos. 24-5.

Borst, Ron. "The Vampire in the Cinema." Photon. No. 18, Filmography in Nos. 19 and 21.

Brower, Brock. "The Vulgarization of American Demonology." Esquire. June, 1964. p. 94.

Caen, Michel. "Entretien avec Barbara Steele." Midi-minuit fantastique. No. 12, p. 29.

Caen, Michel. "Entretien avec Christopher Lee." Midi-minuit fantastique. No. 14. (Interview).

Caen, Michel. "Entretien avec Terence Fisher." Midi-minuit fantastique. Nos. 10-11. p. 1.

Chauffard, R.J. "Qui est Jean Rollin?" Midi-minuit fantastique. No. 24. p. 50.

Cinéfantastique. "Interview with Jean Rollin." Volume III, no. 1.

Cinéma (Paris). "En Tant Que Createur Je Dois Suivre Mon Instinct." Interview with Peter Sasdy. September-October 1972. p. 93.

Cutts, John. "Vampyr." Films and Filming. December, 1960. p. 17+

Degaudenzi, J.L. "Mythe et Realite: Le Veritable Dracula." Midi-minuit fantastique. No. 24. p. 74.

Dyer, Peter John. "Some Nights of Horror." Films and Filming. July, 1958. p. 13.

Evans, Walter. "Monster Movies: A Sexual Theory." The Journal of Popular Film, Volume II, number 4.

Everson, William K. "A Family Tree of Monsters." Film Culture. January, 1955. p. 24.

Everson, William K. "Horror Films." Films in Review. January, 1954.

Everson, William K. "Karloff and Lugosi." Screen Facts. No. 7, p. 40.

Films in Review. "Tod Browning." October, 1953. p. 410.

Fisher, Terence. "Horror is My Business." Films and Filming. July, 1964. p. 7.

Gehman, Richard. "The Hollywood Horrors." Cosmopolitan. November, 1958. p. 38.

Glazebrook, Philip. "The Anti-Heroes of Horror." Films and Filming. October, 1966. p. 36.

Grotjahn, Martin. "Horror—Yes, It Can Do You Good." Films and Filming. October, 1958. p. 9.

Hall, Derek. "The Face of Horror." Sight and Sound. Winter, 1958-9.

Halliwell, Leslie. "The Baron, The Count, and Their Ghoul Friends." Films and Filming. June and July, 1969.

Harrington, Curtis. "Ghoulies and Ghosties." Sight and Sound. April-June, 1952. p. 157.

Kahan, Saul. "Transylvania—Polanski Style." Cinema (American). Volume 3, #4. p. 7.

Losano, Wayne A. "The Vampire Rises Again in the Films of the 70's." The Film Journal. Volume 2, No. 2. p. 60.

Meeker, Oden and Olivia. "The Screamy-Weamies." Collier's. January 12, 1946. p. 42.

Michel, Jean-Claude. "Les Vampires à l'écran." L'écran fantastique. No. 2, 1971.

Midi-minuit fantastique. "Dracula Issue" with various articles on Dracula in literature and films (including a filmography and bibliography). Nos. 4-5.

Midi-minuit fantastique. "Entretien avec Don Sharp." No. 9. p. 77.

Midi-minuit fantastique. "Entretien avec Roman Polanski." No. 20. p. 26.

Midi-minuit fantastique. "Entretien avec Terence Fisher." No. 7. p. 9.

Midi-minuit fantastique. "Erotisme et épouvante dans le Cinéma Anglais." Whole issue has articles, interviews, and filmographies on the English horror film. No. 8.

Midi-minuit fantastique. "Terence Fisher Issue." With various articles, interviews, and filmographies on Terence Fisher, Peter Cushing, and Christopher Lee. No. 1.

Midi-minuit fantastique. "Vamps Fantastiques Issue." No. 2.

Morlot, Jean-Claude. "Impossible Is Not French." Cinéfantastique. Volume III, no. 1. p. 38.

Moss, Morton. "The Devil's Advocate." Los Angeles Herald Examiner. November 28, 1972.

Parish, James Robert and Pitts, Michael R. "Christopher Lee—A Career Article." Cinéfantastique. Volume III, no. 1. p. 4.

Pirie, David. "New Blood." Sight and Sound. Spring, 1971. p. 73.

Polanski, Roman. "Satisfaction—A Most Unpleasant Feeling." Films and Filming. April, 1969. p. 15.

Ringle, Harry. "The Horrible Hammer Films of Terence Fisher." Take One. January-February, 1972. p. 8.

Volta, Ornella. "Entretien avec Mario Bava." Positif. No. 138. p. 44.

Walker, Alexander. "Films." Man, Myth, and Magic. No. 34.

Weinberg, Herman and Gretchen. "Vampyr—An Interview with Baron de Gunzburg." Film Culture. Spring, 1965. p. 57.

White, Dennis. "The Poetics of Horror: More Than Meets the Eye." Cinema Journal. Spring, 1971.

Index to Film Titles

Billy the Kid vs. Dracula 62
Black Sabbath 140
Black Sunday 135, 140, 141
Blood and Roses 102, 105, 107, 109, 110, 111, 119
Blood of Dracula 115
Blood of Dracula's Castle 74
Blood of Nostradamus 78
Brides of Dracula 80, 83, 86, 118, 125
Cave of the Living Dead 135
Count Dracula 62
Count Yorga, Vampire 62, 71, 73, 74, 76, 116
Countess Dracula 98, 101, 102, 103, 106
Curse of Dracula 62
Curse of Nostradamus 77, 78
Curse of the Undead 71
Dance of the Vampires 74
Dark Shadows 51
Dracula (1931) 61, 68, 69, 70, 80, 113, 118, 123
Dracula (1958) 62, 79, 82, 83, 123, 124, 125, 129
Dracula A.D. 1972 62
Dracula A.D. 1974 86
Dracula has Risen from the Grave 62, 126, 128
Dracula, Prince of Darkness 62, 79, 83, 85, 125
Dracula's Daughter 112, 114, 115
Deathmaster, The 62
Daughters of Darkness 101, 102, 103

El Conde Dracula 61
Genie of Darkness 78
Grave of the Vampire 74
Hercules in the Haunted World 138, 140, 141
House of Dracula 62, 89, 91
House of Frankenstein 62
Kiss of the Vampire 126
Lake of Dracula 62
Last Man on Earth 137
Lust for a Vampire 110, 130
Mark of the Vampire 62, 68
Monster Demolishers, The 78
Munsters, The 51
Night Gallery 51
Night Stalker, The 74, 75, 76, 115
Nosferatu 62, 64, 65, 67, 85, 118, 137
Nostradamus 57, 76
Planet of the Vampires 137, 141
Return of Count Yorga 62
Return of Dracula 71
Return of the Vampire 62
Ritual of Blood 102
Santo vs. the Vampire Woman 77, 114
Scars of Dracula 62, 126
Scream, Blacula, Scream 74, 89, 92, 95, 116
Son of Dracula 62, 68, 70, 75, 116
Taste the Blood of Dracula 62, 82, 126, 129, 133
Terror in the Crypt 107, 108, 109, 110, 111
Twins of Evil 114, 130

Uncle was a Vampire 62
Vampire, The 71, 76, 92, 115
Vampire Circus 130
Vampire Lover 110, 112, 129, 130
Vampire's Ghost, The 91
Vampyr 114, 118, 121
Velvet Vampire, The 116
What 140
World of the Vampires 76